Remaking Post-Industrial Cities

Remaking Post-Industrial Cities: Lessons from North America and Europe examines the transformation of post-industrial cities after the precipitous collapse of big industry in the 1980s on both sides of the Atlantic, presenting a holistic approach to restoring post-industrial cities.

Developed from the influential 2013 Remaking Cities Congress, conference chair Don Carter brings together ten in-depth case studies of cities across North America and Europe, documenting their recovery from 1985 to 2015. Each chapter discusses the history of the city, its transformation, and prospects for the future. The cases cross-cut these themes with issues crucial to the resilience of post-industrial cities including sustainability; doing more with less; public engagement; and equity (social, economic, and environmental), the most important issue cities face today and for the foreseeable future.

This book provides essential "lessons learned" from the successes and mistakes of these cities, and is an invaluable resource for practitioners and students of planning, urban design, urban redevelopment, economic development and public and social policy.

Donald K. Carter is Director of the Remaking Cities Institute, Carnegie Mellon University (CMU) in Pittsburgh. He is also Track Chair of the Master of Urban Design program in the School of Architecture. Prior to joining CMU in 2009, Don was President of Pittsburgh-based Urban Design Associates. He is a Fellow of the American Institute of Architects and a Fellow of the American Institute of Certified Planners. He was Co-Chair of the international 2013 Remaking Cities Congress. Don earned a Bachelor of Architecture from CMU and did post-graduate studies in urban design and regional planning at the University of Edinburgh, Scotland.

Remaking Post-Industrial Cities

Lessons from North America and Europe

Edited by Donald K. Carter

Routledge
Taylor & Francis Group

NEW YORK AND LONDON

First published 2016
by Routledge
711 Third Avenue, New York, NY 10017

and by Routledge
2 Park Square, Milton Park, Abingdon, Oxon OX14 4RN

Routledge is an imprint of the Taylor & Francis Group, an informa business

Library of Congress Cataloging in Publication Data
Remaking post-industrial cities : lessons from North America and Europe / edited by Donald Carter.
pages cm
Includes index.
1. Urban renewal--North America. 2. Urban renewal--Europe. 3. City planning--North America. 4. City planning--Europe. 5. Urban policy--North America. 6. Urban policy--Europe. I. Carter, Donald K.
HT178.N69R46 2016
307.3'416097--dc23
2015033969

ISBN: 978-1-138-89928-5 (hbk)
ISBN: 978-1-138-89929-2 (pbk)
ISBN: 978-1-315-70799-0 (ebk)

Typeset in Sabon
by Saxon Graphics Ltd, Derby

MIX
Paper from
responsible sources
FSC® C013056
www.fsc.org

Printed and bound in Great Britain by
TJ International Ltd, Padstow, Cornwall

This book is lovingly dedicated to my wife, Bea, my son, Andrew, and my daughter, Laura, and in memory of my parents, Roberta and William Carter.

Contents

Figures

Tables

Foreword

Bruce Katz

A quarter-century before the Remaking Cities Congress of 2013, a group of urbanists, economists, and policy-makers gathered for the first Remaking Cities conference in Pittsburgh. The situation in 1988 was bleak: the twin forces of suburbanization and deindustrialization had decimated industrial cities across America's Rust Belt. Between 1970 and 1990, Pittsburgh itself had lost one-third of its population and the region shed over 100,000 manufacturing jobs. These were cities that had failed to retrain their workers or retool their factories as the sands of the global economy shifted quickly beneath their feet.

The Congress that convened in 2013 again in Pittsburgh, co-chaired by Don Carter of Carnegie Mellon University, and which I was grateful to attend myself, was another thing entirely—comprised of representatives of post-industrial cities that had endured and, in some cases, such as Pittsburgh, have prospered over the prior three decades. These cases of success are as distinct as the regional economies in which they took place, but taken together they offer lessons and potential models for similar cities throughout the United States and Europe that continue to struggle with economic transition in the twenty-first-century global economy.

That transition is a primary concern and the lesson is clear: those cities that have emerged strongest from this decline have done so by building distinctive advanced economies and quality places atop their industrial base. This does not mean building another Silicon Valley in the American Midwest; rather, it is pivoting legacy assets towards more innovative activity, giving new skills to experienced industrial workers so they can help foster a new era of advanced manufacturing, or encouraging entrepreneurial activity in former one-company towns.

Participants at the 2013 Congress stressed the importance of maintaining and improving upon the solid physical bones in these cities. In many ways, the urban skeleton of older cities in the USA and Europe is a great advantage—with dense, walkable streets, valuable public spaces, attractive waterfronts, authentic neighborhoods, and historic buildings. The challenge is to update these assets to incorporate modern needs—increased public transportation capacity, broadband and technical infrastructure, sustainability improvements, and flexible and shared spaces in both the public and private realm—while retaining their distinctive character, such as in the Ruhr Valley in Germany.

When the development of an advanced economy is married with quality place-making and connectivity in a dense, urban environment, the impact can multiply. Within these potential "innovation districts," advanced research institutions and medical campuses collaborate with corporate R&D divisions, smaller start-up firms and entrepreneurs. By locating within the cores of cities, rather than in far-flung suburbs, this activity offers the promise of greater spillover into other sectors of the economy and adjoining neighborhoods and greater fiscal and economic growth for the cities themselves. At Brookings, we've identified such districts in "strong market" cities such as Boston, New York, San Francisco, and Seattle, but also in older industrial cities such as Baltimore, Buffalo, Cleveland, Detroit, Philadelphia, Pittsburgh, Providence, and St. Louis. Older industrial cities like these offer unique opportunities for innovation, such as the ability to commercialize research generated in universities like Carnegie Mellon University or Drexel University or cheaply convert former industrial buildings into collaborative co-working maker-spaces or to integrate entrepreneurial energy into rethinking municipal service and energy provision to be more efficient and sustainable. The phenomenon is clearly not limited to older industrial cities in the United States; European cities like Barcelona, Belfast, Berlin, Dublin, Eindhoven, Manchester, Sheffield, and Turin have their own distinctive advantages to exploit.

This collection of lessons on remaking post-industrial cities comes at a critical time. Surely, significant challenges remain for these cities as the global economy evolves—climate change, inequality, segregation, and continued global competition were themes that wove throughout the sessions of the Congress—but, given the right tools, they appear better equipped than at any point since the 1960s to tackle these obstacles.

My optimism is fueled in part by shifting global dynamics that have swung back in favor of the city. Household preferences in the developed world are shifting: smaller households are more amenable to urban living; empty nesters are returning to the city. At the same time, the very technological and economic changes that brought down traditional manufacturing are changing business models, advancing a new era of "open innovation," and ultimately leading companies to revalue the density and proximity offered by urban locations.

City responses to these opportunities are also necessitated by a rebalancing of power in the United States and Europe, one both natural and necessary, wherein federal governments are becoming less relevant and local elected leadership—in collaboration with private, civic, and philanthropic actors—is stepping in to harness new market and demographic dynamics. In turn, this has empowered leadership networks in cities from Detroit to Turin, where shared visions and strategic plans have charted a new way forward for written-off cities.

Finally, I'm optimistic because of the sheer volume of innovative and creative problem solving occurring today. Cities are fast, eager learners, ever observant of their peers, able to move quickly to spot innovation elsewhere and apply it at home. While the exact intervention that works in Liverpool won't necessarily work in Milwaukee, there are certainly lessons to be learned across countries and across the world. Especially as cities look beyond traditional urban issues such as housing and begin to experiment with global issues like climate change and sustainability, the "horizontal" replication of innovations across cities will be necessary.

The world is essentially evolving as a network of global cities that trade with each other, learn from each other and come together to solve pressing challenges and bend global, national and state policies to their will.

Thus, the 2013 Remaking Cities Congress and this collection of its lessons that Don Carter has curated are meant to add to the toolbox of solutions available to metropolitan leaders. I urge you to read these not just as interesting urban case studies, but also as practical guides for how to make our cities stronger in the face of continued challenges.

Bruce Katz
Vice President, Brookings Institution
Founding Director, Metropolitan Policy Program

Acknowledgments

I am grateful to the U.S. and European authors who contributed chapters to this book, and in particular to Geraldine Gardner of the German Marshall Fund of the United States, not only for authoring a chapter, but also for her assistance in selecting the European city case studies and recruiting the authors.

I am indebted to Carnegie Mellon University for supporting my research. Olivia Wells, Program Coordinator at the Remaking Cities Institute, was invaluable in helping me with research, editing, and coordinating the work of the contributing authors.

The book would not have been possible without the editorial team at Routledge in New York City, particularly Nicole Solano, Senior Acquisitions Editor, and Judith Newlin, Editorial Assistant, Planning and Urban Design, who guided me through the publishing process.

Finally, I am grateful for the untiring support and encouragement of my wife, Bea, who tolerated my many absent hours over weekends to allow me to write and edit this book.

Introduction

Donald K. Carter

Origins of the Book

In October 2013, three hundred leading urbanists from North America and Europe gathered in Pittsburgh for the Remaking Cities Congress. This was twenty-five years after a previous Remaking Cities Conference had been held in Pittsburgh in 1988. The primary focus in 1988 was the precipitous decline of industrial cities and regions in North America and Europe in the 1980s. Prince Charles was the Honorary Chair and keynote speaker (Figure 0.1).[1]

Figure 0.1 The Prince of Wales with delegates and students at the Remaking Cities Conference in Pittsburgh, 1988
Source: Courtesy of the Remaking Cities Institute.

Figure 0.2 Plenary Session at the Remaking Cities Congress, 2013
Source: Courtesy of the Remaking Cities Institute.

Post-industrial regions in North America and Europe continue to face challenges today, with some achieving a positive transformation and others still in decline. Twenty-five years later was a good time to reconvene in Pittsburgh to assess the past, to share best practices from both sides of the Atlantic, and to craft a new agenda for post-industrial cities. The major sponsors were Carnegie Mellon University and the American Institute of Architects (Figure 0.2). Prince Charles again served as the Honorary Chair and keynote speaker. Eleven city case studies were presented, six from North America (Buffalo, Detroit, Milwaukee, New Orleans, Pittsburgh, and Toronto), and five from Europe (Bilbao, Manchester, Rotterdam, Ruhr Valley, and Turin).[2]

This book, *Remaking Post-Industrial Cities: Lessons from North America and Europe*, is the product of the 2013 Congress. The book includes ten city case studies, expanded and updated to 2015. Several policy chapters document key takeaways from the Congress. All of the chapters were written by authors who attended either one or both Remaking Cities conferences held in Pittsburgh in 1988 and 2013.

The 2013 Remaking Cities Congress

In addition to the city case studies, the 2013 Remaking Cities Congress had plenary presentations by thought leaders from North America and Europe, and panel discussions by leading urbanists. It was primarily a working conference. The core of the Congress was spent in all-day Theme Workshops (Figure 0.3) that dealt with post-industrial cities in five theme areas:

- Re-Positioning the Post-Industrial City in the Global Economy
- Post-Industrialism and the Physical City
- The Twenty-First-Century City as an Innovation Hub

Figure 0.3 Theme Workshop at the Remaking Cities Congress, 2013
Source: Courtesy of the Remaking Cities Institute.

- Urban Systems, Infrastructure, and the Post-Industrial City
- Planning and Social Innovations for Post-Industrial Cities.

Four common themes permeated the five Theme Workshops:

- Sustainability
- Wise Allocation of Resources (Doing More with Less)
- Equity
- Public Engagement.

Equity emerged as the overriding theme of the Congress—equity in all its manifestations: social, economic, and environmental. The equity theme was later reaffirmed in Spain in June 2014 at a follow-up conference (BUILD Bilbao)[3] on post-industrial cities sponsored by the German Marshall Fund of the United States. Equity and innovation were the key themes explored by the speakers and in the workshops in Bilbao.

In 2015, equity, inequality, and the increasing wealth gap are major issues for post-industrial cities on both sides of the Atlantic. Parallel issues of class, race, immigration, segregated urban conditions, and the future workforce are tied to how the equity issue will be dealt with in the future.

Theme Workshops of the Congress

Below is a brief summary of the topics covered in each all-day Theme Workshop.

Re-Positioning the Post-Industrial City in the Global Economy

The global economy has had a profound impact on post-industrial cities. The goal of this workshop was to build a comprehensive economic agenda for post-industrial cities.

Delegates assessed the economic condition of post-industrial cities, explored challenges and successful models for economic revitalization that leverage unique characteristics of place, examined how emerging industries and the new economy were being leveraged in innovative ways to build the post-industrial economy, and discussed issues and opportunities to prepare and equip a workforce capable of taking advantage of new economic opportunities.

Post-Industrialism and the Physical City

The aim of this workshop was to produce a community-building strategy for the post-industrial city. Delegates considered the urban design and patterns of development in post-industrial cities, regions, and neighborhoods that included discussions of housing, preservation, and innovative infill development strategies, as well as the consideration of industrial legacies and their inherent challenges in urban regeneration.

The Twenty-First-Century City as an Innovation Hub

The aim of this workshop was to produce a forward-looking innovation agenda for the post-industrial city. Delegates explored the use of innovative technological applications for creative problem-solving, with technological innovations to aggregate data and engage citizens in the collection and analysis process, the important role of civic innovators and the use of the creative arts in place-making, as well as equitable access to technology, data, and technical jobs, i.e. addressing the Digital Divide.

Urban Systems, Infrastructure, and the Post-Industrial City

The aim of this workshop was to build an integrative strategy for urban systems and infrastructure in the post-industrial city. Delegates developed strategic thinking around value-added infrastructure that includes water, transportation, and other urban systems; the role of energy at the site, district, and city scale; and the place of ecological systems in the post-industrial city, including the reuse of surplus urban land.

Planning and Social Innovations for Post-Industrial Cities

The aim of this workshop was to discuss and develop planning and social innovation strategies for the future of post-industrial cities in the face of population decline, vacant land and abandoned buildings, and economic challenges. Restructuring land use, tackling public education, dealing with distressed municipal finances, transforming an economy, and serving disadvantaged communities are common problems for post-industrial cities in both North America and Europe.

Propositions of the Congress

During the Congress, the delegates developed propositions in the five Theme Workshops. On the concluding day of the Congress, twenty-seven propositions were presented for vote by electronic clickers with five choices: (1) strongly agree; (2) agree; (3) no opinion; (4) disagree; and (5) strongly disagree (Figures 0.4a and 0.4b).

Five propositions had more than 90 percent agreement among the delegates.[4]

Figures 0.4a and 0.4b Voting by electronic clicker on the propositions during the final plenary session, Remaking Cities Congress, 2013
Source: Courtesy of the Remaking Cities Institute.

- *Connect the City (96 percent)*: The post-industrial city of tomorrow must provide transit and alternative modes of transportation to insure all communities have access and connectivity to jobs, education, food, housing, and services.
- *Use Education as Economic Development Strategy (94 percent)*: Post-industrial cities' greatest economic strategy should be to invest in education to cultivate the talent of their people.
- *Grow Entrepreneurial Capacity (92 percent)*: The post-industrial city of tomorrow must cultivate the dormant entrepreneurial capacity of its people to rebuild rich, vibrant, adaptable communities, thus creating a strong sense of place.
- *Develop Adaptive and Flexible Housing (91 percent)*: The post-industrial cities of tomorrow must develop housing and policies that allow for adaptive and changing communities and demographics with the goal of providing different housing opportunities over multiple life stages.
- *Provide Financial Incentives for Reuse (90 percent)*: The post-industrial cities of tomorrow must develop a wider range of creative financial incentives to encourage residents and small developers to reuse existing land, buildings, and neighborhoods.

Other top rated propositions (between 80 percent and 90 percent strongly agree/agree) included: *Provide Wealth Building Investments at the Community Scale*; *Invest in Neighborhoods for Equity*; *Create Innovation Districts*; *Direct Innovation Funding to Underserved Communities*; *Shift Infrastructure Decision Making*; *Prioritize Natural Systems*; and *Cultivate the Soul of the City*.

The Structure of the Book

The book begins with a *Foreword* by Bruce Katz, Vice President and Director of the Metropolitan Policy Program at the Brookings Institution, followed by the *Introduction* by Donald K. Carter, Director of the Remaking Cities Institute at Carnegie Mellon University.

Part I presents *North American City Case Studies*. Chapter 1, *The View from the United States* is by Alan Mallach, Senior Fellow at the Brookings Institution. Mallach starts by looking back "From Industrial to Post-Industrial: A Short History to 1985," followed by "From 1985 to 2015: Era of Change," concluding with "The Challenge of the Future." His chapter is followed by the five city case studies from North America (Figure 0.5):

Figure 0.5 Map of North America with case study cities
Source: Map by Andrea Salomon Gnecco, courtesy of the Remaking Cities Institute.

Chapter 2   *Buffalo, New York* by Robert Shibley and Bradshaw Hovey with Rachel Teaman

Chapter 3   *Detroit, Michigan* by Dan Kinkead

Chapter 4   *Milwaukee, Wisconsin* by Larry P. Witzling

Chapter 5   *New Orleans, Louisiana* by Maurice Cox and Jacqueline Taylor

Chapter 6   *Pittsburgh, Pennsylvania* by Donald K. Carter

Part II presents *European City Case Studies*. Chapter 7, *The View from Europe* is by Geraldine Gardner, Director of Urban and Regional Policy at the German Marshall Fund of the United States. Gardner begins with "Europe: Cradle of Industry," followed by "Europe's Urban Renaissance," concluding with a look at "The Road Ahead." Her chapter is followed by the five city case studies from Europe (Figure 0.6):

Chapter 8   *Bilbao, Spain* by Juan Alayo, Garbiñe Henry, and Beatriz Plaza

Chapter 9   *Liverpool, England* by Erik Bichard

Chapter 10   *Ruhr Region, Germany* by Michael Schwarze-Rodrian

Chapter 11   *Rotterdam, the Netherlands* by Nico Tillie, Luc Boot, Iris Dudok and Roland van der Heijden

Chapter 12   *Turin, Italy* by Anna Prat and Simone Mangili

The *Conclusion* by Donald Carter, editor, synthesizes the key points of the book.

Figure 0.6 Map of Europe with case study cities
Source: Map by Andrea Salomon Gnecco, courtesy of the Remaking Cities Institute.

The City Case Studies: An Overview

Each of the ten city case studies follows the same structure for easy comparison between the case studies:

- Introduction
- Brief History of the City
- The City in 1985
- The City in 2015
- Transformation of the City 1985–2015
- Prospects for the Future.

Each case study section on "Transformation of the City 1985–2015" is organized into sub-sections, "What Went Right?," "What Went Wrong?," and "Lessons Learned," presenting the key takeaways from the book.

Buffalo

Bradshaw Hovey and Robert Shibley with Rachel Teaman, all in the School of Architecture at the State University of New York at Buffalo, co-authored Chapter 2 on Buffalo. Hovey is Co-Director of the Urban Design Project; Shibley is Dean of the School of Architecture; and Teaman is Communications Officer. Buffalo, situated on Lake Erie, the eighth largest city in the US in 1901, was a powerhouse in grain and steel, but like the other cities in this book, lost much of its industrial base in the 1980s. Buffalo's recent economic resurgence is the result of growth in the health, education, and logistics sectors. In late 2011, *A Strategy for Prosperity in Western New York*[5] was published, laying out a comprehensive plan for a dynamic and sustainable economy.

Detroit

Dan Kinkead, Director of Projects for Detroit Future City, wrote Chapter 3 on Detroit, perhaps the most distressed of the cities documented in this book. As a legacy city based on the auto industry, Detroit experienced the boom decades of the 1950s and 1960s of post-World War II America. However, the development of the interstate highway system and the flow of middle-class families to the suburbs, starting in the 1960s, led to an emptying out of the central city of Detroit. The auto industry went through a re-structuring during the Great Recession of 2008–2010, when General Motors and Chrysler declared bankruptcy and were bailed out by the federal government. The City of Detroit itself declared bankruptcy in 2013. *The Detroit Future City: Strategic Framework Plan*, published in 2013, is a roadmap for recovery.[6]

Milwaukee

Larry Witzling, Emeritus Professor at the School of Architecture and Urban Planning, University of Wisconsin-Milwaukee, wrote Chapter 4 on Milwaukee. Like Buffalo, Milwaukee was a Great Lakes industrial powerhouse in 1901 that "feeds and supplies the world." A proud blue-collar town, Milwaukee was known for breweries, tanneries, and food processing, but also for iron, steel, and freight handling. The economic decline began in the 1970s with suburban flight and de-industrialization. However, recent initiatives along the riverfront, including the Calatrava-designed Milwaukee Art Museum, and neighborhood initiatives like "live-make-grow," signified an economic and psychological turnaround by the 1990s and 2000s. In 2014, *Growing Prosperity: An Action Agenda for Economic Development* was published.[7]

New Orleans

Maurice Cox and Jacqueline Taylor, Professors at Tulane University's School of Architecture, co-authored Chapter 5 on New Orleans. The city has received two major hits in the last thirty years: the loss of oil and gas industry jobs in the 1980s and 1990s to Texas; and the devastation of Hurricane Katrina in 2005. Both disasters led to the loss of jobs and population, and reinforced the perception of a city of poverty, crime, and racial disparities. Slowly the city is recovering. New Orleans remains a city of robust tourism, but the overall economy is not strong, with a large proportion of jobs in the low-paying service sector. Investment by the federal government in mixed income housing and infrastructure has softened the blow. Under construction are the new University Medical Center and the adjacent Veterans Administration Medical Center, both viewed as economic generators. *The Plan for the 21st Century*, published in 2013, lays out a framework for New Orleans' physical, social, environmental, and economic future.[8]

Pittsburgh

Donald Carter, Director of the Remaking Cities Institute at Carnegie Mellon University, wrote Chapter 5 on Pittsburgh. Like the other cities in the book, Pittsburgh hit bottom in the 1980s with the collapse of the steel industry and the loss of 133,000 high-paying industrial jobs. Unemployment reached 18 percent, comparable to Great Depression levels, despite being named the most livable city in the United States in 1985. How Pittsburgh became the global poster child for the successful transformation of post-industrial cities is a story of visionary leadership (top down), grass-roots activism (bottom up), a commitment to diversify the economy, and strategic investments in quality of life. However, unlike some cities in this book, Pittsburgh began its comeback with a few unique assets: two major research universities (Carnegie Mellon University and the University of Pittsburgh), a large hands-on philanthropic community, and relatively intact historic neighborhoods. New political leadership is in place to take Pittsburgh to the next level of transformation as a global city of innovation and sustainability.

Bilbao

Juan Alayo, Garbiñe Henry, and Beatriz Plaza, co-authored Chapter 8 on Bilbao. Alayo is an urban planner and former Development Planning Director of Bilbao Ria 2000. Henry is Director of Social Innovation at the University of Deusto. Plaza is on the Faculty of Economics at the University of the Basque Country. The 1980s were especially cruel for Bilbao with the crash of its industrial base in steel and shipbuilding, devastating floods in 1983, and the terrorist activities of ETA, the Basque separatist group. Symbolized by the Gehry-designed Guggenheim Museum, Bilbao has since been transformed from a polluted and economically distressed city to a city known internationally for its comeback. The 1992 *Strategic Plan for the Revitalization of Metropolitan Bilbao* outlined a consensus strategy for air and water cleanup, cultural investments, the development of the Bilbao Metro transit system, and urban regeneration projects, funded by national, regional, and municipal investments and implemented by new organizations such as Bilbao Metropoli 30 and Bilbao Ria 2000.

Liverpool

Erik Bichard, Professor of Regeneration and Sustainable Development at the University of Salford, Manchester, wrote Chapter 9 on Liverpool. In the eighteenth, nineteenth, and early twentieth centuries, Liverpool was one of the busiest ports in the world, at one point handling almost 40 percent of the world's trade in cotton. Travelers and immigrants arrived by ships, creating a multi-ethnic and prosperous city. Major civic and institutional buildings were constructed with the wealth of the trans-Atlantic trade. However, after World War II, the port of Liverpool suffered a decline due to competition from India for cotton imports and increasing air travel. By 1985, Liverpool had lost 33 percent of its jobs since the 1960s. Unemployment was high. Perhaps the only bright spot was the emergence in the 1960s of the Liverpool music scene, epitomized by the Beatles. Revitalization of the central area of Liverpool at the beginning of the twenty-first century was the start of the transformation of the city, followed by the redevelopment of the dock areas. Liverpool once again became a destination city, culminating in the city being designated the European Capital of Culture in 2008.

Rotterdam

Nico Tillie, Iris Dudok, Peter M. J. Pol, Luc Boot, and Roland van Heijden co-authored Chapter 11 on Rotterdam. Tillie is a researcher and lecturer in the Landscape Architecture Faculty at the Delft University of Technology. Dudok is with the Rotterdam Department of City Planning. Pol is an urban strategist and lecturer at the Rotterdam School of Economics at Erasmus University Rotterdam. Boot is Process Manager for the Rotterdam

Metropolitan Region, and van Heijden is an urban strategist with the City of Rotterdam. During World War II, like the Ruhr region, Rotterdam was heavily bombed. Rebuilding the city was a major initiative, and as a significant port for Europe, Rotterdam began to come back quickly. However, in the 1980s, port activities moved further from the city center, and national policy designated smaller towns around Rotterdam as centers for population growth, resulting in depopulation of the central city and the emergence of unused brownfields in the port area. In 2013, *The National Program for Rotterdam South (NPRZ)* was published with a twenty-year implementation strategy for social, economic, and physical renewal of the most challenged section of the city.[9]

The Ruhr Region

Michael Schwarze-Rodrian, Director of European and Regional Networks at the Regional Association Ruhr (RVR), wrote Chapter 10 on the Ruhr Region. Like Rotterdam, the Ruhr Region, an agglomeration of medium and small industrial towns, was heavily bombed in World War II, losing 30 percent of its industrial capacity. The resurgence of the Ruhr Region in the 1950s and 1960s was the center of the German economic miracle. However, in the 1970s with demand for coal dropping drastically, and in the 1980s with steel production moving to Asia, the Ruhr Region fell into an economic depression. The Ruhr Region chose to embrace its industrial past and to rebuild the region based on sustainability principles. The internationally renowned Emscher Landscape Park is exemplary of those efforts. An updated *Regional Plan Ruhr* will be released in 2016.

Turin

Anna Prat and Simone Mangili, both of Torino Internazionale, co-authored Chapter 12 on Turin. Torino Strategica is a regional planning association with eighty-nine members, including public bodies, institutions, universities, cultural centers, companies, unions and trade associations. The oil crisis of the 1970s led FIAT, the major employer in the region, to cut production, lay off workers, and move production out of Italy. By the mid-1980s Turin was in severe economic decline with attendant social issues. In 2000, Turin was the first Italian city to adopt its *Strategic Plan*. A second *Strategic Plan* was prepared in 2006. The 2006 Winter Olympics was a major catalyst in the transformation of the city with over $4 billion of public investments in transit, parks, and housing, combined with private investments in the historic heart of the city. In July 2014, Torino Strategica presented the Interim Report of the *Metropolitan Torino 2025 Strategic Plan*.[10]

Conclusion

The book concludes with a summary by Donald K. Carter of "Lessons Learned" from the ten city case studies.

Notes

1   Barbara Davis, ed., *Remaking Cities: Proceedings of the 1988 International Conference in Pittsburgh* (Pittsburgh, PA: University of Pittsburgh, 1989).
2   "Remaking Cities Congress," available at: www.cmu.edu/rci/congress/Home.html (accessed July 7, 2015).
3   "Build Bilbao Urban Innovation Leadership Dialogues 2014," available at: www.gmfus.org/sites/default/files/GMF-BUILD-2014-Report-For-Web-Upload.pdf (accessed July 7, 2015).

4   "Remaking Cities Congress Concluding Plenary Propositions," available at: www.cmu.edu/rci/congress/dms/pdf/RCC_Propositions_final.pdf (accessed July 7, 2015).

5   UB Regional Institute and the Urban Design Project, *A Strategy for Prosperity in Western New York* (Buffalo, NY: WNY Regional Economic Development Council with support from the Brookings Institute, 2011).

6   City of Detroit, *The Detroit Future City: Strategic Framework Plan*, available at: http://detroitfuturecity.com/framework/

7   For Milwaukee, see *Growing Prosperity: An Action Agenda for Economic Development*, available at: http://city.milwaukee.gov/GrowingProsperity#.VjNSkGrZ_IU

8   The New Orleans master plan, *The Plan for the 21st Century*, available at: www.nola.gov/city-planning/master-plan/

9   For Rotterdam, see *The National Program for Rotterdam South (NPRZ)*, available at: www.eukn.eu/e-library/project/bericht/eventDetail/national-programme-rotterdam-south/

10 For Turin, Torino Strategica, Interim Report, *Metropolitan Torino 2025 Strategic Plan*, available at: www.torinostrategica.it/en/metropolitan-turin-2025/

Part I

North American City Case Studies

1   The View from the United States

Alan Mallach

Driven by the simultaneous disruptive processes of migration, economic readjustment, and demographic change, cities in the United States have undergone a profound transformation since the end of World War II. Through the 1980s, that transformation was a negative one for most cities as they lost jobs, wealth, and population. Since the 1990s, a growing number of cities, although far from all, have begun to rebuild themselves by finding new economic roles and reconfiguring their physical form. Even in more successful cities, regeneration has been spatially and economically uneven in its effects on different places and sectors of the population, leaving many neighborhoods and their residents behind. As cities today grapple with post-industrial realities, they face the challenges of finding new roles in the global economy, rebuilding their physical fabric, systems, and infrastructure, and re-emerging as the hubs of innovation that they once were.

From Industrial to Post-Industrial: A Short History to 1985

America's older cities embody the remarkable rise of the United States from the mid-1800s to the early twentieth century from a largely agrarian nation into the world's economic and industrial powerhouse. Dozens of cities, large and small, were part of that transformation. Many of them have become iconic, with Detroit becoming a synonym for the car industry and Pittsburgh for steelmaking. By 1920, Detroit was the fourth largest city in the United States, Cleveland the fifth largest, and Pittsburgh the ninth.

These cities were not only industrial powerhouses, but were also centers of government, arts, learning and culture. Even today, universities like Johns Hopkins, Carnegie Mellon University, the University of Pittsburgh, and Case Western Reserve are among America's greatest. The recent controversy over selling the collection of the Detroit Institute of Arts serves to remind us of its importance, not only to the world of art, but to its community. They were also centers of upward mobility, as generations of immigrants—from inside and outside the United States—came there, found decent-paying, albeit dirty and sometimes dangerous work, and propelled their children into the American middle class. The cities were polluted and far from pretty, yet they were vital centers of unprecedented opportunity (Figure 1.1).

As early as the 1920s, automobile ownership and suburban growth were already beginning to erode urban supremacy. The Great Depression, which froze pre-existing patterns for over a decade, was followed by World War II, when the conversion of American industry into a powerful war machine gave cities a new, but brief lease on vitality and prosperity. As the nation demobilized at the end of the war, industrial cities

Figure 1.1 Southside Pittsburgh, circa 1940
Source: Photo by Jack Delano, Library of Congress, Prints and Photographs Division, FSA/OWI Collection.

were in many respects tired, run-down places, which had seen little growth or investment for nearly two decades. As the nation embraced the automobile with a passion, the stage was set for their collapse.

Between the late 1940s and the 1980s, a series of radical changes transformed cities from the nation's powerhouse to its urban problem. Many different factors contributed to that transformation. Suburbanization took off soon after the end of World War II, with thousands of new homes built on former cornfields and apple orchards across the country. Nassau County, east of New York City, saw its population grow from 400,000 to nearly 700,000 during the late 1940s and to 1.3 million by 1960. Simultaneously, America's population center moved from the north and east to the south and west. Since 1950, as the population of the United States has roughly doubled, that of Florida, California, Arizona, and Texas has quadrupled. Phoenix has gone from a city of 100,000 to one of nearly 1.5 million.

Although urban manufacturing in the Northeast and Midwest was still strong at the end of World War II, its days were numbered. Obsolete plants and equipment, coupled with competition from the suburbs, the South, and eventually overseas, led to the collapse of historic industries from the 1960s through the 1980s, as not only large-scale heavy industries such as steel or automobiles, but also much smaller-scale manufacturing, largely disappeared from the cities. These industries not only had provided the jobs for the city's population, but also had occupied large parts of each city's land mass. The collapse of manufacturing left the cities not only with widespread unemployment, but with the vast physical residue of their historic industrialization.

Overlaid on these changes is the pervasive effect of race, the seemingly permanent elephant in the national living room. Black in-migration and white flight paralleled the collapse of the urban industrial base. Although racial conflict was an undercurrent in America's urban history long before the riots of the 1960s, the riots moved it into the open, as the Kerner Commission warned: "Our nation is moving toward two societies, one black, one white—separate and unequal."[1] Fifty years later things have changed in many respects, but have remained much the same in others.

Government was not indifferent to these changes. The Urban Renewal program pumped some $60 billion (in 2014 dollars) into the redevelopment of older cities in the 1950s and 1960s, while a host of other short-lived initiatives, including the War on Poverty, Model Cities, and Urban Development Action Grants (UDAG) were rolled out during the 1960s and 1970s. Some were useful, but modest in their scale and impact. The Urban Renewal program was far more ambitious, but grounded in flawed premises about the reasons for urban decline and misguided prescriptions for its reversal, thus, it was largely ineffective. As John Teaford has written:

> By the early 1960s, however, skeptics were questioning the merits of federally subsidized urban renewal, and ten years later the program generally evoked images of destruction and delay rather than renaissance and reconstruction. By the time it died in 1974, the federal urban renewal program was much maligned and could claim at best mixed results.[2]

When the first Remaking Cities Conference took place in Pittsburgh in 1988, the view from the United States was not a promising one. Almost every older city had lost population since the 1950s, and abandonment of old buildings had become endemic. Their manufacturing bases had sharply declined, much of their middle class had decamped for suburbia, and the remaining population was far poorer than that of their suburban neighbors. While many participants in the conference presented scattered revitalization success stories, usually sustained with public funds, the overall picture was one of sustained decline.

From 1985 to 2015: Era of Change

There is no way to pinpoint an exact moment when the trajectories of America's older cities began to change, but it is clear that the decades of the 1990s and 2000s saw a dramatic change. While a few older cities, most notably New York City and Boston,[3] had already shown strong revival, since the 1990s, revival has spread to city after city, including many that had been all but left for dead in earlier years. In the late 1980s, Washington, D.C., was widely known as "the murder capital of the world" with a downtown that was "dull, dirty, and dangerous."[4] Today not only downtown, but large parts of the district are vibrant and exciting. In a dramatic reversal, the city's population is growing by 10,000–15,000 people per year.

Washington, D.C., as the center of government for the wealthiest and most powerful nation in the world and a mecca for lobbyists, non-profit organizations, government contractors, and think tanks, may be an extreme case, but is far from unique. Pittsburgh has become the poster child for Rust Belt revival, but Baltimore, Philadelphia, and St. Louis are also experiencing highly visible change. Buildings have been restored and new ones constructed, new stores and restaurants open, and thousands of people are moving into these cities to live and work.

Like their earlier decline, the reasons for the cities' turnaround are complicated, and reflect economic, generational, and other forces. One factor has been the growth in what is often called the knowledge economy. As universities and medical centers have grown into behemoths, they have drawn billions of dollars and thousands of highly-skilled people to them; Johns Hopkins in Baltimore and the University of Pittsburgh Medical Center (UPMC) in Pittsburgh have become the dominant economic engines of those two cities. Over the past decade, Baltimore has added 25,000 jobs in health care and education, to the point where they now make up almost two out of every five jobs in the city. Counting the multipliers generated by spending, spin-offs, and secondary employment, it is likely that these two sectors account for two-thirds or more of the urban economy, with tourism and entertainment likely to account for much of the rest. The picture is similar in Pittsburgh, where education and health care have grown by 30,000 jobs over the past decade. UPMC has become not only the largest employer in Pittsburgh, but in all of Western Pennsylvania. In Buffalo, the health care sector provides nearly one-quarter of all the jobs in the city.[5] These once-industrial cities have truly become post-industrial cities.

The economic shift is paralleled by an even more significant change in how generations of Americans see their cities. The mindset that led middle- and upper-income families to flee the cities in the 1960s and 1970s has changed; younger people today, largely raised in the suburbs, see cities as desirable and a destination of choice. Well-educated, highly-skilled people who have reached adulthood during the past ten to fifteen years, members of what has come to be known as the millennial generation, are flocking to the cities in unprecedented numbers. While Washington, D.C., grew by 13 percent between 2000 and 2013, its population aged 25–34 with BA/BS or higher degrees more than doubled, going from 51,000 to nearly 113,000. Although that demographic makes up only 4 percent of the nation's population, they were 17 percent of Washington's entire population in 2013 and at the current rate of increase will exceed 20 percent of the city's population by 2020. The same trend is visible in other formerly-industrial cities. Pittsburgh has seen that demographic increase by 60 percent or 12,000 since 2000; millennials with college degrees now make up 11 percent of the city's population.

Millenials seek out distinctive urban assets: high density, walkability, historic and architectural character, and a rich mixture of land and building uses. Areas that share those features have been transformed. For example, Washington Avenue, once St. Louis' garment district and all but abandoned twenty years ago, is now a vibrant shopping and entertainment district with thousands of residents living in restored factories and warehouses (Figure 1.2). Transformation is not without its problems; as the New Orleans case study describes, it can be a daunting challenge to preserve the valued features of a city's culture and traditions in the face of change.

These urban assets were there all along, but it took new eyes to see them. It also took increased safety and reduced crime to make urban assets more approachable to these new populations. Violent crime has plummeted in many cities: Washington, D.C., saw nearly five hundred murders annually during the 1980s and early 1990s, but in 2012 there were fewer than one hundred. The reduction in crime in many industrial cities is less dramatic, but still significant. For example, the number of violent crimes has declined by over 50 percent since the early 1990s in both Baltimore and Pittsburgh.

Figure 1.2 Washington Avenue in St. Louis, MO
Source: Google Earth, 2013.

However real this transformation appears, it is inconsistent, uneven, and unequal. Pittsburgh is doing far better than Cleveland and Detroit in its ability to attract new populations and new investment, while many small cities like Flint, MI, and Youngstown, OH, that lack the research universities and medical centers that fuel growth in Pittsburgh and Baltimore, are faring far worse.[6] In these cities the transformation is spatially uneven. Downtowns and areas around major universities and medical centers, along with a few nearby neighborhoods with exceptional historic or architectural features, are seeing dramatic revival. However, these areas typically make up less than 10 percent of a city's land area; most neighborhoods in cities like Buffalo and Milwaukee are declining, or at best holding their own.

In most post-industrial cities only a few areas offer what are widely seen as distinctive urban assets. Most cities are made up of neighborhoods of single family houses, which may be row houses in Baltimore or Philadelphia, or detached houses in Cleveland, Buffalo, and Detroit (Figure 1.3). These areas lack the density and variety of uses, as well as public transportation that draw millennials to the central core. As the core revives, the historically working-class and middle-income neighborhoods are more likely to experience decline than gentrification.

While jobs are created primarily within the central core, they are often filled by new in-migrants or suburban commuters rather than city residents. Of 267,000 jobs in Pittsburgh in 2011, 200,000 or 75 percent are held by commuters. Since 2002, as the city gained over 20,000 jobs, the number of Pittsburgh residents working inside the city has fallen by 5,000. Meanwhile, the number of jobs in most cities outside the central core, including what's left of their manufacturing base, is declining. Among large post-industrial cities, only Milwaukee has as much as 10 percent of its job base today in manufacturing. As the Milwaukee case study in Chapter 4 describes, that city is now using the remaining manufacturing base as a strategy to rebuild its economy.

Figure 1.3 Neighborhoods like Woodbridge in Detroit, MI, are at risk
Source: Photo by Andrew Jameson, Wikimedia Common.

US cities are becoming more and more polarized. An increasingly affluent central core is ringed by struggling and often declining single family neighborhoods. The polarization is racial as well as spatial and economic. Since 2000, the income gap between African-American and Caucasian households in reviving post-industrial cities, exacerbated by the accelerating flight of middle-class black households from the cities to the suburbs, has widened into a chasm. It is important to celebrate the revival that has taken place, but equally important to recognize its limitations and the very real challenges that have come in its wake.

The Challenge of the Future

The challenge facing America's post-industrial cities is whether or not they can build on the successes of recent years and find a path to becoming cities that are sustainable centers of economic activity in the global economy. Will they be able to restore their physical fabric, rebuild their infrastructure, create governance systems that are appropriate to today's conditions, and above all, build an equitable social and economic fabric that enables all of their residents to benefit from their restored growth and prosperity? Can post-industrial cities play a role in the twenty-first century that parallels the role they played under very different circumstances in the nineteenth and early twentieth centuries?

The first challenge is that of repositioning the city in the global economy. The most successful cities are those that have done so, although often in ways not replicable by others. New York City, the global crossroads, and Washington, D.C., the center of national power, are truly *sui generis*, and offer few lessons for other cities. The questions are twofold: (1) will an economic base built primarily on universities and medical centers, and secondarily on tourism and entertainment, provide a sustainable basis for urban repositioning?; and (2) are there viable alternatives to those sectors as a basis for the post-industrial urban economy?

The answers are as yet unclear. Those robust sectors may be able to foster sustainable economic success in a handful of cities graced with institutions that are indeed globally competitive, such as Pittsburgh and Baltimore. Whether that success is replicable in cities that lack such institutions is doubtful; a community college or community hospital creates few spin-offs and little secondary economic activity. While small cities located close to a major metropolis can sometimes piggy-back on regional growth, like Lancaster, PA, or Lowell, MA, cities that lack the assets to compete globally may be unable to escape long-term distress unless they can either develop those assets, a difficult proposition, or re-establish their historic status as the economic center of their region, perhaps even more difficult.[7]

Alternate economic options seem limited. Manufacturing, while reviving in the United States, is far more technology-intensive than labor-intensive today, and is unlikely to provide more than a handful of the jobs needed for urban revival. Similarly, technology sectors, while growing in a handful of cities, are still modest. No post-industrial city has a high-tech sector remotely comparable to those in cities like San Francisco, Seattle, and Austin. Moreover, as Berkeley economist Enrico Moretti argues, technology and innovation today are not locationally neutral, but are drawn to hubs that offer an entire supportive eco-system.[8]

The second challenge is to rebuild the physical form of the city in the fashion that best responds to the emerging needs and demands of twenty-first-century economic and demographic realities. Much of the physical form of the Victorian city is exceptionally well suited to those demands. High-density, walkable downtowns with buildings that are adaptable to a variety of uses and compact, distinctive neighborhoods like St. Louis' Central West End or Buffalo's Allentown are well positioned for success in a post-industrial world. The industrial buildings of that era have proven readily adaptable to a host of twenty-first-century uses (Figure 1.4). The Buffalo case study in Chapter 2 describes how that city is changing both its physical form and economic engines to respond to emerging realities.

Figure 1.4 An 1890s warehouse converted into lofts, St. Louis, MO
Source: Photo by Publichall, Wikimedia Commons.

At the same time, these areas typically make up only a small part of the land mass of the post-industrial city. Buffalo may have Allentown, but it also has areas like Broadway-Fillmore, with hundreds of boarded-up houses and vacant lots, where the remaining homes have little architectural or historical value. In addition to derelict areas that are no longer neighborhoods by any serious criterion, and growing expanses of vacant land with little apparent reuse value, cities like Buffalo have numerous neighborhoods that remain at risk, where the physical and social fabric is fraying and abandoned houses are appearing on once-intact blocks. Non-residential areas, particularly neighborhood shopping streets that served most residents before car ownership became widespread, and industrial sites left over from these cities' manufacturing heyday, are their own distinct challenge. Reusing vacant land (Figure 1.5), rebuilding disinvested areas, and stabilizing areas at risk of market collapse are all far more challenging tasks than revitalizing downtowns and the nearby architecturally distinguished neighborhoods.

When one thinks about the challenges facing post-industrial cities, it becomes apparent that the difficulties are compounded by obsolete, dysfunctional systems of finance, governance, and planning through which cities are being forced to confront their challenges. While cities are no longer self-contained economic or physical entities, they have become parts of ever-growing regions made up of a multiplicity of interdependent entities, and their governing structures have not changed to reflect this reality. Few regions in the United States, particularly those that include post-industrial cities, have any effective regional governance. Fragmentation and a philosophy of "beggar thy neighbor" are still the norm. Allegheny County, with a population of 1.2 million, contains 130 separate cities, boroughs, and townships (Figure 1.6), with median house values ranging from nearly $600,000 in Sewickley Heights to barely $10,000 in Braddock. Despite the political fragmentation of its region, Pittsburgh has been able to build strong regional links and public–private partnerships, which have played a significant role in its revitalization.

Figure 1.5 Monterey Street in Detroit, MI
Source: Image by Google Earth, 2013.

Figure 1.6 Allegheny County in Pennsylvania with 130 separate municipalities
Source: Map by Marantha Dawkins, courtesy of Remaking Cities Institute.

The absence of effective regional governance hampers efforts to build strong economic engines, to address the need for greater resilience in the face of climate change and the increasing risk of natural disaster, and to rebuild obsolete, crumbling infrastructure. At the same time, fiscal and civic considerations dictate that the need for municipal reform is great in terms of empowering city residents, neighborhood organizations and community development corporations to take greater responsibility for reshaping their communities.

Cities in the United States operate under fiscal constraints that make it difficult for them to provide the basic services their citizens need, let alone invest meaningful resources in the future. Despite their low property values and their residents' low incomes, cities are almost entirely dependent on local property taxes, supplemented in some states by modest wage or sales taxes, to cover their costs. In contrast to the United Kingdom, where equalization of fiscal conditions is a major central government commitment, few states make more than token gestures in this direction. The limited vestiges of federal revenue sharing in the form of the Community Development Block Grant program continue to shrink; this past year, Pittsburgh received $13 million compared to $22 million in 2001, a 56 percent cut when adjusted for inflation.[9]

At the same time, all of America's post-industrial cities face the overarching challenge of how to become not only a more prosperous city, but a more just city, a city, as Susan Fainstein puts it, which fosters democracy, diversity, and opportunity.[10] As America's older cities have moved toward the post-industrial future, they have also become more unequal with respect to their distribution of income, their spatial segregation by economic status, the economic disparities of their neighborhoods, and access of their residents to the jobs being created through their post-industrial transition. These cities risk becoming bipolar cities, in which a few areas grow and thrive while much of the remainder of the city continues to decline, and in which symbolic rather than physical walls (as was the case in medieval Europe) are erected to separate the two.

Countering the forces pushing cities toward polarization is a daunting task for America's post-industrial cities. Not only is much of the trend driven by national and global, rather than local forces, but the ability of the cities to address even those forces that may be within their control is hampered by fiscal and legal constraints, regional fragmentation, as well as fragmentation among the institutions that must come together. Collaboration among such disparate institutions as school districts, community colleges, planning agencies, financial institutions, corporations, and more will be necessary if this challenge is to be successfully addressed. It is heartening that growing numbers of mayors like Pittsburgh's Bill Peduto and New York's Bill de Blasio, as well as other public and private sector leaders, are no longer just talking about these issues, but are taking steps to address them.

Notes

1   *Report of the National Advisory Commission on Civil Disorders* (New York: Bantam Books, 1968), 1–29, available at: www.eisenhowerfoundation.org/docs/kerner.pdf (accessed August 3, 2015).
2   John C. Teaford, "Urban Renewal and its Aftermath," *Housing Policy Debate* 11(2) (2000), 443. While a great deal was written about the urban renewal program *in medias res*, particularly in the 1960s, and while a number of monographs have been published about the workings of the program in individual communities, I find it amazing that despite the massive scale of this program and its impact on urban America, no serious extended study of the program has ever been written.
3   Although both New York and Boston had strong manufacturing bases, neither had been predominately industrial cities. Still, it is important to remember, when looking at their current vitality, that both cities were in severe crisis during the 1960s and 1970s.
4   Gerry Widdicombe, "The Fall and Rise of Downtown DC," *The Urbanist*, Issue 488, January 2010.
5   Data for jobs and workers comes from the US Census Longitudinal Employer-Household Dynamics Program and covers the period from 2002 to 2011. Available at: http://onthemap.ces.census.gov/
6   Although even Flint and Youngstown are seeing flickers of similar investment; by 2014, both cities sported at least one downtown espresso place (although no Starbucks), and a smattering of new restaurants, serving the small pool of homegrown members of the "creative class" in those cities.
7   It is important to remember that in their heyday, American industrial cities were not only manufacturing centers, but were also regional centers of business, finance, and retail trade and services, a role that diminished dramatically as well between the 1950s and the 1980s, as large parts of those sectors suburbanized.
8   Enrico Moretti, *The New Geography of Jobs* (Boston, MA: Houghton Mifflin Harcourt, 2012).
9   US Department of Housing and Urban Development, "CPD formula program allocations." Available at: http://portal.hud.gov/hudportal/HUD?src=/program_offices/comm_planning/about/budget
10 Susan Fainstein, *The Just City* (Ithaca, NY: Cornell University Press, 2010), p. 165.

2   Buffalo Case Study

Robert Shibley and Bradshaw Hovey
with Rachel Teaman

Introduction

Buffalo in 2015 is experiencing near-euphoria over what seems like a sudden change in fortune. The national media produced a spate of stories about Buffalo's comeback. Cranes are in the air in Buffalo's "Eds and Meds" hub, the Buffalo Niagara Medical Campus and at HarborCenter, a new hockey-oriented waterfront attraction. Neighborhoods are being reborn, long-time expatriates are coming home, newcomers are arriving, housing values are up, unemployment is down and businesses are being created. Suddenly, Buffalo is hip (Figure 2.1).

Writing comeback stories, however, is a tricky business. Such stories can make it seem like everything has changed, that it has changed overnight, and that it has changed for

Figure 2.1 Buffalo's resurgence is defined by a return to the urban core, the revitalization of its neighborhoods, and the restoration and public reconnection to its waterways
Source: Photo by Douglas Levere, provided by the University at Buffalo.

everyone. Buffalonians have been working on the remaking of their city for decades, yet it remains a work in progress and is delivering benefits quite unevenly to the citizens of the city and region.

Comeback stories can obscure rather than explain how change occurs. In Buffalo, there was no single charismatic leader who led the charge, no corporate or philanthropic angel who paid the way, no single catalytic project and no single, historic turning point. Instead, there was a confluence of deeply embedded civic movements, public planning and implementation work, government policies and programs, fine-grained private initiatives and broad national and global trends that continue to make Buffalo more livable again.

If there was a single-leading factor, perhaps it was simply that there were people who loved the City of Buffalo so much, who believed it was like no other place anywhere else, that they stayed through the hard times and devoted themselves to making it better. It is hard to quantify such devotion to community, but Buffalo's experience suggests it is real nonetheless.

A series of powerful civic discourses drive planning, policy and action. Those conversations—over kitchen tables, in taverns and coffee shops, in thousands of planning meetings and public forums—have been persistent, repetitive, and hortatory. They have taken on organizational structure and became movements. They made the call for Buffalo to rebuild its urban core, save its historic architecture, restore its great Olmsted parks, reconnect to its vast waterfront, rebuild its neighborhoods, and reenergize its economy. They set the agenda for Buffalo's transformation (Figure 2.2).

These civic discourses inform and gain strength from enlightened public sector planning. In the 1990s and 2000s, the City of Buffalo prepared for and then created an ensemble of plans for its downtown, waterfronts, Olmsted parks, and citywide redevelopment that continue to guide decision-making.[1] Anchor institutions banded together to plan the Buffalo Niagara Medical Campus, now a burgeoning reality.[2] The region planned to manage its metropolitan growth in a more rational way, develop waterfront greenways, promote cultural tourism, and protect watersheds.[3] The University at Buffalo created a three-campus plan and has already committed over $1 billion in its implementation, making higher education and public transit the spine of a regenerating region.[4] The governor demanded that the region come together to create a homegrown economic development strategy and rewarded the plans that emerged.[5]

There were major policies and programs as well. The Joint Schools Construction Fund invested $1.5 billion in Buffalo's aging public school buildngs. State and federal historic preservation tax credits (worth 40 percent of eligible costs) spurred reuse of dozens of other buildings. State and federal brownfields programs have paid for planning and the cleanup of many sites damaged in the region's industrial heyday.

Anchor institutions played major roles. The University at Buffalo (UB) grew rapidly after its absorption into the State University of New York system, exploding in the 1960s, stabilizing in the 1970s, joining the prestigious Association of American Universities in the 1980s, and maturing into a major public research university today. In the past ten years, UB has strengthened its relationship with the community and expanded its role in the growth of the region. Buffalo's health care systems struggled through the wrenching changes of the past three decades and with UB became key elements in the restructuring regional economy. Small firms, neighborhoods, civic groups, and individuals, impatient with the pace of change, created their own initiatives.

The city also began to leverage larger national or global trends that had long worked against it. Alan Ehrenhalt's "great inversion"[6] describes a back-to-the-city movement in the US that Buffalo is also experiencing. Local firms got the hang of selling to a global market. Advanced manufacturing began to fill the gap left by the demise of the old

Figure 2.2 More than forty years of aggressive and inclusive planning dialogue underlie the resurgence unfolding in Buffalo today
Source: Image courtesy of Urban Design Project, School of Architecture and Planning, University at Buffalo.

manufacturing. Capital that once had fled Buffalo began to return from higher-cost locations. Refugees and immigrants from around the globe animated the city's neighborhoods. Climate change may bring still more immigrants, both foreign and domestic. Buffalo has come back a long way from the depths of deindustrialization and decay. The story of how and why is not simple, and it still has a long way to go.

Brief History of the City

Buffalo's story is America's story. The city grew with the young nation, from frontier outpost to border village, canal town to rail town, commercial entrepot to industrial powerhouse. For much of the nineteenth century, Buffalo was gateway to the American West. In the twentieth century Buffalo was, like Detroit and Pittsburgh, part of the "arsenal of democracy" in the fight against fascism. Also like Detroit, Buffalo suffered the great agonies of racial division, suburban sprawl, and deindustrialization.

Buffalo was a tiny trading post when George Washington was elected President in 1789. It was a village of fewer than 2,000 when British soldiers gave it the torch in the War of

1812. After the Erie Canal opened in 1825, however, the village grew rapidly, quadrupling in population from 1820 to 1830 to nearly 8,700. Buffalo was incorporated as a city in 1832 and its growth continued, roughly doubling in population each decade through 1860. On the eve of the Civil War, Buffalo was the tenth largest city in the nation, just behind Chicago.

Like Chicago, Buffalo was transformed again and again by the rapid changes in economy and technology chronicled in William Cronon's magisterial *Nature's Metropolis*.[7] No sooner had canal transport created Buffalo than railways changed it again. The first non-stop rail service connecting New York to Buffalo opened in 1842, the same year Buffalonian Joseph Dart invented the grain elevator, an innovation that allowed wheat to be moved, not in burlap sacks, but in bulk in lake freighters and railway cars.

The same concatenation of raw goods, bulk transport, and finished products that made Buffalo a center of grain milling and brewing also gave it advantages in iron and steel making. Ore from Minnesota and coal from the Appalachians came together on ships and rails in Buffalo. In 1900, Lackawanna Iron and Steel Company moved its headquarters from Scranton, PA, to West Seneca, NY, where they would make steel for the next eighty-two years.[8]

Waves of European immigration fueled Buffalo's commercial and industrial growth, first Germans and Irish, later Italians, Poles and other Eastern Europeans. Buffalo emerged as an ethnically segregated city—English, Scots and Canadians on one side, Germans on another, Irish on another, Poles and Italians landing in their own enclaves. The city added roughly 100,000 new residents in each of the last two decades of the century. In 1901, when Buffalo hosted the Pan-American Exposition, the population was 350,000, making it the eighth largest city in the US.

Buffalo's growth continued through mid-twentieth century, powered in part by hydro-electricity generated at Niagara Falls. The city became a hub for rail and lake shipping and a center of auto and aircraft manufacturing. During World War II, workers at the Curtiss-Wright Company built thousands of P-40 Warhawk fighter and C-46 cargo planes.

Buffalo's population peaked at 580,000 in 1950, but trends that would push the city's long decline had already taken hold. Suburbanization, often understood as a phenomenon of the 1950s and later, began in Buffalo in the 1920s with the growth of "streetcar suburbs" in Kenmore and Snyder. The move to the Sunbelt, widely recognized by the 1970s,[9] was apparent by the 1960 census when Los Angeles, Houston, San Francisco, Dallas, San Antonio, San Diego, and Seattle all surpassed Buffalo, ranked twentieth in population. Likewise, manufacturers there worked to substitute technology for labor long before there was talk of "deindustrialization."

There are those who locate the critical hinge in Buffalo history at the opening of the St. Lawrence Seaway in 1959. That feat of infrastructure engineering steered water-borne freight away from Buffalo and its archipelago of concrete grain silos. One of the bitter ironies in Buffalo's history was that the Skyway, an elevated highway bridge, intended to let lake freighters pass below car traffic, was completed about the same time large ships stopped coming altogether.[10] But many other factors contributed to the decline after the Seaway hinge. The ruthless mobility of capital, the bitter racial conflicts that fed white flight, the entropic path of suburbanization all ate away at the heart of Buffalo.

Local leaders struggled through much of the latter twentieth century to find a way to stop the slide. Highway building, slum clearance, public housing, downtown redevelopment schemes, industrial development agencies, federal community development subsidies, downtown stadia and arenas—all the supposedly forward-looking policies of those eras—failed to stop the loss of jobs, people, and homes. By the 1990s, however, the downward spiral began to slow and is actually starting to trend up in the second decade of the twenty-first century. The city and region have come to understand how to build on their assets and attend to the basics to establish a better quality of life.

The City in 1985

Physical Form and Conditions

Buffalo in mid-1985 was part of a region shrinking overall, growing at the edges, decaying in the middle, and seeing the first green shoots of rebirth at the center. Unfortunately, at that moment in the city's history the balance of these contradictory forces still leaned in favor of decay and dispersion.

The fundamental character of the city, nevertheless, remained intact. The street plan designed in 1804 by Joseph Ellicott, colleague of Pierre Charles L'Enfant, master planner of Washington, DC, provided a robust armature for nearly two centuries of growth. Great radial streets connected the city with its hinterland and converged on two grand central squares. The grid that intersected Ellicott's hub and spokes reliably oriented the city to the Buffalo River, Lake Erie, and the Niagara River waterfronts.

The plan, however, suffered a variety of insults over the years. A parking garage, a convention center and, in 1984, a hotel atrium amputated Genesee Street, one of the city's great vistas to the waterfront. The urban renewal projects of the 1960s had done similar damage, cutting a second radial to facilitate office tower and shopping mall construction, and obliterating the once vital Shelton Square.

Buffalo's citywide park and parkway system, designed in the 1870s by Frederick Law Olmsted, also remained what it had been—with several egregious exceptions. The park system constitutes a system of spaces that gave the city its distinct phenomenology, its unique character. But the post-war urgency to reduce traffic congestion, to save the declining center city, and paradoxically to "open" up the suburbs for development took its toll. A new expressway took tree-lined Humboldt Parkway as a path of least resistance to the suburbs, cutting neighborhoods in two in the process. The Scajaquada Expressway displaced the Bridle Path in Delaware Park. And the construction of the Niagara Thruway separated the community from the Niagara River for miles.

For all this, the planners' mantra of "Ellicott, Olmsted and the water" described much of what still made the City of Buffalo special. It made the city legible and coherent, as well as connecting one neighborhood to another, to downtown, and to the water. It provided dynamic views and because of the varied parcel geometries they produced, invited great architecture, not only great commercial and public buildings by celebrated designers but also a beautiful vernacular building stock (Figure 2.3). "The Best-Planned City in America" was Olmsted's boast about his (and Ellicott's) designs but also an aspiration for twentieth-century citizens.

In 1985, Buffalo's $500 million light-rail line opened for passengers. It was to be the spine of a stronger rail and bus transit system and the link between the city center and the new university campus in suburban Amherst. But funding fell short and so did the light rail. When federal transit operating subsidies were cut under President Reagan, resources were spread even thinner. The proportion of commuters using transit plummeted from 29 percent in 1980 to 11 percent in 1990.[11]

A downtown business improvement district, Buffalo Place Inc., was created to manage, maintain, and promote the new 1.2-mile pedestrian transit mall and to provide new leadership for a downtown revival still in its infancy. But the five big department stores closed one by one throughout the 1980s, victim as much to trends in the retail industry as anything going on downtown.

Elliott, Olmstead, and the Water

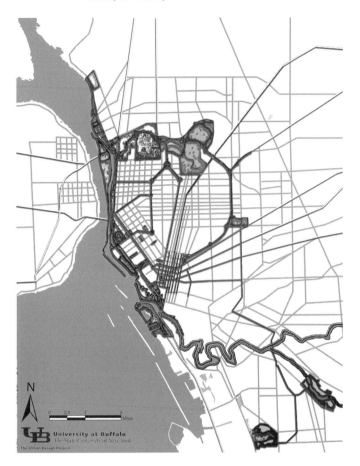

Figure 2.3 The City of Buffalo is built on the structure of Ellicott's radial and grid street plan, Olmsted's network of parks and parkways, and its location on the water, a combination resulting in what Olmsted called "the best planned city in America."
Source: Image provided by The Urban Design Project, School of Architecture and Planning, University at Buffalo.

City government underwrote a "retail design competition" to understand the potential for downtown retail redevelopment and to restore Lafayette Square.[12] Fifty-two teams entered designs from over twenty states and four countries in 1986. But the prizes were barely awarded before Pyramid Corp. built a huge mall on a suburban highway interchange. Walden Galleria, still the region's largest and busiest retail destination, opened in 1989, extinguishing hopes for a downtown shopping revival. The new Lafayette Square, however, became home for a long-running Thursday in the Square concert series that reintroduced tens of thousands of people to downtown, especially young people.

Efforts continued to create a "Theater District" a few blocks north of Lafayette Square on Main Street. The projects were initially framed in the late 1970s by a graduate urban design studio led by Harold L. Cohen, Dean of the UB School of Architecture and Environmental Design. The keystone property, the historic Shea's Buffalo Theater, had been saved from the wrecker's ball only a few years before. Development of apartments in an adjacent building and restoration of the Market Arcade, a 1990s shopping mall, among other projects, went forward.

Planning was underway in 1985 to build a new downtown baseball stadium for the minor league Buffalo Bisons. The ballpark, opened in April 1988, was designed to grow from 21,000 seats to more than 40,000 in the event team owners were able to land a major league franchise. However, the cost of acquiring franchises escalated, and Buffalo was priced out of the competition.

City government sunk federal dollars into residential infill projects, starting with high quality single-family homes near City Hall in Georgia-Prospect. A more scattered development in the Pratt-Willert neighborhood offered frame houses with a more suburban image. Hundreds of new homes followed but none with the quality of architecture, site design or lasting impact of Georgia-Prospect.

In Waterfront Village developers offered upscale condos with lakefront vistas within walking distance of downtown. In the late 1970s huge stones were sunk in the harbor to create a spit of solid land where years before bulk cargo ships had docked. The marina they created became one of the most popular summertime locations in town, but the homes nearby have private frontages on the water limiting public access.

In the same year, the first leg of Interstate I-990, a northern spur of Buffalo's suburban beltway, opened, making possible several more decades of residential, office and retail development on the periphery of the metropolis. The decision to build UB's new campus in suburban Amherst was perhaps the most controversial development decision in the history of Buffalo. Many believed—and still believe—it should have been built downtown or on Buffalo's waterfront.

The region continued to sprawl (Figure 2.4). City infill projects were a drop in the bucket compared to suburban developments and not enough to offset ongoing abandonment

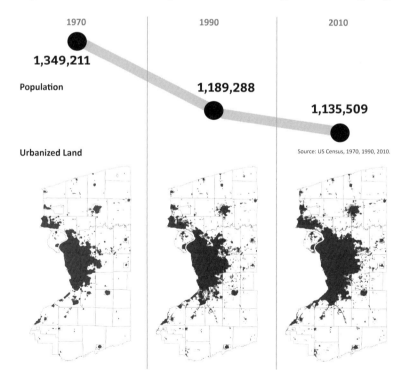

Figure 2.4 The region's decades-long population slide combined with a 166-square-mile increase in urbanized land compounded the challenge of sprawl between 1970 and 2010

Source: Image provided by UB Regional Institute, School of Architecture and Planning, University at Buffalo.

and demolition. Nearly 1,500 single-family homes were built in the two-county region in 1985, but less than 2.5 percent of those were in the city. Indeed, through 2015, the city share of regional single-family housing starts was never much above 5 percent and usually below.

Demographics

In the 1950s and 1960s, the population of metropolitan Buffalo—Erie and Niagara Counties—continued to grow rapidly as soldiers returned from World War II and Korea, moved to the suburbs, and had children. The regional population grew by nearly 218,000 by 1960, with another 42,000 people added by the 1970 census. During the same period, the population of the central city declined by more than 117,000[13] even as the proportion of African-Americans more than doubled to about 20 percent.

After 1970, what had been a move to the suburbs also became a migration to other parts of the nation. Buffalo lost another 105,000 people during the 1970s but the two-county region had a net loss almost as great.[14] Even before Bethlehem Steel closed, industrial enterprises were cutting back or closing down. By 1985, the regional population was about 1.2 million, down from nearly 1.35 million just fifteen years earlier; and Buffalo's population was now less than three-fifths what it had been at its peak in 1950.[15] By 1985, Buffalo was more than one-quarter African-American—up from just 3 percent before World War II and an influx of Hispanic residents, mainly from Puerto Rico, had begun.

Economy

The final shutdown at Bethlehem Steel in 1982, in the teeth of the Reagan recession, punctuated a much broader-based transition in the Buffalo economy, one it shared, not only with other "Rust Belt" cities but also with the nation and the western industrialized world. Manufacturing jobs as a proportion of all employment had been declining since the last quarter of the nineteenth century, more steeply since World War II, and still more precipitously after about 1980. Bethlehem Steel's closure was a shock but not a surprise. Workers knew the company had quit reinvesting in the Lackawanna plant years before and had shifted capital for new equipment to other locations. Other factories closed. In 1985, windshield-wiper maker Trico Products Corp. began to shift production to the Texas-Mexico border, and a few years later all 3,000 jobs had been shipped out of Buffalo.

These upheavals were traumatic for Buffalo and other legacy cities that had invested heavily in industry, but the changes should be understood in the context of an evolving economy, not merely a shrinking one. The relative decline of manufacturing was accompanied by growth in the "service sector." This was exemplified in 1985 by the entry of historic hometown banks—Liberty National, Buffalo Savings Bank and Erie County Savings Bank—into the national banking market as Norstar, Goldome, and Empire. Their growth gave rise to the mid-1980s Main-Genesee urban renewal project that produced several new office towers, Fountain Plaza, and the hotel atrium on the Genesee radial street. Buffalo's emergence as a financial center, unfortunately, was cut short by the savings and loan crisis of the late 1980s and early 1990s.

The City in 2015

There is an undeniable mood of optimism across the city and region in 2015. Governor Andrew Cuomo delivered $1 billion in economic development. Ground was broken on Solar City, the largest production facility of photovoltaic panels in the western hemisphere, located on the site of the former Republic Steel plant. Even Buffalo's most skeptical citizens see fundamental change.

The most recent population estimates for Erie County showed that the net change from the year before was positive, if only by a few hundred residents.[16] For a county that has been losing population steadily for forty-five years, that is good news. Over 6,000 jobs were created in the region in 2014.[17] It is a trend that, if continued, could turn around the population decline. The West Side of Buffalo—not long ago seemingly doomed to fatal abandonment and demolition—is a seller's market in 2015. It is plausible that Buffalo, as well as the region's historic town centers and villages, will become denser, more vibrant and more sustainable.

That said, everything is not great. Nearly 1,000 Buffalo Public School students fail to graduate each year.[18] An unemployment rate that is the lowest in seven years masks the reality of thousands who have fallen out of the labor force entirely. Huge swaths of Buffalo's East Side are mostly vacant with empty lots, tall weeds, and opportunistic trees. Buffalo remains one of the poorest cities in the nation.[19] High rates of obesity, diabetes, heart disease, and other chronic illness are concerning.

Physical Form and Conditions

Buffalo today truly is "a city of two tales," as one citizen said at a public meeting early in 2015 (with apologies to Charles Dickens). Parts of the city are booming with construction and brimming with new people and energy. Other parts of the city are dormant, decaying, or vacant. Still others are waiting for the day when—perhaps if—the wave of reinvestment hits them. Buffalonians are in a position to worry about gentrification and abandonment simultaneously.

Every day in 2015 seems to bring another positive story about a project to retrofit old industrial buildings for apartments, develop a new hotel, open a new restaurant, or purchase an apartment complex for renovations and higher rents. While the 1980s and 1990s saw federally subsidized residential infill projects, such as HOPE VI, the trend in 2015 is toward reuse of old industrial buildings for up-scale apartments supported by historic preservation tax credits. Often, these projects are in locations previously thought undesirable.

Perhaps the most striking example of such change has been the emergence of Larkinville. What had been in 2000 a collection of vacant or underused industrial, warehouse, and related neighborhood buildings with the canal-era moniker of "The Hydraulics," Larkinville in 2015 is a vibrant node of office employment a mile east of downtown with restaurants, food trucks, special events, a post-modern town square, and a few thousand workers daily—all orchestrated by developer and civic leader Howard Zemsky.

Buffalo was in the midst of a hotel boom in 2015 with several recently opened, including an Embassy Suites in the comprehensive retrofit of a former federal office building. Several are under construction, including one in the new headquarters for Delaware North Companies, another at HarborCenter, and several more planned or proposed. The Hyatt Regency that occupied a block of Genesee Street in 1985 was up for a major renovation—but not to remove the offending atrium unfortunately.

Capital investment in the Buffalo Niagara Medical Campus in 2015 is robust with UB's new medical school, a new Children's Hospital, clinical facilities for Roswell Park Cancer Institute and a new medical office building all being built at the same time (Figure 2.5). This followed construction of a new joint UB-Kaleida Health facility to house a Clinical and Translational Research Center, the Gates Vascular Institute, and two other major new medical buildings. At the same time, Kaleida Health is planning the redevelopment of two vacant

Figure 2.5 Construction progresses downtown on the University at Buffalo's state-of-the-art medical
          school, set to open in 2017. UB's emerging downtown campus on the Buffalo Niagara
          Medical Campus has played a major role in revitalizing the urban core.
Source: Image by Douglas Levere, provided by University at Buffalo.

century-old hospital complexes. In a less vibrant real estate market—any other time in the
past forty years—the two properties would have sat vacant for a long time. Instead, interest
is high in developing major mixed-use projects led by housing.

Overall, $9 billion in capital projects were completed, under construction, or planned in
or near downtown in 2015.[20] More than half of those projects were residential or mixed-
use. The solar-panel facility at Riverbend accounted for $5 billion.[21] That project symbolizes
the progress the region has made in redeveloping brownfields. More than 1,200 acres of
contaminated land on 113 sites—including the 100-acre Solar City site—have been
reclaimed.[22]

Unfortunately, centrifugal forces continue to offset development in the core. The same
proportion of new housing units is projected for construction in the suburbs—95 percent
or more—in 2015 as thirty years ago in 1985.[23] Suburban office and retail expansion also
contributed to the trend. Sprawl, as noted earlier, was a feature of regional development
from the 1950s, if not before. After 1970, however, outward expansion continued even as

the region lost residents. The population of Erie County and its neighbor, Niagara County, fell 16 percent from 1970 to 2010 while the urbanized area grew by 78 percent.[24]

The impacts of "sprawl without growth" have been severe. Suburban development and center-city abandonment left the City of Buffalo with a huge overhang of vacant homes, massive demolition costs, and a growing inventory of vacant land. Between 1970 and 2010, 55,000 new households were created while 185,000 new homes were built.[25] Approximately 45,000 units were demolished in the same period and there may still be as many as 45,000 units of vacant housing. This left many neighborhoods pockmarked with boarded-up houses and vacant lots and gouged a huge hole in the East Side that is now reverting to an urban prairie. Buffalo's first-ring suburbs may be the next to decline with homes built in the 1950s and 1960s showing their wear, lacking contemporary amenities, and many occupied by older residents anxious to cash out and move. Who will buy their homes? To reverse these declines new investments in infrastructure and maintenance will be required, but unfortunately on a shrinking municipal tax base.

Demographics

The good news is that Buffalo's population decline, precipitous in the 1970s, slowed throughout the 1980s and 1990s and has more recently flattened out. There are signs—the 2015 Erie County population estimate, for example—that the trend may be reversing. The Buffalo Niagara region reached its peak population of more than 1.35 million in 1970.[26] By 2010, the figure had dropped to about 1.13 million. Notably, half of that decline occurred during the 1970s[27] and three-quarters before 1990. Since 2010, the region's population has stabilized, a trend for the city, as well.

There are other signs of life. Recent analysis of the Telestrain data set suggests that Richard Florida's "creative class" workers grew faster between 2000 and 2012 than in many other cities. Buffalo's share of people aged 20–29 years old, of young people with college education, of people with graduate degrees, and of high earners all increased relative to competing cities.

Buffalo has become more diverse. The population is about 50 percent Caucasian, 37 percent African-American and 10 percent Latino.[28] The foreign population has grown since 2000 with an influx of refugees from Burma, Nepal, Somalia, Iraq, Sudan, and elsewhere. Especially on Buffalo's West Side, immigrants are bringing new life to the city, stabilizing residential neighborhoods and commercial districts.[29] The region's international student population soared between 1985 and 2015. In 2013, the region's colleges and universities awarded more than 2,800 international student degrees, more than four times as many as conferred in the mid-1980s.[30]

Economy

The regional economy is also more diverse, moving away from over-reliance on manufacturing and toward a workforce that looks more like the country as a whole. The continuing transformation of the manufacturing economy—the sector is still relatively strong in Buffalo[31]—has combined with growth in health care, education, financial services, hospitality and tourism, and other sectors. However, employment in government has contracted.[32]

This was before Governor Andrew Cuomo advanced his initiative to support rebuilding the Western New York and Buffalo area economy. He first awarded the region's economic development strategy, *Plan for Prosperity*, over $100 million in state investments, followed by the "Buffalo Billion" to stimulate further growth in sectors like renewable energy. By early 2015, the state's $1 billion was projected to leverage an additional $7 billion in private capital with a total five-year economic impact of $11.3 billion and new employment of 14,000 (direct, indirect, and induced). So successful has been the Buffalo initiative that Cuomo has proposed a similar, competition-based economic development initiative for seven other regions across upstate New York. The state will award the winning regions with a total of $1.5 billion in state economic development funding. The Governor has clearly committed to the revitalization of the upstate New York economy.

Still, poverty remains an intractable problem for Buffalo. A 2013 Census estimate showed half of all children under 18 are living in poverty. Moreover, Buffalo's poverty profile has a distinct ethnic and racial tilt. The poverty rate for all households was 31.4 percent, but for African-Americans it was 41.2 percent, for Hispanics 46.9 percent, while for Caucasians is was only 19 percent.[33]

Transformation of the City (1985-2015)

What Went Right?

Buffalo's successes came from an alignment of civic discourses, official planning, major policies and programs, a fine-grain of do-it-yourself civic and business action, and national and global trends shifting in Buffalo's favor. Civic discourse led the way, setting the agenda for planning, policy, program, and action.

All of the major planning efforts of the 1980s, 1990s, and beyond include significant public participation. The public participated as individual citizens but also as advocates speaking for parks, watersheds, transit riders, downtown, ethnic groups, economic justice, fair housing, neighborhoods, architectural preservation, and good design. The dialogue with the now-educated public went on continuously, in conventional media, social media, and in "third places" like bars, and coffee shops.[34] The dialogue never stops and it continues to set the urban agenda.

People often say how they hate planning. Buffalonians have done a lot of it. It clarifies values. It organizes agreements to act. And it provides benchmarks against which to measure progress in implementation. It has become a cliché to say that plans gather dust on the shelf but to promise this new plan will not. But for all the skepticism, Buffalonians believe deeply in planning—not as an alternative to actions but as a way to organize for right actions.

The dialogues have the power to move controversy to consensus and to avoid error. Buffalo has what some consider a litany of past planning mistakes—highways, stadiums, university campuses, all in the wrong place or of the wrong design—that might not have been made had there been adequate public discourse.

Planning follows the citizens' lead. Starting in 1994, the City of Buffalo, Buffalo Place Inc.,[35] and the Urban Design Project at the University at Buffalo teamed to host a series of agenda-setting "summits" for downtown, neighborhoods, and waterfronts[36] that ultimately led to a full ensemble of plans under the rubric of the *Queen City in the 21st Century: Buffalo's Comprehensive Plan*. Adopted in 2006, the Comprehensive Plan gave rise to the Buffalo Green Code, a new unified development ordinance with a form-based zoning ordinance poised for adoption in 2015.

District planning supported public aims for economic development and diversification in the Theater District, Buffalo Niagara Medical Campus, the Erie Canal Harbor, Downtown, Larkinville, and the PUSH Green Development Zone. Billions in capital investments have been targeted for these specific projects thus avoiding the opportunist "throw paint on the canvas" development patterns of previous decades. Many projects were conceived first by University at Buffalo students, like the Theater District concept in 1978 or study for downtown housing in 1993.[37]

The medical campus, now emerging as a center of health care, innovation, and commercialization, was particularly important to the economic turnaround. Employment rose from 7,000 to 12,000 between 2002 and 2012 with 5,000 more expected by 2017. Leaders from Kaleida Health, Roswell Park Cancer Institute, the University at Buffalo, and other entities worked together to accomplish things they could not achieve by themselves.

The story of the Buffalo Olmsted Parks Conservancy illustrates how civic discourses led from talk to organization to planning to action. Citizens demanded a role in park planning in the early 1970s; the Delaware Park Steering Committee evolved into an advocacy group, Friends of Buffalo Olmsted Parks, and then into an operating not-for-profit that contracts with the City to maintain the parks and guides implementation of their restoration and management plan.

The Buffalo Niagara Riverkeeper is another example, evolving from a volunteer advocacy organization over several decades to become a mid-sized not-for-profit with the capacity to conduct research, oversee implementation of a greenway plan, guide green infrastructure development, and manage the implementation of the Buffalo River Remedial Action Plan, a plan to dredge toxic sediments from the Buffalo River. Since the cleanup, public infrastructure dollars have been invested in converting a 1.4-mile stretch of Ohio Street into a tree-lined, riverfront parkway linking Buffalo's inner and outer harbors.[38] Ongoing public discourse about expanding public access to the waterfront and repairing the environment drove the work during each phase of the process.

The Erie Canal Harbor Development Corporation heard the same discourse and responded with $300 million invested in the Canalside entertainment and cultural district, museum, recreation, hotel, restaurant, and retail development.

Anchor institutions each took their own pieces of the transformation. UB, for example, worked to build its research capacity, make its campuses better, and participate in development of the medical campus. UB leadership understood its efforts in the broader context of the civic conversation about the economic future of the city.

Similar work was undertaken by the Buffalo Urban Development Corporation for brownfield remediation; by the Richardson Center Corporation to instigate, plan and implement the reuse of H.H. Richardson's historic Buffalo State Hospital Complex; and by a special-purpose not-for-profit to restore and recreate a Frank Lloyd Wright masterpiece, the Darwin Martin house. All contributed to a metropolitan environment that is more competitive, healthier, more appealing, and more supportive of the good life for its citizens.

What Went Wrong?

One of the region's most vexing problems is the chronic poor performance of students in the Buffalo Public Schools. Graduation rates have hovered around 50 percent. The proportion of those who enter college is even smaller. Unemployment among poor and minority residents is high. The prospect of continuing—even deepening—intergenerational poverty looms large.

Unfortunately, the response from the community has been to engage in the bitterest kind of civic combat. Since 2014, the by-play on the board of education has been vicious, frequently personal and with racial undertones. While the daily newspaper conducted a crusade against "failing schools," corporate and philanthropic forces campaigned for charter schools, and the teachers union dug in its heels.

What is not widely acknowledged is that "failing schools" are coterminous with concentrations of poverty. The most reliable predictor of success in school is the socio-economic status in households of the students, but there is no remedy on the horizon that would break the city-suburban segregation of public education.[39] At this point it is not clear who or what will break the crippling public education stalemate facing Buffalo and other cities with high concentrations of poverty.

Equitable housing and economic policy are prerequisites for quality education. To be fair, the gap between affluent, highly educated professionals and poor and working-class people besets the US and the world. There may not be a local or regional solution. Then again, success with the Buffalo Niagara region's jobs-based economic strategy and job-training programs is a good place to start.

The Buffalo Niagara region has failed to contain the "sprawl without growth" that has persisted for nearly half a century. Local plans and zoning ordinances, for the most part, continue to allow development on the periphery of the region (Figure 2.6). There is no policy that addresses the imbalances among households formed, housing units built, and homes left vacant or demolished. A previous attempt to solve the problem in *The Erie-Niagara Regional Framework for Growth* (2006) foundered upon resistance to the idea of a two-county planning agency. The more recent effort, *One Region Forward* (2015), is a performance-based plan rather than a prescriptive plan that depends on voluntary action by municipalities and others to restrain sprawl. It is too soon to tell whether builders will continue to create new homes without worrying what happens to the old ones or that they are creating new energy and infrastructure maintenance demands in the form of larger homes with longer commutes. The regional Metropolitan Planning Organization embraces the plan but a stronger connection between politics, policy, and performance called for in *One Region Forward* is required.

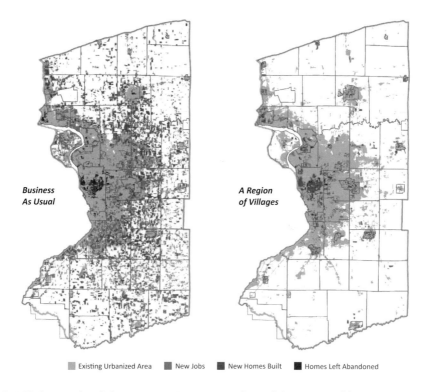

Business As Usual

A Region of Villages

Existing Urbanized Area   New Jobs   New Homes Built   Homes Left Abandoned

Figure 2.6 If the trends of the past continue, new jobs and homes would continue to grow on rural land with homes in first-ring suburbs and central cities abandoned. Alternatively, a "strong towns and villages" approach would put new jobs and homes in our city, town and village centers, strengthen transit connections and preserve open space and farmland.

Source: Image provided by UB Regional Institute, School of Architecture and Planning, University at Buffalo.

Lessons Learned

A number of conclusions can be drawn about the thirty years of downtown development, brownfield cleanup, neighborhood revitalization in Buffalo. These lessons are threaded throughout the chapter. Several stand out, however.

Engage the Public, Honor the Discourse, and Embrace Controversy

This is a truism in planning and, in many cases it's the law. Public participation is essential. When citizens set it, the public agenda has real clout and staying power. Planners and their elected bosses say they are all for public engagement. That doesn't mean they like it, but they depend on it. The ongoing civic conversations about downtown, neighborhoods, waterfront, parks, and architecture are what gives Buffalo's plans their power, strengthened by processes of engagement that inform planning. Also, because of transparency, decision-makers are kept honest. Controversy inevitably will come, but when embraced with openness in a public process, it can lead to better decisions.

Planning Works

The process of planning, even when it is redundant, allows the public and leaders to think through problems, clarify values, expand constituencies, influence politics and focus attention setting the stage for appropriate action. Plans, when published, are valuable but the planning process itself is the critical element.

Use the Tools at Hand

Use existing powers and authorities while creating new ones. The *One Region Forward* plan will not depend on a new regional governmental structure to implement it. Instead of fighting a losing battle to create "another layer of government," the plan asks everyone to implement the ideas and values of the plan in their own spheres of action in ways specific to their mission. The plan's implementation council is benchmarking progress annually, coordinating where possible and, more importantly, continuing programs of public education and engagement. Regional governance may yet organically evolve.

It's Not Either-Or

Harvard economist Edward Glaeser famously asked "Can Buffalo ever come back?" and went on to suggest we stop investment in buildings, rather investing in people.[40] But place-based and people-focused strategies are not in competition, they are complementary. Buffalo's successes, which belie Glaeser's implicit prediction that Buffalo will not come back, depended on leveraging the commitment people have to each other and to the places they share.

Understand What Makes Cities Great

Buffalo made many mistakes by not knowing how cities work or why they are inherently valuable and priceless. Like the planners of the 1950s and 1960s, professionals today are confident they know what they are doing. Thus, the current planning orthodoxy in dialogue with local knowledge from citizens has created a civic agenda for Buffalo that is more likely to succeed than using the conventional wisdom of the 1950s and 1960s.[41]

Take the Long View

The smallest relevant unit of analysis for successes and failures of city making might be the decade. It is not hard to change something in a year, but it is hard to tell if the changes will make for a lasting recovery and a better quality of life. Buffalo's most effective citizens and leaders are those who are in it for the long haul and who recognize and embrace that decades are built one year at a time.

Align Federal, State and Local Programs

In Buffalo, for example, *One Region Forward* is closely coordinated at the federal level with the *Prosperity* and *Buffalo Billion* initiatives that are supported by the State of New York, and with the City of Buffalo's comprehensive suite of plans.

Prospects for the Future

Buffalo in 2015 looks promising. But history demonstrates that prosperity is never guaranteed and threats can come from within or without. The quintuple-disaster that befell Buffalo and other legacy cities—deindustrialization, racial conflict, suburban dispersion, capital flight, and globalization—was something Buffalonians should have seen coming. Instead they watched the catastrophe as if through the rear-view mirror and struggled for decades to mount an effective response. Buffalo's future prospects depend on its ability to anticipate the oncoming challenges and respond ahead of the curve.

For starters, continued progress toward a more sustainable way of life requires that Buffalo mount even more aggressive efforts to address its current and historic problems. This means continuing to build key economic sectors while respecting environmental imperatives,[42] improve educational outcomes, redress economic disparities, control sprawl, manage the surplus of vacant homes and empty lots, clean up the toxic legacy of our industrial era, improve public transit, and invest in downtown, waterfronts, parks, neighborhoods and architecture to make great places people love. The agenda is clear and action is underway on all these agendas. The question that remains to be answered is whether the kind of distributed implementation process that was designed to enact the *One Region Forward* plan will let Buffalo and its region reverse the tendency to sprawl.

There are new challenges ahead, some unseen beyond the horizon: Buffalo's cohort of aging citizens is tied to issues in housing, health care, labor markets, and the future economy; poverty is increasing in the first-ring suburbs; the influx of international refugees could be an asset or a burden; climate change could bring a new wave of immigrants, foreign and domestic, and new pressures to address the development of renewable energy sources.

The response to these and other challenges will depend on whether Buffalonians can sustain the kind of work they have already done in "persuasive story-telling about the future."[43] It depends on whether they can find a way to act, each in their own spheres, to advance a common agenda. The fundamental challenge for citizens of Buffalo is the same one John Dewey identified in *The Public and Its Problems* in 1927, namely to constitute itself and to sustain and enlarge its democratic voice in response to the economic, social and environmental problems it will confront. The strength of community and love of place manifested in the work of the last thirty years suggests this is possible.

Notes

1 The ensemble of nationally award-winning plans was produced for a variety of clients, all including the City of Buffalo. The Urban Design Project at the School of Architecture and Planning, University at Buffalo, The State University of New York, led all the planning teams.

2 Chan Krieger Associates, *Buffalo Niagara Medical Campus Plan* (Buffalo, New York: Buffalo Niagara Medical Campus, 2002); Gamble Associates and Chan Krieger Associates, *Buffalo Niagara Medical Campus Master Plan Update: A Scoping Document for the Future* (Buffalo, New York: Buffalo Niagara Medical Campus, 2010).

3 A plan library has been created by the University at Buffalo Regional Institute, *One Region Forward: A New Way to Plan for Buffalo Niagara* (Buffalo, New York: The Greater Buffalo Niagara Regional Transportation Council, 2015), available at: www.oneregionforward.org/data-tools/plan-library/ (accessed March 28, 2015).

4 The State University of New York at Buffalo and Beyer Blender Belle Architects, *Building UB: The Comprehensive Physical Plan* (Buffalo, New York: State University of New York at Buffalo, 2010).

5 UB Regional Institute and the Urban Design Project. *A Strategy for Prosperity in Western New York* (Buffalo New York: WNY Regional Economic Development Council with support from the Brookings Institute, 2011); UB Regional Institute, *The Buffalo Billion Investment Development Plan* (Buffalo, New York: Western New York Regional Economic Development Council, with support from the Brookings Institute and McKenzie Global, 2013).

6 Alan Ehrenhalt, *The Great Inversion and the Future of the American City* (New York: Random House, 2012).

7 William Cronon, *Nature's Metropolis: Chicago and the Great West* (New York: Norton, 1991).

8 The company later pushed for the incorporation of part of West Seneca as a city and in 1919 Lackawanna Iron and Steel was acquired by Bethlehem Steel under which name steelmaking would continue in Lackawanna, NY, until 1982 when the plant was closed.

9 David C. Perry and Alfred J. Watkins, eds., *The Rise of the Sunbelt Cities* (Beverly Hills, CA: Sage, 1977).

10 William Graebner, "Ribbon of Steel and Concrete: A Cultural Biography of the Buffalo Skyway (1955)," *American Studies* 48(1) (2007): 77–100.

11 US Census Bureau, Decennial Census, *Means of Transportation to Work* (Washington, DC: Government Printing Office, 1980, 1990). Note: Includes workers within the City of Buffalo.

12 Robert G. Shibley, *Buffalo, New York: Design Research on the Retail Core: The Buffalo Urban Retail Core Design Competition* (Buffalo, New York: State University of New York at Buffalo, 1988).

13 US Census Bureau, Decennial Census, *Total Population* (Washington, DC: Government Printing Office, 1950, 1960, 1970).

14 US Census Bureau, Decennial Census, *Total Population* (Washington, DC: Government Printing Office, 1970, 1980).

15 US Census Bureau, Decennial Census, *Total Population, Race* (Washington, DC: Government Printing Office 1970, 1980).

16 US Census Bureau, Decennial Census, *Population Estimates Program*, available at: www.census.gov/popest/ (accessed March 12, 2015).

17 *Buffalo Business First*, "Labor Report: Buffalo Added 6,200 Jobs in Past Year," available at: www.bizjournals.com/buffalo/news/2015/03/05/labor-report-buffalo-added-6-200-jobs-in-past-year.html (accessed March 12, 2015).

18 New York State Education Department, "New York State School Report Card," 2014, available at: https://reportcards.nysed.gov (accessed March 12, 2015).

19 US Census Bureau, American Community Survey, "Poverty Rate," 2013, available at: www.census.gov/acs (accessed March 12, 2015).

20 Buffalo Niagara Partnership, *Downtown Buffalo Development Projects* [map]. available at: www.buffaloniagara.org/files/content/Marketing/Brochures/DTdevMap-ByStatus.pdf. Note: Data source is the Buffalo Niagara Enterprise. Downtown capital project totals for *proposed* and *ongoing* development activity are current as of September 22, 2014. Completed development projects are included back through 2003: available at: www.buffaloniagara.org/files/content/Marketing/Brochures/DTdevMap-ByStatus.pdf and www.buffaloniagara.org/files/content/Marketing/Brochures/DTdevMap-ByType.pdf

21 Ibid., 8.

22   New York State Department of Environmental Conservation, "Brownfield Cleanup Program" database, available at: www.dec.ny.gov/cfmx/extapps/derexternal/index.cfm?pageid=1 (accessed March 12, 2015).

23   US Census Bureau, Building Permits Survey Database, "Building Permits Issued by Census Place, Monthly Data," 2015.

24   US Census Bureau, Decennial Census, *Total Population* (Washington, DC: Government Printing Office, 1970, 2010); US Census Bureau, Decennial Census, *Urbanized Land Area* (Washington, DC: Government Printing Office, 1970, 2010).

25   US Census Bureau, Decennial Census, *Homes by Year Built* (Washington, DC: Government Printing Office, 1980, 1990, 2000 and 2010); US Census Bureau. American Community Survey, 1-year estimates, *Homes by Year Built* (Washington, DC: Government Printing Office, 2012).

26   US Bureau of Census and Real Estate Center at Texas A&M University, available at: http://recenter.tamu.edu/data/pop/ (accessed March 12, 2015). Note: Decade years represent April 1, Census data, not the mid-year estimates.

27   US Census Bureau, Decennial Census, *Total Population* (Washington, DC: Government Printing Office, 1970, 1980, 1990, 2000, 2010).

28   US Census Bureau, American Community Survey, "Race, Hispanic or Latino by Race," 2013.

29   US Census Bureau, Decennial Census and American Community Survey, "Foreign Born," 1970, 1980, 1990, 2000, 2010, 2013.

30   Integrated Postsecondary Education Data System, "Completions Database," 1987, 2013. available at: http://nces.ed.gov/ipeds/

31   In 2014, 12 percent of jobs within the Buffalo-Niagara MSA, were in the manufacturing sector. Source: U.S. Bureau of Labor Statistics, NYS Department of Labor, Quarterly Census of Employment and Wages, 2014.

32   Employment grew in the biomedical (6.9 percent), financial services (0.4 percent), and tourism (6.3 percent) economic clusters between 2011 and 2013. Sources: New York State Department of Labor, Quarterly Census of Employment and Wages (2011 and 2013 annual average employment). Clusters are defined by Empire State Development Corp.

33   Citywide and Children Poverty Rates: US Census Bureau. American Community Survey 1-year estimates, "Poverty Status in 2013 for Children Under 18," 2013; US Census Bureau, American Community Survey 1-year estimates, 2013; "Ratio of Income in 2013 to Poverty Level," 2013; Poverty by Race: US Census Bureau. American Community Survey 3-year estimates, "Poverty Status in 2013 (White Alone)," 2013; "Poverty Status in 2013 (Black or African American Alone)," 2013; "Poverty Status in 2013 (Hispanic or Latino)," 2013.

34   Ray Oldenburg, *The Great Good Place: Cafes, Coffee Shops, Bookstores, Bars, Hair Salons, and Other Hangouts at the Heart of a Community* (New York: Marlowe, 1987).

35   Buffalo Place, Inc. is the Buffalo Downtown improvement district that was initially established to manage the pedestrian mall after the free-fare zone was established, available at: www.buffaloplace.com/home (accessed March 29, 2015).

36   Robert G. Shibley and Bradshaw Hovey. *The Buffalo Summit Series: Experiments in Democratic Action: 1994 to 98* (Buffalo, New York: The Urban Design Project, 1998).

37   Robert G. Shibley, Alex Morris, et al., *A New Downtown Neighborhood in Buffalo* (Buffalo, New York: The Urban Design Project, 1993).

38   The riverfront parkway has complemented new investments in neighborhoods on the east side of the city that have not seen development pressure for decades.

39   Gerald Grant, *Hope and Despair in the American City: Why There Are No Bad Schools in Raleigh* (Cambridge, MA: Harvard, 2009).

40   Edward L. Glaeser, "Can Buffalo Ever Come Back? Probably Not—And Government Should Stop Bribing People to Stay There," *City Journal*, Autumn 2007.

41   Clifford Geertz, *Local Knowledge: Further Essays in Interpretive Anthropology* (New York: Basic Books, 1983).

42   Consider the formation of the Western New York Environmental Alliance, a consortium of more than 100 organizations finding common cause in setting priorities for environmental action as another source of community engagement gaining traction in Buffalo—they are at the table in One Region Forward and members are active at the state and local level in Buffalo, available at: http://216.92.20.139/organizations (accessed March 28, 2015).

43   James Throgmorton, *Planning as Persuasive Storytelling: The Rhetorical Construction of Chicago's Electric Future* (Chicago: University of Chicago Press, 1996).

References

Buffalo Business First (2015) "Labor Report: Buffalo Added 6,200 Jobs in Past Year," March 5, 2015. Available at: www.bizjournals.com/buffalo/news/2015/03/05/labor-report-buffalo-added-6-200-jobs-in-past-year.html (accessed March 12, 2015).

Buffalo Niagara Partnership. *Downtown Buffalo Development Projects* [map]. 2015. Available at: www.buffaloniagara.org/files/content/Marketing/Brochures/DTdevMap-ByStatus.pdf (accessed March 12, 2015).

Byers, Jim, "Shocked and Awed by Rebirth of Buffalo," *Toronto Star*, April 30, 2014. Available at: www.thestar.com/life/travel_blog/2014/04/shocked_and_awed_by_the_rebirth_of_buffalo.html (accessed January 26, 2015).

Chan Krieger & Associates (2003) *Buffalo Niagara Medical Campus Master Plan.* Buffalo, New York: Buffalo Niagara Medical Campus.

Chan Krieger Sienewicz Architects and Planners et al. and Richardson Center Corporation (2009) *Master Plan for the Richardson Olmsted Complex, Buffalo.* Buffalo, New York: Richardson Center Corporation.

Cronon, William (1991) *Nature's Metropolis: Chicago and the Great West.* New York City: Norton.

Dewey, John (1927) *The Public and Its Problems.* New York: Holt.

Ehrenhalt, Alan (2012) *The Great Inversion and the Future of the American City.* New York: Random House.

Gamble Associates and Chan Krieger Associates (2010) *Buffalo Niagara Medical Campus Master Plan Update: A Scoping Document for the Future.* Buffalo, NY: Niagara Medical Campus.

Geertz, Clifford (1983) *Local Knowledge: Further Essays in Interpretive Anthropology.* New York: Basic Books.

Graebner, William (2007) "Ribbon of Steel and Concrete: A Cultural Biography of the Buffalo Skyway (1955)." *American Studies* 48(1): 77100.

Grant, Gerald (2009) *Hope and Despair in the American City: Why There Are No Bad Schools in Raleigh.* Cambridge, MA: Harvard Press.

Greater Buffalo Regional Transportation Council (2011) "Vehicle Miles Traveled for Erie and Niagara Counties."

HOK Planning Group. *The Erie and Niagara County Framework for Regional Growth.* Buffalo, NY: State University of New York Press, 2006.

Institute for Local Governance and Regional Growth (2005) *A Cultural Tourism Strategy: Enriching Culture and Building Tourism in Buffalo Niagara.* Buffalo, New York: Buffalo Niagara Cultural Tourism Initiative.

Integrated Postsecondary Education Data System (2013)"Completions Database" 1987, available at: http://nces.ed.gov/ipeds/ (accessed March 12, 2015).

Kaplan, Melanie D.G. (2014) "In Buffalo, N.Y., a New Vitality Is Giving the Once-Gritty City Wings," *Washington Post*, July 24, 2014, available at: www.washingtonpost.com/lifestyle/travel/in-buffalo-ny-a-new-vitality-is-giving-the-once-gritty-city-wings/2014/07/24/f8ff6156-1126-11e4-98ee-daea85133bc9_story.html (accessed January 22, 2015).

Kowsky, Francis R.(2013) *The Best Planned City in the World: Olmsted, Vaux, and the Buffalo Park System.* Boston: University of Massachusetts Press and Library of American Landscape History.

Lovine, Julie V. (2014) "The Best Architecture of 2014," *The Wall Street Journal*, December 24, 2014, available at: www.wsj.com/articles/the-best-architecture-of-2014-sense-and-sensitivity-1419478663 (accessed March 28, 2015).

New York State Department of Education (2014) "New York State School Report Card," 2014, available at: https://reportcards.nysed.gov (accessed March 12, 2015).

New York State Department of Environmental Conservation, "Brownfield Cleanup Program" database, available at: www.dec.ny.gov/cfmx/extapps/derexternal/index.cfm?pageid=1 (accessed March 12, 2015).

New York State Department of Labor (1980) "Summary Population and Housing Characteristics," available at: www.labor.ny.gov/stats/

New York State Department of Labor, "Quarterly Census of Employment and Wages," available at: www.labor.ny.gov/stats/lsqcew.shtm (accessed March 12, 2015).

Oldenburg, Ray (1987) *The Great Good Place: Cafes, Coffee Shops, Bookstores, Bars, Hair Salons and Other Hangouts at the Heart of a Community.* New York: Marlowe.

Schneekloth, Lynda, Robert G. Shibley, and Thomas Yots (2011) *Olmsted in Buffalo and Niagara.* Buffalo, New York: Urban Design Project, The University at Buffalo School of Architecture and Planning, University at Buffalo/SUNY.

Schneider, Keith (2013) "Once Just a Punch Line, Buffalo Fights Back," *New York Times*, July 30, 2013, available at: www.nytimes.com/2013/07/31/realestate/commercial/once-a-punch-line-buffalo-fights-back.html?pagewanted=all&_r=0 (accessed January 22, 2015).

Shibley, Robert G. (1988) *Buffalo, New York: Design Research on the Retail Core-The Buffalo Urban Retail Core Design Competition.* Buffalo, New York: University at Buffalo, State University of New York Press.

Shibley, Robert G. and Bradshaw Hovey (1998) *The Buffalo Summit Series: Experiments in Democratic Action: 1994 to 98.* Buffalo, New York: The Urban Design Project.

Shibley, Robert G. and Bradshaw Hovey with David Carter and John Sheffer (2006) *Queen City in the 21st Century: Buffalo's Comprehensive Plan.* Buffalo, New York: City of Buffalo.

Shibley, Robert G., Bradshaw Hovey, with Buffalo Place Inc. and the City of Buffalo (2002) *The Queen City Hub: Regional Action Plan for Downtown Buffalo, Overview: A Context for Decision Making.* vol. 1. Buffalo, New York: City of Buffalo.

Shibley, Robert G., Bradshaw Hovey, with Buffalo Place Inc. and the City of Buffalo (2003) *The Work Plan,* vol. 2, Buffalo, New York: City of Buffalo.

Shibley, Robert G. and Alex Morris with Buffalo Place Inc. and Urban Design Project Staff (1993) *A New Downtown Neighborhood in Buffalo.* Buffalo, New York: The Urban Design Project.

Shibley, Robert G. and Lynda Schneekloth (2010) "Olmsted Park and Parkway System for the 21st Century," in *Proceedings of Fabos Conference on Landscape and Greenway Planning.* Budapest: Budapesti Corvinus Egyetem, Tájtervezési és Területfejlesztési Tanszék, pp. 179–86.

Shibley, Robert G. and Lynda Schneekloth (2008) *The Olmsted City—The Buffalo Olmsted Park System: Plan for the 21st Century.* Buffalo, New York: Buffalo Olmsted Parks Conservancy and The Urban Design Project.

Shibley, Robert G., Lynda Schneekloth, Bradshaw Hovey, eds. (2007) *Queen City Waterfront—Buffalo Waterfront Corridor Initiative: A Strategic Plan for Transportation Improvements.* Buffalo, New York: City of Buffalo.

Throgmorton, James (1996) *Planning as Persuasive Storytelling: The Rhetorical Construction of Chicago's Electric Future.* Chicago: University of Chicago Press.

UB Regional Institute (2011) *A Strategy for Prosperity in Western New York.* Buffalo, New York: Western New York Regional Economic Development Council, with support from the Brookings Institution.

UB Regional Institute (2013) *The Buffalo Billion Investment Development Plan.* Buffalo, New York: Western New York Regional Economic Development Council, with support from the Brookings Institution and McKenzie Global.

UB Regional Institute (2015a) "The Plan." One Region Forward. February 1, 2015, available at: www.oneregionforward.org/the-plan/ (accessed March 11, 2015).

UB Regional Institute (2015b) "Drafting the Plan." One Region Forward, available at: www.oneregionforward.org/the-plan/drafting-the-plan/ (accessed March 11, 2015).

UB Regional Institute and the Urban Design Project (2011) *A Strategy for Prosperity in Western New York.* Buffalo, New York: WNY Regional Economic Development Council, with support from the Brookings Institution.

UB, State University of New York and Beyer Blender Bell Architects (2010) *Building UB: The Comprehensive Physical Plan.* Buffalo, New York: University at Buffalo, State University of New York Press.

Urban Design Project with Kevin Connors and Associates, Trowbridge Wolf Michaels Architects and Hiroaki Hata (2006) *The Larkin District Plan.* Buffalo, New York: City View Properties, updated 2015.

US Bureau of Census and Real Estate Center at Texas A&M University, "Population," available at: http://recenter.tamu.edu/data/pop/ (accessed March 12, 2015).

US Census Bureau (1951) Decennial Census, *1950: Total Population*. Washington, DC: Government Printing Office.

US Census Bureau (1961) *1960: Total Population*. Washington, DC: Government Printing Office.

US Census Bureau (1971a) *1970: Total Population*. Washington, DC: Government Printing Office.

US Census Bureau (1971b) *Total Population, Race*. Washington, DC: Government Printing Office.

US Census Bureau (1971c) *1970: Commute Modes to Work*. Washington, DC: Government Printing Office.

US Census Bureau (1971d) *Urbanized Land Area*. Washington, DC: Government Printing Office.

US Census Bureau (1981a) *1980: Total Population*. Washington, DC: Government Printing Office.

US Census Bureau (1981b) *1980: Homes by Years Built*. Washington, DC: Government Printing Office.

US Census Bureau (1981c) *Means of Transportation to Work*. Washington, DC: Government Printing Office.

US Census Bureau (1981d) *Total Population, Race*. Washington, DC: Government Printing Office.

US Census Bureau (1985) *Building Permits Survey Database, Building Permits Issued by Census Place, Annual Data*. Washington, DC: Government Printing Office.

US Census Bureau (1991a) *1990: Total Population*. Washington, DC: Government Printing Office.

US Census Bureau (1991b) *1990: Homes by Years Built*. Washington, DC: Government Printing Office.

US Census Bureau (1991c) *Means of Transportation to Work*. Washington, DC: Government Printing Office.

US Census Bureau (2001a) *2000: Homes by Years Built*. Washington, DC: Government Printing Office.

US Census Bureau (2001b) *2000: Total Population*. Washington, DC: Government Printing Office.

US Census Bureau (2011a) *2010: Commute Modes to Work*. Washington, DC: Government Printing Office.

US Census Bureau (2011b) *2010: Homes by Years Built*. Washington, DC: Government Printing Office.

US Census Bureau (2011c) *2010: Total Population*. Washington, DC: Government Printing Office.

US Census Bureau (2011d) *Urbanized Land Area*. Washington, DC: Government Printing Office.

US Census Bureau (2012) *Homes by Years Built*. Washington, DC: Government Printing Office, available at: www.census.gov/acs (accessed March 12, 2015a).

US Census Bureau (2013a) *Ratio of Income in 2013 to Poverty Level*. Washington, DC: Government Printing Office, available at: www.census.gov/acs (accessed March 12, 2015).

US Census Bureau (2013b) American Community Survey 1-year estimates, "Poverty Status in 2013 for Children Under 18," available at: www.census.gov/acs (accessed March 12, 2015).

US Census Bureau (2015) Building Permits Survey Database. "Building Permits Issued by Census Place, Monthly Data," available at: http://censtats.census.gov/bldg/bldgprmt.shtml (accessed March 12, 2015).

US Census Bureau, "Poverty Rate, 2013," available at: www.census.gov/acs (accessed March 12, 2015).

US Census Bureau, Dicennial Census. "Population Estimates Program," available at: www.census.gov/popest/ (accessed March 12, 2015).

Wendel Duchscherer Architects & Engineers (2007) *Niagara River Greenway Plan and Final Environmental Impact Statement*. Erie and Niagara Counties, New York: Niagara River Greenway Commission.

3   Detroit Case Study

Dan Kinkead

Introduction

For many, Detroit maintains a seemingly unrivaled position as the iconographic post-industrial legacy city. Its bona fides have come from actual long-term disinvestment, depopulation, and economic decline, as well as a symbolic and breathtaking fall from the aspirational "Arsenal of Democracy" to the universally recognized "Tragedy of Detroit."[1] The reality and symbolism of Detroit have intertwined to create a powerful and consumable narrative that can mask important historic contributions, existing challenges, and emerging opportunities for the future. Unpacking these often-complex aspects reveals important insights into how Detroit arrived at its current condition, and most importantly, how it can begin to move forward to transform itself and deliver a fundamental, sustainable, and unique value proposition for residents and businesses.

While Detroit's overall narrative is not unique, it is superlative, and emerging scholarship regarding American post-industrial "legacy cities," along with renewed appreciation for their importance, means that Detroit can offer salient insight to other cities. Such insight is not relegated to a dissection of the city's past, but also to a robust discussion about its present and future. As the city emerges from the largest municipal bankruptcy in US history and decades of decline, Detroit has the opportunity to develop and implement an equitable, sustainable, and innovative recovery, and to become a global leader for post-industrial transformation. Detroit's historical role as an economic and social bellwether will be reinforced as it seeks to update policy, drive investment, stabilize neighborhoods, and create competitive assets from longstanding liabilities such as vacant land and buildings. Detroit is poised to create a new urban narrative. Thoughtful and strategic decision-making will be essential to achieving it.

Brief History of the City

Detroit's strategic position along the Detroit River, a strait between the upper and lower Great Lakes and the St. Lawrence Seaway, made it an essential trading port. From its founding in 1701 as a French trading outpost, to its dominance as an industrial hub in the middle of the twentieth century, Detroit has been defined by its connectivity for industrial production, similar to many other post-industrial cities. By combining raw materials from waterborne and rail transportation systems to create finished products for retail, Detroit ultimately cultivated the quintessential model of vertical integration, achieving remarkably high productivity and eventual market dominance.

To drive such robust production, Detroit was also a great importer of human capital. It provided an array of employment opportunities for foreign-born immigrants, then Appalachian whites, and ultimately Southern blacks escaping Jim Crow laws. Detroit's population began to surge in the late nineteenth century with growing industrial production, and from 1900 to 1950 the city's population mushroomed from 285,704 to 1,849,568, fueled by the explosive growth of the auto industry. While Detroit did not register among the largest ten cities in the United States by population until 1910, by 1920, it had the fourth largest population, and would retain that title until falling to fifth largest in 1950 (Table 3.1).[2]

The industrial production that drove Detroit's economy in the twentieth century was increasingly based on divisions of labor and mass production, meaning there was a range of tasks available to workers with limited education and training. While many of Detroit's jobs would become vulnerable to markets with lower costs, Detroit's overall growth through the middle of the twentieth century was actually reinforced because it offered typically strong wages to secure a necessary workforce.

This growth also resulted in Detroit's overall land area expanding by nearly five times from 1900 to 1926. During this time period the city grew from a relatively small footprint of 28 square miles to a sprawling city of 138.75 square miles. Achieved primarily through annexation, Detroit's land area grew from its working riverfront northward, radiating out from the central thoroughfare of Woodward Avenue. While other cities with similar growth aspirations may have encountered topographical barriers, Detroit had very few, allowing it to expand quickly and relatively easily. Detroit's robust growth was not just linked to industrial automotive production, but also to its consumption, and to federal policy that would enable an exponential increase in auto use and auto-dominant transportation systems.

By the middle of the twentieth century Detroit made the vehicles that Americans drove, and it began to model an urban form to accommodate them. This included the rapid development of single-family homes, supported by robust autoworkers' incomes and the Servicemen's Readjustment Act of 1944 (the GI Bill) for returning veterans of World War II, which favored new construction over existing rehabilitation.[3] This, combined with the Eisenhower administration's Federal-Aid Highway Act of 1956,[4] leveraged by then Mayor Albert Cobo, began to augment and even supplant Detroit's pre-existing Beaux-Arts radial network of avenues from Judge Augustus Woodward's 1805 plan, and the overlapping grid-iron of the rectilinear Northwest Ordinance of 1787. Not coincidentally, Detroit's once expansive streetcar line ran its last cars down Woodward Avenue in 1956. While most of Detroit's streetcars were offloaded to Mexico City, Detroit had created a virtually limitless network of infrastructure and housing that expands to this day.

While Detroit's growth trajectory had long been geared toward outward expansion, such development had become the domain of the suburbs by the mid-1950s, and early signs of resulting disinvestment near the city's core became evident. Attempts at revitalization were catalyzed by federal programs such as Title I of the Housing Act of

Table 3.1 Population of Detroit, 1880–1950

Year	1880	1890	1900	1910	1920	1930	1940	1950
Total	116,340	205,876	285,704	465,766	993,678	1,568,662	1,623,452	1,849,568
Change (%)		+77	+39	+63	+113	+58	+3	+14

Source: Adapted from US Census (1998).

1949. This compromised policy combined predominantly single-use residential development programs with public housing provisions and private developer delivery systems that prioritized middle-income populations and displaced low-income, often African-American, populations. Concentrated in the oldest parts of the city, adjacent to downtown, these areas were often the focus for renewal from business and civic leaders.

As Detroit's African-American population continued to grow and experience dislocation from historical population centers, many sought opportunities in Detroit's expanding neighborhoods. Here, the city's archetypal American landscape of single-family homes became sites of spatialized racism where "redlining" and covenants became common tools to protect the "integrity" of certain neighborhoods against the perceived threat of integration. While many African-Americans had escaped unjust treatment in the American South, they found aspects of it again in Detroit.

As large-scale civic improvements such as Cobo Hall (named for the controversial mayor who initiated many mid-century renewal efforts) were developed downtown, construction of expressways quickened with the promise of improved connectivity. Lobbied by the auto industry, and supported by continued federal funding and powerful civic leaders, freeways would soon proliferate across Detroit, and its neighborhoods. Ironically, for all of the aspiration for civic improvement in Detroit, the 1950s saw Detroit's population first begin its decline. While many leaders were focused on the operations of urban renewal, Detroit's economy became more dominated by the automotive industry, just as the industry itself seemed to be moving out. According to June Manning-Thomas, "Between 1947 and 1955, Chrysler, Ford, and GM built twenty new plants in the Detroit region, employing a total of 72,000 workers. Not a single one of these plants was located within Detroit …"[5]

While many firms would cite city taxes, codes, and requirements for their reasons to invest elsewhere, the reality was a shifting model of auto-production that valued large expansive sites for modern assembly production. Here, Detroit's previously abundant land area had become entirely built out, in many cases with low-density single-family homes, and without additional annexation (which would not happen) Detroit's ability to attract and maintain such auto-production facilities was slipping away. Moreover, the residents in the single-family homes, many of whom were also employed in the factories that were relocating to the suburbs, would soon find their way out too.

By the 1960s, Detroit's struggles were becoming more evident, and as institutionalized racism toward an increasingly African-American population was growing, hostilities would ultimately flash in the summer of 1967 as police officers raided an after-hours bar with mostly African-American patrons. Crowds gathered outside the establishment as violence erupted. Before it was over, more than 17,000 police officers, National Guardsmen, and federal troops were called in, forty-three people lost their lives, more than 2,500 buildings were burned and looted, and more than 7,200 people were arrested.[6] The riots of 1967 were not the first for Detroit, but they were by far the largest and most destructive, and they came at a vulnerable moment when many African-Americans sought proper housing and opportunity after decades of struggle, and when many whites were weighing their options to stay or go.

As Detroit became identified with the "Motown" sound, the city was starting to come apart. The following two decades saw further declines in overall population, particularly the white population, and by 1974 Detroit had elected its first African-American mayor, Coleman Young. Young, a brash, unapologetic, and frank leader was Detroit's mayor for twenty years. During that time, white flight, fueled by violence, ignorance, and unchecked regional growth, was facilitated by cheap land, rapid construction, growing crime, and an expanding expressway system.

The result was expansive, unchecked regional growth that attracted businesses and residents at a remarkably high rate. It is no coincidence that this regional growth was directly proportionate to Detroit's decline. From 1969 to 2013, Detroit would have fits and starts of new development, but with its inability to attract or retain residents and businesses, less than 30,000 new building permits would be pulled in that forty-four-year span. Over the same time frame nearly 190,000 demolition permits would be released in the city, and a staggering 828,000 new construction permits would be released across southeast Michigan.[7]

Detroit's decline became irrefutable, and while many other cities also struggled over the last few decades of the twentieth century, Detroit faltered more significantly, and in many cases, more precipitously, than many other post-industrial cities. For this, Detroit transcended its identity as a city, and became part of an increasingly dystopian American narrative.

The City in 1985

While the antecedents and contributors—if not the recognizable characteristics—of Detroit's decline had begun much earlier, the 1980s marked a noteworthy waypoint along the city's downward trajectory. As in so many other post-industrial cities, the 1980s conveyed the reality of a global economy, the fragile nature of population dynamics, and resulting impacts on urban centers. The 1980s would see Detroit and its leaders come to terms with its decline and attempt a recovery through large-scale redevelopment that ranged from industrial complexes to grand civic gestures. Many will debate the impact of such projects on Detroit's physical form and its economy, but Detroit remained on its declining course long after they were complete.

Physical Form and Conditions

For Detroit, the 1980s were defined by deteriorating physical condition manifest by disinvestment and depopulation. As less revenue was available to maintain the city, and more property was abandoned, Detroit's physical characteristics declined rapidly. Interwoven into this decline were an increasing number of arson cases, including homeowners and business owners interested in claiming insurance money that often dwarfed the diminished market value of the structure. In the 1980s, such activity was culturally institutionalized into an annual ritual of "Devil's Night" fires in which typically older abandoned housing stock would be burned the night before Halloween. The mid-1980s marked the peak with nearly 800 fires in one night.[8] The result was an increasingly burnt-out hulk of a city that negatively impacted the quality of life for residents and businesses while conveying a message through local and national media that dissuaded investment and exacerbated Detroit's negative identity.

While the challenges facing Detroit's physical condition seemed to be at a more decentralized scale across the city, to stem the tide of decline in the late 1970s and early 1980s the city and its civic leaders would pursue a range of large-scale and high profile projects with mixed success. The development of the massive hotel, commercial, and office complex downtown known as the Renaissance Center, and its adjacent park space, Hart Plaza, became recognizable fixtures of a new Detroit. While the Renaissance Center operated with some success, its heavy-handed and fortress-like design, from the prolific and relatively repetitive John Portman, created massive floor area in a city with ample commercial space, and was dissociated from the city's streets. Built for $350 million, it opened in 1974, and ultimately sold for $80 million to General Motors nearly two decades later.[9]

At the same time, General Motors and Mayor Coleman Young used eminent domain in a controversial redevelopment to land a sprawling manufacturing complex on the Detroit-Hamtramck border (Hamtramck is a small municipality set within Detroit's geographic footprint). It would compose land previously part of the Dodge Main factory, and a relatively intact Polish neighborhood, referred to as Poletown.[10] The means and methods to bring the project to fruition stretched the definition of "public good" and vividly demonstrated just how desperate Detroit's leaders had become to retain the industrial jobs that were slipping through their hands.

While projects such as these moved forward, the city continued to decline. Families left, stores closed, and opportunities were lost. For those who remained—increasingly poor African-Americans—the disparate and granular representations of Detroit's struggles, from unemployment, crime, residential blight, and commercial vacancy were symptomatic of larger issues that had been developing for decades.

Demographics

By 1980, Detroit's overall population had declined 35 percent from 1,849,568 in 1950 to 1,203,339.[11] As many other major US cities struggled to maintain population over the same time period, Detroit only fell from being the fifth most populous city in the United States to the sixth in the same time period.[12] Nearly all Detroit's population decline from 1950 to 2000 was Caucasian. During most of Detroit's population decline, until 2000, the overall African-American population in the city grew. By 1980, the city's total African-American population had risen to 63 percent, and by 2010 it would reach 82.7 percent (Table 3.2).[13] The net result was a staggering decline in population density across the city, from 13,330 people per square mile in 1950 to 8,673 in 1980. The resulting loss in population and Detroit-based employment led to a substantial decline in property tax and income tax for the city.

As the Detroit region continued to grow, inner and outer suburb development increased by nearly 30 percent from 1950 to 1970. Enabled by the lack of any regional growth coordination or control, the diaspora has continued to today. Where Detroit's population was 55 percent of the total five county region's population in 1950, by 1970 it had fallen to 32 percent, and by 2000 it was only 20 percent.[14]

The undeniable reality of residential market collapse in Detroit also came into focus in the 1980s. Detroit's housing production had historically lagged behind demand for over ten years, meaning Detroit's total housing unit peak came in the early 1960s, nearly ten years after the city's population began to decline. As Detroit's population continued to

Table 3.2 Population of Detroit, 1950–2010

Year	1950	1960	1970	1980	1990	2000	2010
Total	1,849,568	1,670,144	1,511,482	1,203,339	1,027,974	951,270	713,777
White	1,545,847	1,182,970	838,877	413,730	222,316	116,599	75,758
Black	300,506	482,223	660,428	758,939	777,916	775,772	590,226
Other	3,215	4,951	12,177	30,670	27,742	58,899	47,793
Density (per sq. mi.)	13,330	12,037	10,894	8,673	7,409	6,856	5,144

Source: Adapted from US Census (1990, 2000, 2010).

Table 3.3 City and regional total employment, 1970–2000

Year	1970	1980	1990	2000
Region	1,938,512	2,105,879	2,350,310	2,673,052
Detroit	735,104	562,120	412,490	345,424
Percentage of total	38	27	18	13

Source: Adapted from SEMCOG (2002).

decline into the 1980s, the housing market plummeted with huge supply and little demand. By 1990, Detroit had 36,170 vacant housing units—8.8 percent of its 410,000 total unit count. The trajectory was set in the 1980s and by 2010 the vacant housing unit count would grow by over 120 percent.[15] The resulting vacancy, particularly in the 1980s, led to further market struggles, and diminished quality of life, and exacerbated a fundamental imbalance between cost and revenue. As the city borrowed more money to fund necessary services, this imbalance would lead to Detroit's bankruptcy.

Economy

On the heels of the OPEC oil crises, mounting market capture by overseas competitors, and growing lethargy within all aspects of American industrial production, the speed and breadth of Detroit's decline in automotive production grew. As the tide of automotive fabrication went out from Detroit, the islands that remained were increasingly focused on corporate leadership, engineering, and design. This often continued to include professional services, such as legal and advertising, but many such firms had begun to move to outlying suburbs. While the region experienced modest gains in employment from 1970 to 1980, Detroit's share of total regional employment decreased significantly from 38 to 27 percent (Table 3.3).[16]

The region's employment distribution was becoming increasingly decentralized. In 1970, the region's top ten employment centers contained 64.7 percent of the total regional employment, and by 2000 the top ten employment centers contained only 47.1 percent.[17]

The City in 2015

If 1985 was a waypoint for decline in Detroit, then 2015 has been its moment of reckoning. Detroit's struggles during the last half of the twentieth century have continued, impacting every measurable indicator from population decline to poverty and foreclosure rates. Some might say Detroit's struggles have become existential. By 2010, even among its post-industrial legacy city peers, Detroit ranked at or near the bottom for all performance indicators.[18]

Marked by its emergence from the largest municipal bankruptcy in US history, the birth of a strategic framework to guide the city's transformation, unprecedented federal engagement, and a newly elected Mayor, Detroit has entered 2015 with unparalleled challenges, and less recognized—but transformational—opportunities.

In July 2013, $18 billion in debt, the City of Detroit filed for bankruptcy. While the filing symbolized Detroit's generational struggles, posed great challenges to residents and municipal employees, and impacted local pride, it also meant the start—albeit a painful one—to a new dimension for the city. While economists evaluated potential impacts on pensioners and creditors, many others considered the fate of the city and its residents, who bear the greatest burden in any debt restructuring. Ultimately, most recognized Detroit's unsustainable reality, where four out of every ten dollars in municipal revenue is dedicated to debt service. In the end, with 100,000 creditors and 20,000 retirees, the process would be completed remarkably fast, by December 2014.[19]

In the midst of the process, a "grand-bargain"—achieved through philanthropic, corporate, and governmental entities—drastically limited impacts on services and pensioners, and protected important Detroit assets such as its remarkable art collection. The great unraveling that laid bare Detroit's failures also yielded threads of opportunity for viable, informed, and strategic renewal.

Such threads are bound together for many within the Detroit Future City Strategic Framework Plan (DFC Framework). Developed from 2010 to 2013, before the City's bankruptcy, the DFC Framework's initial research not only recognized the depths of Detroit's struggles, it developed an informed, strategic, and shared platform for change that moved well beyond the ubiquitous "vision" plans the city had seen for decades. If Detroit's resulting bankruptcy allowed the city to restart in the present, the DFC Framework provides an important shared resource for the city's future.

The genesis of the DFC Framework came from many of Detroit's civic leaders—from institutions, philanthropy, government, faith-based, community, and business—who had thoughtfully worked through the city's decline, recognized business as usual was no longer viable, and determined that a bold, comprehensive, participatory, and evidence-based strategy would be necessary. This was not a time for small-scale incremental strategies, or curious visions, but rather, something transformational. In one of the city's darkest moments they joined with then Mayor Dave Bing to create a new future.

The DFC Framework (then known as the Detroit Works Project) was launched in mid-2010, and embarked on a two and a half-year planning and civic engagement process that resulted in the Detroit Future City Strategic Framework Plan. The planning process was driven by a stakeholder-led Steering Committee that worked with planners, economists, and designers, led by Toni Griffin to incorporate 163,000 stakeholder interactions and conversations with innovative strategies and actions to create a comprehensive and action-oriented blueprint for near- and long-range decision-making. To ensure action is catalyzed, a DFC Implementation Office was formed shortly after the launch of the Strategic Framework in 2013, and serves under a stakeholder-led Executive Committee and Steering Committee structure. Focused on innovative projects, policy, strategy, and capacity building, the Implementation Office works hand-in-hand with residents, as well as neighborhood, institutional, governmental, and philanthropic leaders to bring the Strategic Framework to life.

The formation of the DFC Implementation Office coincided with the creation of a White House team to better coordinate federal action, investment, and policy in Detroit. Brokered through coordination with philanthropic and business leaders, the federal team has acted as an advocate and strategist for funding and action.

In many cases, their collaboration is directly with newly elected Mayor Mike Duggan's leadership team. Elected by popular vote in the fall of 2013 after mounting a successful write-in campaign, Mayor Duggan worked side by side with the City's Emergency Manager, Kevyn Orr until his departure at the close of the bankruptcy. In a short time Mayor Duggan and the City Council have begun to create public sector capacity and impact Detroiters have not seen in decades.

It is within this context that Detroit finds itself precariously balancing between the realities of fiscal insolvency, indications of its continued struggles, and emerging signs of a transformational future. It is a contested and complicated space.

Physical Form and Conditions

The result of generations of disinvestment and depopulation, with limited means and capacity to address what remained, has left Detroit with increasingly lower densities, high vacancy, and noteworthy scars. Today, the vacant land area of the city totals over 23.4 square miles, just larger than the land area of Manhattan (Figure 3.1).[20] An additional 9.7 square miles of land area includes vacant and often blighted structures. Many of these structures are likely to come down in the next few years through the City of Detroit's increasingly robust blight elimination efforts.

While Detroit's density is low, it is also remarkably uneven, with some areas of considerable density, with retail services present. Other areas are extremely low. Here quality of life can be extremely challenged, with an older, often poor, population with limited access to amenities and services. These are also areas where density levels are as much as one-fifth of their historic peak (Figure 3.2), making the cost to serve each household overwhelmingly and unsustainably expensive.[21] These are the realities that have contributed to Detroit's bankruptcy, and limited the ability for Detroit to convey an effective value proposition to many residents. These realities, however, if viewed differently, may be the seeds for Detroit's transformation. Where vacant land shifts from being a liability to an unparalleled asset, and where thoughtfully guided growth can achieve sustainable densities throughout the city, providing the amenities, residential density, and proximity for a flourishing urban economy are fundamental objectives of the Detroit Future City Framework.

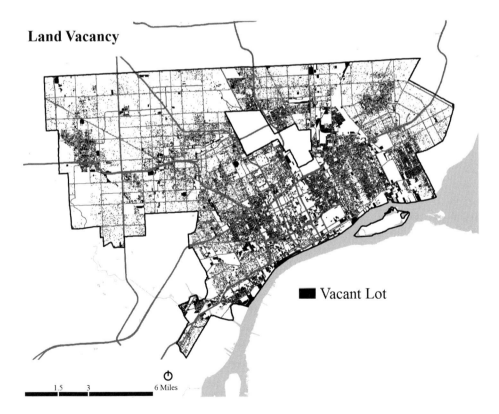

Figure 3.1 Land vacancy, Detroit
Source: Adapted from Motor City Mapping (uncertified results) (2014).

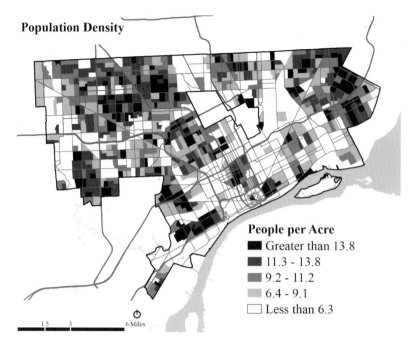

Figure 3.2 Population density, Detroit
Source: Adapted from US Census (2010).

Demographics

In 2015, Detroit's population is estimated to be 688,000, less than the 713,000 of 2010.[22] Detroit's population declined 40 percent from 1980 to 2010 while the regional population continued to grow. The regional transformation created one of the most racially polarized metropolitan areas. Striking differences exist between the predominantly African-American city and its surrounding, predominantly Caucasian suburbs (Figure 3.3).

More recent concerns about property values, service delivery, fees, relocation, and poor quality of life have persisted and contributed to a quickening pace of population decline between 2000 and 2010, especially as the national economic downturn made adjacent suburban properties much more attainable. However, where white flight had defined Detroit's decline through the second half of the twentieth century, from 2000 to 2010 Detroit's African-American population declined nearly 24 percent from 775,772 to 590,226. This represented 78 percent of the city's total population decline.[23]

At the same time, emerging employment opportunities and renewed interest in urban centers have seen estimates of an increase in a young, educated, Caucasian population in 2014, particularly within the center of the city. As this small population grows, so too are equity and opportunity concerns. The result has been growing popular mistrust of some reinvestment, and an appeal for community benefits agreements.

Economy

Exacerbated by the financial collapse of 2008, Detroit's lingering economic misfortunes crystalized by 2010 with an unemployment rate, housing vacancy rate, and poverty rate ranked worst among post-industrial "legacy city" peers (Table 3.4), and a 2013 labor force participation rate that is less than half the national average for 22–54-year-olds.[24]

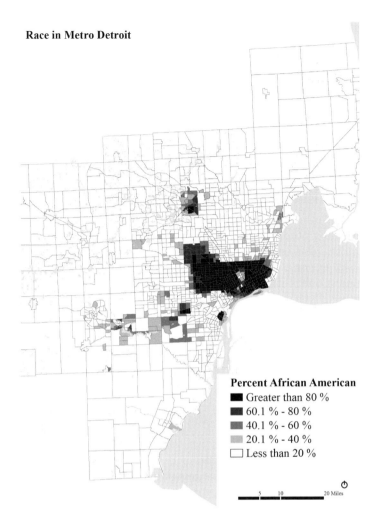

Figure 3.3 Regional race distribution, Detroit
Source: Adapted from US Census (2010).

Table 3.4 Peer post-industrial "legacy city" comparative table

	Baltimore, MD	Newark, NJ	Philadelphia, PA	Buffalo, NY	Cleveland, OH	Detroit, MI	Milwaukee, WI	Pittsburgh, PA	St. Louis, MO	Youngstown, OH
Unemployment rate (2010)	2	7	5	4	8	10	3	1	6	9
Crime rate (2009)	8	1	5	7	6	9	3	2	10	4
Housing vacancy rate (2010)	6	4	2	5	8	10	1	3	8	7
Population living in poverty (2011) (%)	1	4	3	7	8	10	5	2	6	9

Source: Adapted from Brachman and Mallach (2013), pp. 20–1.

Contributing to these realities was a Detroit economy exhibiting significant job sprawl, where only 38 percent of working Detroiters actually worked in Detroit,[25] well below the national average, and where 77 percent of its metropolitan jobs in 2010 were located between 10 and 35 miles from the central business district.[26] Today, while many residents from outside the city fill professional service jobs in the city's center, many Detroiters fill roles, often service sector, in the suburbs. The resulting commute demands resources, including time and money. For many in the city without viable private transportation, employment opportunities are limited.

Overall, Detroit's economy lost 21 percent of its tax base between the fourth quarter of 2000 and the first quarter of 2014, however, Detroit is battling back, recording 4 percent job growth since the start of 2010.[27] This uptick in employment may be too small to claim an inflection point in the city's economy, particularly because most gains were made in the downtown and midtown areas only. Still, it's a remarkable statistic given Detroit's long-running decline. Other noteworthy positive signs include an unemployment rate that has fallen faster than regional or national rates, and an employment rate in the city growing while regional and national rates have stalled. To do this, Detroit has regained private sector jobs at almost one and a half times the national rate (9.4 percent vs. 6.5 percent).[28]

Detroit's newest challenge is to make sure the gains it is making today can have a broader impact on all Detroiters tomorrow. Developments, including the American Lightweight Materials Manufacturing Innovation Institute (ALMMII), led by Detroit's Mayor, Mike Duggan, will bring new innovative industrial growth to a previously vacant 100,000 square foot industrial structure, and may point to a broader buoying of Detroit's economy with a deeper impact for more Detroiters.

Transformation of the City (1985–2015)

What Went Right?

Detroit's overarching trajectory of decline remains profound, but it appears that the city has reached a turning point that for a long time seemed out of reach. A number of important facets, each of them relatively recent, have not only helped Detroit navigate its decline, but may also help to define a new direction.

Leadership from Detroit's Civil Society

Innumerable individuals and organizations have provided essential capacity and leadership as elected officials were increasingly beset with existential challenges. From philanthropic leaders, to community, faith-based, business, and educational leaders, critical initiatives such as the DFC Framework, Blight Removal Task Force, and the bankruptcy's "grand bargain" have been made possible. Here the depth and breadth of Detroit's human and financial capital, much of it with ties back to the mass-production and consumption economy of Detroit's past, have emerged to outline a new future for the city.

A Diversifying Economy

Amidst Detroit's declining automotive industrial economy, linked to mass production and divisions of labor, a more diverse array of economic contributors have emerged. Present throughout the city's history, but now in sharper relief, Detroit's spectrum of employment includes not only a more diversified industrial base, including food processing and logistics, it also includes major medical and educational anchor institutions, and an emergent "new economy," tied to technology, creative enterprise, and light-scale fabrication. This organically grown economy is now being more carefully cultivated with planning and investment, yielding important job growth.

Bankruptcy

The ability of Detroit to emerge from bankruptcy free of crushing debt service, while maintaining the integrity of commitments to pensioners, is essential not only for its recovery, but for its existence. Remarkably poor past decisions may have compounded the city's challenges, but the pace of disinvestment and depopulation has cemented them. The work of the city's state-appointed Emergency Manager, Kevyn Orr, helped the city navigate the process quickly and effectively with full leadership now restored within the Mayor's office and City Council.

What Went Wrong?

Innumerable factors played into Detroit's continued decline over the last thirty years, but few had as much impact as the city's inability to maintain sufficient densities, employ enough Detroiters, and coordinate regional growth management. Business as usual, deploying the same capital and operational approaches to the city, compounded its cost-revenue imbalance, and diminished quality of life for Detroiters.

Unmanaged Declining Density

As precipitous depopulation and disinvestment dramatically reduced residential and employment densities across the city, land use designations, capital and operational programs, and city systems and services were not re-evaluated and strategically adjusted. Over time, this led to poorly considered reinvestment strategies, and diminished quality of service. Overall, Detroit's historic densities fell from twenty-one people per acre to eight by 2010, while the land area, conventional systems, and services remained the same, the total property tax revenue plummeted.[29]

Insufficient Employment

Detroit's economy has shown strong signs of increased diversification, yet its sprawling regional employment market, limited spatial strategies to drive employment opportunities, and mounting educational and mobility challenges for Detroiters, have all led to very poor labor force participation rates and high unemployment. By 2010, for every one hundred Detroiters, there were only twenty-seven private-sector jobs in the city.[30] Over time this has eroded a significant part of Detroit's tax revenue, and universally compromised its citizens' quality of life.

Lack of Regional Urban Agenda

Detroit's population decline, and its robust regional population growth, began in the middle of the twentieth century, and have increased in pace and magnitude. Sprawl can be attributed to cheap land, federal policy, and racial intolerance as well, but the nonexistence of any meaningful growth coordination has resulted in a population and capital investment sprawl that has wasted fixed infrastructure in the city, stressed natural resources, and reinforced a highly auto-dependent transportation system that limits opportunity for poorer residents.

Lessons Learned

The reality of Detroit's calamitous decline over the course of the last half of the twentieth century, and its resulting bankruptcy, have ensured that business as usual is no longer a foregone conclusion. The sobering clarity of Detroit's insolvency, the commitment of a range of leaders to move the city forward, and the presence of effective strategies, unprecedented data, and committed federal partners have changed Detroit's trajectory. The insight gained during these transformative years may be the city's most durable and impactful legacy.

The result of declining population, increased joblessness, and poor regional cooperation have hobbled Detroit, but its inability over the last thirty years to establish necessary strategy, policy, and regulatory measures to realistically address these challenges has exacerbated Detroit's decline. Instead, budget adjustments, grand projects, and a long list of vision plans have been the response. While Detroit's challenges would have remained, their most venomous impacts may have been mitigated sooner through more thoughtful and nuanced responses that sought not to fulfill a conventional and arguably irrelevant canon of urbanity, but rather to seed:

- innovative new land utilization patterns that would leverage Detroit's condition to achieve sustainable densities;
- deliberate strategies to establish shared ownership of the city's future;
- the political will to confront challenges as they arose.

Innovative Land Utilization

Detroit's future land use spectrum must become a sustainable mix of different densities and functions that will allow the city to deliver a higher quality of life to all Detroiters, and become a more resilient and dynamic global model for post-industrial transformation.

Shared Ownership

Whether by corporate or governmental elites, Detroit's efforts to redefine itself through the decisions and valuation of a few, often have limited (or negative) impact for the many. More voices will be necessary in the discussion to shape a shared future in which thousands of new, diverse owners, can develop an equitable and collective narrative.

Political Expedience Can Hide Truth

Historically, the compulsion to satisfy political interests has limited the ability of key decision-makers to effectively confront the hard realities they have faced. This is a contributory factor to Detroit's municipal bankruptcy. Future leadership of all kinds must be unafraid to have the difficult, but productive, conversations necessary to shift away from business as usual. This is a moment for Detroit's "Profile in Courage."

Prospects for the Future

The Detroit that emerges in the next thirty years will be fundamentally different from the Detroit of the past, and for it to succeed, it will need to develop more relevant and innovative approaches to guide investment, reduce cost, and increase revenue. Strategic areas for focused growth, neighborhood stabilization, and vacant land transformation will allow the city not only to sustain itself, but to differentiate and lead. Informed by robust community input, research, and data analyses, a range of ongoing planning efforts, including Detroit Future City, can help to collaboratively outline these geographies, and support decision-makers to shape the policy and regulation to fulfill them.

Focused Growth

Detroit must focus investment for maximum impact citywide by leveraging existing assets and densities, and identifying emerging markets. Including the greater downtown, a range of mixed-use neighborhood centers, and employment centers (including industrial areas) can foster critical employment and residential gains to generate more efficient densities, desirable mixtures of use, and critical revenue for the city as a whole. Such areas can also utilize existing robust infrastructure systems.

While many have remarked that Detroit must "shrink" to meet its current conditions, instead its economy must grow to enable future opportunities. More Detroiters must be able to contribute to the city's labor force, and contribute to its revenue generation to support citywide functions.

Mixed-use areas can leverage Detroit's only present market demand to target development for multi-family mixed-use projects and stimulate emerging agglomeration economies that thrive in density. Detroit's pipeline of development for multi-family units has exponentially grown over the last few years, and will likely increase. Current occupancy rates for multi-family residential in Detroit's greater downtown average between 95 to 100 percent.[31] At the same time, many new and smaller-scale firms are emerging, and interest in Detroit's industrial land is growing. Finally, neighborhood mixed-use areas provide ripe opportunities for early reinvestment to increase residential densities and provide commercial and retail services to capture aspects of Detroit's annual retail leakage. Detroit must strategically guide investment, and stoke emerging markets to raise up and strengthen the city overall.

Neighborhood Stabilization

As Detroit's vast residential areas have suffered significant depopulation, degrading markets, and increased blight, the reason for many to stay has become less and less clear. Detroit must work to stabilize its traditional residential neighborhoods by strengthening localized mixed-use centers and commercial corridors, to re-occupy existing housing where possible, to focus home repair loans and other tools, and to eliminate blight. In some cases, where moderate degrees of land vacancy exist, side-lot disposition programs can allow neighbors to maintain property and eliminate a cost burden for the city.

Vacant Land Transformation

Detroit has the opportunity to transform its massive and growing vacant land portfolio—which is often plagued by illegal dumping and blight—from a costly liability that implicitly defines its failures, into an innovative open space network that can provide spaces for food production, renewable energy generation, green and blue infrastructure, and recreation. Here, Detroit's most symbolic image of devastation can be a globally significant site for urban ecological transformation, so long as the prospects for the future are not bound by the conventional wisdom of the past. Past mindsets have driven conventional reinvestment strategies only to see them fail, squandering increasingly precious resources, exacerbating the city's broad cost-revenue imbalance, and ultimately facing municipal bankruptcy.

Areas that today exist as codified "neighborhoods" through regulatory designations bear little resemblance to actual neighborhoods. While all Detroiters should be given the opportunity to remain where they live if they choose, over time the prevailing land use designation in Detroit's highest vacancy neighborhoods must include open space functions. Today, regulation upholds uses in these areas that many Detroiters have rejected, while denying emerging uses being promoted by Detroiters that can help all residents of the city. From simple tree plantings that can reconstitute Detroit's tree canopy, helping to mitigate heat island effect that claims lives every year, to food production sites that yield jobs and nutritious foods for a city dominated by food deserts and high death rates due to heart disease, Detroit does not need to look any further than the vacancy it has today to realize a new, sustainable future for tomorrow. All such innovative land uses can also create more hospitable environments for residents (Figure 3.4).

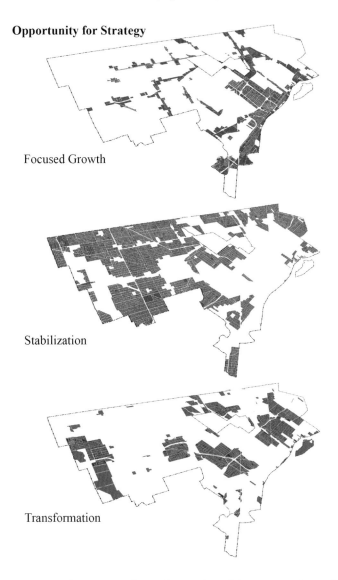

Figure 3.4 Opportunity for strategy: focused growth, stabilization, and transformation
Source: Adapted from Detroit Future City.

Grow the Economy

Detroit ranks as one of the strongest cities in the United States across a range of employment clusters. From digital and creative industries that catalyze innovation, to medical and educational anchor institutions with large workforces and procurement budgets, to automotive production and food processing, Detroit's economy can be cultivated to generate more jobs, and to create a more resilient and diverse employment spectrum.

Drive Agglomeration in Detroit's Innovation District and Beyond

Detroit's greater downtown, including its midtown area, and parts of the Corktown neighborhood has over 110,000 jobs, and has seen significant growth over the last ten years, even as the city as a whole saw jobs decline.[32] Detroit's Innovation District embodies the city's diverse economy and provides densities that foster entrepreneurial collaboration associated with agglomeration economies. Efforts must be made to catalyze other areas that may foster similar economic advantages over time, achieving greater penetration of economic growth into the city's neighborhoods.

Ensure Equitable Growth Outcomes

Detroit's economy must work for everyone, and with the current poverty rate of 39.3 percent and unemployment rate of 6.6 percent, that is a significant challenge.[33] Balanced and inclusive growth among Detroit's employment centers and economy should be thoughtfully connected with education, workforce, and capital access development programs.

Transform the Master Plan of Policies

Detroit's existing Master Plan has little relevance to Detroit's existing conditions or its potential future. Accordingly, it is a relatively unused tool, leaving municipal leaders and investors to often navigate an anecdotal and Byzantine process of redevelopment that exacerbates the tendency of weak market cities such as Detroit to accommodate actions that may serve only short-term gains at the cost of long-term vision and sustainability. Current community planning, and larger stakeholder-led strategic plans such as Detroit Future City offer remarkably informed and well-composed starting points for a new Master Plan.[34]

Update Zoning

To fulfill the objectives of a new Master Plan of Policies, current regulatory devices in the city—particularly zoning—must be updated to move beyond the existing Euclidean zoning that dominates. Given the spatialized dimension of Detroit's challenges (vacancies, low-density, auto-dependent single-uses, and adjacency of residential areas to industrial areas) updates including mixed-use, open space, and form-based provisions can reinforce the link between Detroit's urban form and its performance.

Strategically Renew Detroit's Systems

In many cases, Detroit's infrastructure systems and services will need to be modified to reflect and efficiently serve the changing densities and activities across the city. Today, some parts of the city have insufficient infrastructure capacity to support essential growth while others have expansive systems that cost much more than the revenues they generate, contributing to poor performance citywide. Poor service and cost-revenue imbalances must be addressed together.

Reduce Impact on the Great Lakes

Detroit is at the center of 84 percent of North America's fresh surface water supply, and 22 percent of the global supply,[35] but each year Detroit's combined sewer overflow system—similar to many other US cities of the same vintage—releases untreated waste into the Detroit River when rainfalls are heavy. In 2011, Detroit had thirty-six discharges.[36] Each year Detroit-area beaches are regularly closed due to high e-coli levels and the ecology of the Great Lakes is threatened. Rather than sinking billions of dollars into concrete storage vaults, as some cities are forced to do, Detroit has the opportunity to utilize its available land area to manage storm water through retention, detention, and direct conveyance systems while improving the quality of a globally significant natural resource, and reducing reliance on expensive fixed gray infrastructure systems. The Detroit Water and Sewerage Department has begun important pilot projects to fulfill this objective.[37]

Buffer Residents from Noxious Sources

With Detroit's industrial areas and high capacity roadways and freeways adjacent to neighborhoods, available vacant land area can be used to plant trees that provide carbon buffers from fugitive dust and diesel particulate matter. With a childhood asthma rate three times greater than the national average, these simple and cost-effective measures can improve quality of life for Detroiters citywide.[38]

Fuel Detroit's Dense Employment and Residential Growth

Greater density in Detroit is essential for its long-term viability, sustainability, and attractiveness to new investment and agglomerating economies. More robust systems will be both necessary to support this densification, and fiscally sustainable due to the supporting revenues.

Conclusion

Detroit has the opportunity to shape a new future where existing and often unrecognized assets can be leveraged, and long-running liabilities can be transformed. Rather than pursuing an elusive and irrelevant urban aspiration of the "conventional city," Detroit can blaze a new trail as a preeminent post-industrial "legacy city" providing globally significant lessons for others to follow. From the lumbering "tragic" laggard to the international center of innovative urbanism, Detroit's fundamental shift in mindset can set a new, and most importantly, sustainable trajectory. Where Detroit's past was defined by singular characteristics of industry, race, and land, its future will be defined by its ability to thoughtfully and strategically integrate an increasingly diverse array of opportunities, challenges, and ideas.

Detroit did not arrive at its current condition—nor will it emerge from it—overnight, but important shifts are already surfacing in the city that can be coordinated through shared city-wide strategic tools, while capitalizing on a revived and driven city government and motivated citizenry.

Notes

1   Daniel Okrent, "Detroit: The Death—and Possible Life—of a Great City." *Time*, September 24 2009.
2   US Census Bureau (1998) "Population of the 100 Largest Cities and Other Urban Places in the United States: 1790 to 1990." Available at: www.census.gov/population/www/documentation/twps0027/twps0027.html (accessed January 18, 2015).
3   Kenneth T. Jackson, *Crabgrass Frontier: The Suburbanization of the United States* (New York: Oxford University Press, 1985).
4   Richard F. Weingroff, "Federal-Aid Highway Act of 1956: Creating the Interstate system." 60(1) (1996). Available at: www.fhwa.dot.gov/publications/publicroads/96summer/p96su10b.cfm (accessed January 10, 2015).
5   June Manning-Thomas, *Redevelopment and Race: Planning a Finer City in Postwar Detroit* (Baltimore, MD: Johns Hopkins University Press. 1997).
6   Thomas J. Sugrue, *The Origins of Urban Crisis: Race and Inequality in Postwar Detroit* (Princeton, NJ: Princeton University Press, 1996).
7   SEMCOG (2015) "Residential Building Permits." Available at: http://archive.semcog.org/Data/Apps/permits.cfm?mcd=8999 (accessed January 5, 2015).
8   Dave Fornell, "Even Devils' Night Has Fallen On Hard Times." *Firehouse.com*, November 6, 2012. Available at: www.firehouse.com/blog/10825365/even-devils-night-has-fallen-on-hard-times (accessed March 15, 2015).
9   "Coleman A. Young, 79, Mayor of Detroit and Political Symbol for Blacks, Is Dead." *The New York Times*, December 1, 1997. Available at: www.nytimes.com/1997/12/01/us/coleman-a-young-79-mayor-of-detroit-and-political-symbol-for-blacks-is-dead.html (accessed January 10, 2015).
10 Jenny Nolan, "AutoPlant vs. Neighborhood: The Poletown Battle," *The Detroit News*, January 26. 2000. Available at: http://blogs.detroitnews.com/history/2000/01/26/auto-plant-vs-neighborhood-the-poletown-battle/ (accessed January 10, 2015).
11 SEMCOG (2002) "Historical Population and Employment by Minor Civil Division, Southeast Michigan." Available at: http://library.semcog.org/InmagicGenie/DocumentFolder/HistoricalPopulationSEMI.pdf
12 US Census Bureau (1998) "Population of the 100 Largest Cities and Other Urban Places in the United States: 1790 to 1990." Available at: www.census.gov/population/www/documentation/twps0027/twps0027.html (accessed January 18, 2015).
13 US Census Bureau (1990) "Table 23. Michigan—Race and Hispanic Origin for Selected Large Cities and Other Places: Earliest Census to 1990." Available at: www.census.gov/population/www/documentation/twps0076/MItab.pdf (accessed January 17, 2015.) US Census Bureau (2010) "Profile of General Demographic Characteristics: 2010." Available at: http://factfinder.census.gov/faces/tableservices/jsf/pages/productview.xhtml?src=bkmk (accessed March 14, 2015).
14 SEMCOG (2002) "Historical Population and Employment by Minor Civil Division, Southeast Michigan." Available at: http://library.semcog.org/InmagicGenie/DocumentFolder/HistoricalPopulationSEMI.pdf
15 Alan Mallach, ed., *Rebuilding America's Legacy Cities: New Directions for the Industrial Heartland* (New York: The American Assembly, Columbia University, 2012).
16 SEMCOG (2002) "Historical Population and Employment by Minor Civil Division, Southeast Michigan." Available at: http://library.semcog.org/InmagicGenie/DocumentFolder/HistoricalPopulationSEMI.pdf
17 Ibid.
18 Lavea Brachman and Alan Mallach, *Policy Focus Report: Regenerating America's Legacy Cities* (Cambridge, MA: Lincoln Institute of Land Policy, 2013).
19 "Detroit Bankruptcy Expert: City's Top Priorities Are Improved Information Systems, Highly Skilled Employees," *Crain's Detroit Business*, July 23, 2014. Available at: www.crainsdetroit.com/article/20140723/NEWS01/140729930/detroit-bankruptcy-expert-citys-top-priorities-are-improved (accessed January 16, 2015).
20 Motor City Mapping (2014). Available at: http://d3.d3.opendata.arcgis.com/datasets/7cfed5afb7654e2495ef4c1ead320aa5_0 (accessed January 20, 2015).
21 Detroit Future City, "2012 Strategic Framework." *The Detroit Future City: Strategic Framework Plan* (Detroit, 2013).

22 US Census Bureau (2010) "Profile of General Demographic Characteristics: 2010." Available at: http://factfinder.census.gov/faces/tableservices/jsf/pages/productview.xhtml?src= bkmk (accessed March 14, 2015).

23 US Census Bureau (2000) "Profile of General Demographic Characteristics: 2000." Available at: http://factfinder.census.gov/faces/tableservices/jsf/pages/productview.xhtml?src= bkmk (accessed March 14, 2015). US Census Bureau (2010) "Profile of General Demographic Characteristics: 2010." http://factfinder.census.gov/faces/tableservices/jsf/pages/productview. xhtml?src=bkmk (accessed March 14, 2015).

24 Mass Economics. Adapted from US Census Bureau 2000 Decennial Census, American Community Survey, 2013. US Census Bureau. "Profile of General Demographic Characteristics: 2010." http://factfinder.census.gov/faces/tableservices/jsf/pages/productview.xhtml?src=bkmk (accessed March 14, 2015).

25 Mass Economics. Adapted from Longitudinal Employer-Household Dynamics. 2011.

26 Elizabeth Kneebone, "Job Sprawl Stalls: The Great Recession and Metropolitan Employment Location." Brookings Metropolitan Policy Program. Available at: www.brookings.edu/research/ reports/2013/04/18-job-sprawl-kneebone (accessed March 14, 2015).

27 Mass Economics. Adapted from Quality of Workforce Index, All Jobs, 2000–2014.

28 Mass Economics. Adapted from Quality of Workforce Index; Quarterly Census of Employment Wages.

29 Detroit Future City, "2012 Strategic Framework." Detroit.

30 Ibid.

31 Zimmerman/Volk Associates. *Main Tables/Maps.* "Update: Residential Market Demand for Greater Downtown Detroit." Available at: http://downtowndetroit.org/wp-content/uploads/ 2014/04/Main-Tables-plus-maps.pdf

32 Detroit Future City, "2012 Strategic Framework."

33 US Census Bureau. "Profile of General Demographic Characteristics: 2010" Available at: http://factfinder.census.gov/faces/tableservices/jsf/pages/productview.xhtml?src=bkmk (accessed March 14, 2015).

34 Detroit Future City, "2012 Strategic Framework."

35 US Environmental Protection Agency. "Great Lakes Basic Information: Geography & Hydrology" Available at: www.epa.gov/greatlakes/basicinfo.html?_ga=1.61732076.17924692 35.1426428078 (accessed March 15, 2015).

36 Detroit Future City, "2012 Strategic Framework."

37 Khalil, AlHajal, "After the Flood, Expanded Green Infrastructure Could Help Absorb Rain, Planners Say," *Michigan Live*, August 16, 2014. Available at: www.mlive.com/news/detroit/ index.ssf/2014/08/after_the_flood_expanded_green.html

38 Detroit Future City, "2012 Strategic Framework."

References

Anon (1997) "Coleman A. Young, 79, Mayor of Detroit and political symbol for blacks, is dead." *The New York Times*, December 1, 1997. Available at: www.nytimes.com/1997/12/01/us/ coleman-a-young-79-mayor-of-detroit-and-political-symbol-for-blacks-is-dead.html (accessed January 10, 2015).

Anon (2014) "Detroit bankruptcy expert: City's top priorities are improved information systems, highly skilled employees," *Crain's Detroit Business*, July 23, 2014. Available at: www. crainsdetroit.com/article/20140723/NEWS01/140729930/detroit-bankruptcy-expert-citys-top-priorities-are-improved (accessed January 16, 2015).

Brachman, Lavea and Alan Mallach (2013) *Policy Focus Report: Regenerating America's Legacy Cities.* Cambridge, MA: Lincoln Institute of Land Policy.

Detroit Future City (2013) "2012 Strategic Framework." Detroit.

Fornell, Dave (2012) "Even Devils' Night Has Fallen On Hard Times." *Firehouse.com*, November 6. Available at: www.firehouse.com/blog/10825365/even-devils-night-has-fallen-on-hard-times (accessed March 15, 2015).

Jackson, Kenneth T. (1985) *Crabgrass Frontier: The Suburbanization of the United States.* New York: Oxford University Press.

Kneebone, Elizabeth (2013) "Job Sprawl Stalls: The Great Recession and Metropolitan Employment Location." Brookings Metropolitan Policy Program 2015. Available at: www.brookings.edu/research/reports/2013/04/18-job-sprawl-kneebone (accessed March 14, 2015).

Mallach, Alan, ed. (2012) *Rebuilding America's Legacy Cities: New Directions for the Industrial Heartland.* New York: The American Assembly, Columbia University.

Manning-Thomas, June (1997) *Redevelopment and Race: Planning a Finer City in Postwar Detroit.* Baltimore, MD: Johns Hopkins University Press.

Mass Economics (2015a) Adapted from Bureau of Labor Statistics, Local Area Unemployment Statistics Program and Current Population Survey, 1980–2014.

Mass Economics (2015b) Adapted from Longitudinal Employer-Household Dynamics. 2011.

Mass Economics (2015c) Adapted from Quality of Workforce Index, All Jobs, 2000-2014.

Mass Economics (2015d) Adapted from Quality of Workforce Index; Quarterly Census of Employment Wages.

Mass Economics (2015e) Adapted from US Census Bureau 2000 Decennial Census; American Community Survey, 2013 Single Year.

Motor City Mapping (2014) Available at: http://d3.d3.opendata.arcgis.com/datasets/7cfed5afb7654 e2495ef4c1ead320aa5_0 (accessed January 20, 2015).

Nolan, Jenny (2000) "Auto plant vs. neighborhood: The Poletown battle," *The Detroit News,* January 26. Available at: http://blogs.detroitnews.com/history/2000/01/26/auto-plant-vs-neighborhood-the-poletown-battle/ (accessed January 10, 2015).

Okrent, Daniel (2009) "Detroit: The Death—and Possible Life—of a Great City." *Time,* September 24, 2009.

SEMCOG (2002) "Historical Population and Employment by Minor Civil Division, Southeast Michigan." Available at: http://library.semcog.org/InmagicGenie/DocumentFolder/Historical PopulationSEMI.pdf

SEMCOG (2015) "Residential Building Permits." http://archive.semcog.org/Data/Apps/permits. cfm?mcd=8999 (accessed January 5, 2015).

Sugrue, Thomas J. (1996) *The Origins of Urban Crisis: Race and Inequality in Postwar Detroit.* Princeton, NJ: Princeton University Press.

US Census Bureau (1990) "Table 23. Michigan—Race and Hispanic Origin for Selected Large Cities and Other Places: Earliest Census to 1990."Available at: http://www.census.gov/population/www/documentation/twps0076/MItab.pdfwww.census.gov/population/www/documentation/twps0076/MItab.pdf (accessed January 17, 2015).

US Census Bureau (1998) "Population of the 100 Largest Cities and Other Urban Places in the United States: 1790 to 1990." Available at: www.census.gov/population/www/documentation/twps0027/twps0027.html (accessed January 18, 2015).

US Census Bureau (2000) "Profile of General Demographic Characteristics: 2000." Available at: http://factfinder.census.gov/faces/tableservices/jsf/pages/productview.xhtml?src=bkmk (accessed March 14, 2015).

US Census Bureau (2010) "Profile of General Demographic Characteristics: 2010." Available at: http://factfinder.census.gov/faces/tableservices/jsf/pages/productview.xhtml?src=bkmk (accessed March 14, 2015).

US Environmental Protection Agency (2015) "Great Lakes Basic Information: Geography & Hydrology." Available at: www.epa.gov/greatlakes/basicinfo.html?_ga=1.61732076.179246923 5.1426428078 (accessed March 15, 2015).

Weingroff, Richard F. (1996) "Federal-Aid Highway Act of 1956: Creating the Interstate System." 60(1). Available at: www.fhwa.dot.gov/publications/publicroads/96summer/p96su10b.cfm (accessed January 10, 2015).

Zimmerman/Volk Associates (2014) *Main Tables/Maps.* "Update: residential market demand for Greater Downtown Detroit." Available at: http://downtowndetroit.org/wp-content/uploads/2014/04/Main-Tables-plus-maps.pdf

4   Milwaukee Case Study

Larry P. Witzling

Introduction

An iconic poster from 1901 (Figure 4.1) celebrates Milwaukee as the place that "feeds and supplies" the world. A welcoming goddess on the poster convinces the viewer that Milwaukee is the epicenter of the globe's cultural, agricultural, and industrial footholds. When created, the poster may have been ahead of its time in marketing circles, but in a way, it serves as a history lesson that gives direction to Milwaukee's economic future. That history lesson teaches us how Milwaukee's resilience has been tested and survived, especially during the last three decades of economic decline. While Milwaukee shares many

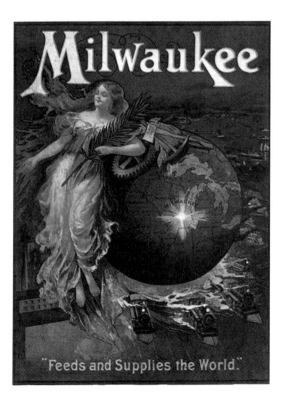

Figure 4.1 Milwaukee's iconic industrial poster, which captures today's reindustrialization of the city
Source: Artist unknown. "The Book of Milwaukee," Evening Wisconsin, 1901.

attributes with other Great Lakes cities, it retains unique characteristics as a "right-size" community poised for twenty-first-century transformation.

Today, Milwaukee's reindustrialization is energized by several factors, including partnerships for job training, downtown investments, neighborhood planning, reuse of vacant land, new approaches to expanding businesses, an entrepreneurial spirit, and people who embrace their city's traditions. In recent years Milwaukee has remediated environmental problems, implemented a Riverwalk, demolished an underused freeway, invigorated its beaches and lakefront, and opened up sites for housing and businesses that were previously unthinkable. However, challenges still abound regarding transit, public schools, the city's relationship to outer suburbs, chronic social and economic inequity, and public funding for infrastructure and civic uses. Within this milieu, Milwaukee began to reindustrialize through collective action of the public and private sectors.

Brief History of the City

Milwaukee's future is inescapably linked to its past. Milwaukee embraces an industrial heritage as an asset that needs strengthening—not just for short-term economic reasons, but also as part of a long-term view of a city that can thrive in a complex world economy. Reuse of past traditions helps Milwaukee become a more resilient city. Put another way, a city that does not embrace local manufacturing as an integral component of its economic life may not be sustainable in the long run.

At the turn of the twentieth century, the city produced steel and iron, and supported a full range of industries including tanneries, sausage factories, lithographers, and brewers. Rail lines and a commercial harbor shipped agricultural goods in addition to industrial products. Milwaukee was working like a well-oiled machine, with waterways, nearby farms, and access for goods and services.

In the 1920s and into the 1930s, Milwaukee was a strong city despite the challenges of the Great Depression. Work relief programs were initiated, but attention was also given to growth of the public park system, libraries, and other cultural needs.

After World War II, the sheen of the iconic poster faded as city neighborhoods suffered from economic disinvestment and were then brutally fractured by urban renewal in the 1960s. Suburbs grew, and like other cities, Milwaukee began experiencing a population loss in the 1970s. Heavy industry was on the decline. Skilled workers in the city lost their jobs. Factories moved first to suburbs (with cheap land and subsidies) and then to other states or offshore (with cheap labor). Social and economic equity worsened, as seen in Tables 4.1, 4.2 and 4.3.

Today, reversing economic decline continues to be the collective mission for many organizations as the revitalization of neighborhoods and industrial districts continues. Milwaukee once seemed mired in blue-collar traditions of "sausage and beer." Today, Milwaukee embraces those values, and still enjoys a "post-industrial" beer (sometimes found in the basements of arts and crafts bungalows or a host of new microbreweries). The Milwaukee Brewers baseball team adopted five racing sausages as mascots. The park system revived a nineteenth-century tradition of beer gardens, including "traveling" beer gardens operating at multiple sites. Figure 4.2 includes several icons that represent Milwaukee today.

From a more material economic perspective, key "driver" industries form the foundation of Milwaukee's current wave of reindustrialization. These drivers include the food and beverage, equipment manufacturing, energy production and delivery, and water management sectors (all with location quotients well above 1.0). New, and less predictable, opportunities have emerged from Milwaukee's traditions. Today, entrepreneurial activity goes beyond the arts, to include creativity in manufacturing start-ups, ongoing manufacturing shops, and larger industries considering expansion.

Table 4.1 Shift in place of work for residents in the city of Milwaukee

Place of work for residents of Metro Milwaukee (%)	1970	2011
Downtown Milwaukee	8.5	8.7
Rest of the City	47.2	25.3
Milwaukee County Suburbs	33.9	20.7
Waukesha County	11.9	24.6
Outside Metro Area	2.1	11.3

Table 4.2 Shift in household income for residents in the city of Milwaukee

Race	Change in real household income in Metro Milwaukee adjusted for inflation, 1979–2010 (%)
Metro – all households	−12
City of Milwaukee – all households	−25.4
Black households	−28.9
White non-Hispanic households	−2.2
Hispanic households	−20.7

Table 4.3 Shift in inequality for residents in the city of Milwaukee

Growing inequality in household income in the City of Milwaukee: % households in income classes adjusted for inflation	1979	2010
under 15,000	13.6	20
15,000-29,999	17.5	22.1
30,000-75,000	43.4	40.1
75,000-150,000	23.3	15.5
150,000 and above	2.2	2.4

Along with manufacturing, Wisconsin has a strong agricultural history. The preeminent goddess in the 1901 poster is prominently holding a sheath of wheat. In more recent times, urban agriculture has taken root in home gardens, community gardens and orchards, grounds around restaurants, and in urban farming sites like Will Allen's Growing Power projects, which have gained national attention. Urban agriculture grew exponentially in the last decade, changing the interrelationship of local farms, urban areas, and industry. It is impossible to view Milwaukee's neighborhoods today without recognizing many of the critical agricultural and food-related initiatives related to health, local economics, and long-term sustainability.

Conflicts over Urban Form: Milwaukee's Grid Wars

Change in Milwaukee, like many cities, did not occur without conflict. European colonization began just two hundred years ago with French traders. Pre- and post-European forms of development collided and then adjusted to create a city with new opportunities.

Figure 4.2 Milwaukee's high-art icon—the Art Museum addition—is shown here with two items that were part of an industrial design exhibit—the Oscar Meyer Weinermobile (designed by Milwaukee's Brook Stevens) and the Talgo train car—built, but not used in Milwaukee, due to a City-State political controversy

Source: Photo by author.

One of the more curious, but enduring events in Milwaukee's physical history, is the fight over urban form bordering the Milwaukee River. The river, which divides and unites Milwaukee's downtown, engendered a bitter dispute between two early settlers, Solomon Juneau and Hiram Kilbourn. Juneau founded his settlement east of the Milwaukee River, while Kilbourn settled on the west side. The two settlers intentionally misaligned their respective community streets to diminish the movement of goods and services, both across the river and between settlements. This was particularly evident when the Wisconsin territorial government erected a bridge that connected misaligned streets on opposing sides of the River. In 1845, a violent feud broke out and several bridges were destroyed or damaged. In response, a city charter was approved in 1846, which permanently united the settlements with three bridges, all at unique angles.

Ongoing Collisions of Form, Politics, and Economics

Battles over urban resources have never ended. When Milwaukee boasted a socialist mayor, Frank Ziedler (who inspired "sewer socialism"), Senator Joe McCarthy brought national notoriety to Wisconsin with his accusations of suspected Communists and homosexuals in the State Department. Years earlier Milwaukee's labor conflicts boiled over into the deaths of rolling mill workers—a tragedy memorialized in Bay View, one of Milwaukee's fastest improving districts. In the 1960s, Father Groppi's civil rights march from the north side to the south side marked another battle that had an eerily familiar congruence with Milwaukee's splits in city form, this time created by the Menomonee Valley.

The City in 1985

Physical Form and Conditions

After World War II, Milwaukee adopted many of the practices, some ill-fated, found in other Great Lakes cities. Freeways were built, suburbs expanded, urban renewal imposed, and deindustrialization increased (Table 4.4). Milwaukee's power and prominence diminished. As a city languishing in Chicago's shadow, it became harder for Milwaukee to gain stature as part of the region's economic engine. Today Milwaukee's smaller size may actually make it the "right-size" for reindustrialization and long-term sustainability.

Other pervasive conflicts that intertwined with urban form included the massive urban renewal projects that replaced great neighborhoods with architectural experiments derived from misguided architectural theories. At the same time, freeways destroyed highly functional systems of streets and blocks, which destabilized some of Milwaukee's poorest neighborhoods, as seen in Figure 4.3.

During the 1980s, much of the urban form slowly stabilized (not necessarily in a good way) and discussions became focused on improving Milwaukee's physical condition. In previous times Milwaukee had boasted a reputation for maintaining a high quality of public infrastructure and services (nicknamed the center of "sewer socialism"). These civic virtues reawakened, although funding, as always, remained a struggle. The value of urbanism was recognized by 1985 but no changes had yet occurred. Reinvestments were a topic of discussion for areas along Lake Michigan and even outside the city limits in older inner ring suburbs abutting Milwaukee.

In the 1980s, the Milwaukee development community would not build anything but large single-family detached homes. Multi-family housing—even townhouses—was considered unpopular, undesirable, and unmarketable. Not even "upscale townhouse" had been accepted and common usage of the word "condominium" had not changed from segregated suburban multi-family units to higher-end apartments in urban centers. Infrastructure suffered from deferred maintenance and lack of regional support. Even older traditional suburbs abutting the Milwaukee boundary began to stagnate. New development was considered feasible primarily in outer suburbs where the new infrastructure and tax base were subsidized, greenfield development cost less, and legacy problems had not emerged.

Table 4.4 Shifts of manufacturing employment in the Milwaukee region

Manufacturing employment and the deindustrialization of Milwaukee, 1963–2009

Year	City of Milwaukee	Milwaukee County Suburbs	Exurbs	% of MSA manufacturing in the City of Milwaukee
1963	119,284	56,051	24,858	59.60%
1967	118,600	62,500	35,400	54.80%
1977	91,400	62,200	50,500	44.80%
1982	77,900	51,400	51,100	43.20%
1987	63,900	43,100	57,000	40.00%
1997	46,467	40,466	78,210	28.10%
2002	34,957	32,654	71,386	25.10%
2009	27,253	26,342	63,025	18.90%
% change, 1963–2009	−77.2%	−53.0%	153.60%	

1910

1966

1996

Figure 4.3 Three figure-ground maps of Milwaukee's downtown showing the grain of streets, blocks and small lots prevalent through the 1910s (top), with minor degradation in the 1950s (middle) and destroyed in the 1960s (bottom) by new freeways, urban renewal, and superblock developments

Source: Adapted from UWM student drawings.

Demographics

Always a diverse city, post-suburbanization problems persisted with segregation, classism, poverty, and inequality. Population declined alongside property values. The social and economic statistics noted earlier in Tables 4.2 and 4.4 will not surprise anyone. The same demographic shifts that impacted other cities also impacted Milwaukee. Some of these changes reflected a major downward trend. As recently as the mid-1970s Milwaukee's worst neighborhoods were better than those of comparable cities. Yet by 1985 these neighborhoods were in trouble. As these neighborhoods continued to languish, major community-based efforts focusing on neighborhood planning and reinvestment began. Initially in conflict with overall city plans of the 1970s, these neighborhood-scale planning efforts were eventually integrated with overall planning policies and practices.

Economy

The neighborhood changes impacted Milwaukee's oldest industrial areas. Industrial districts had grown along rail lines that were built bordering riverine topography. This geographic legacy created a loosely linked, well-distributed pattern of industrial districts and its residential areas, seen in Figure 4.4.

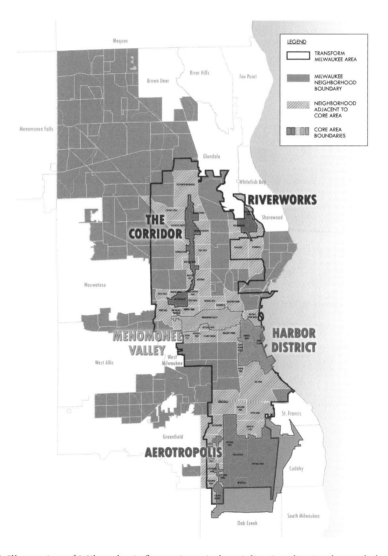

Figure 4.4 Illustration of Milwaukee's five major reindustrialization districts located along rail lines, linked with walkable residential neighborhoods that grew in the surrounding system of streets and blocks

Source: Drawings by GRAEF.

Milwaukee's industrial districts display a formal structure, however, that is not easily perceived on the ground. Most industrial areas do not have a single name or identity. Few offer easily perceived or coherent street systems and some of these industrial areas extend beyond the city boundaries.

Over decades, industrial areas lost their initial economic luster. Early twentieth-century pictures of cities with smokestacks implied strength and pride. At the end of the twentieth century, like other Great Lakes cities, Milwaukee's smokestacks became symbols of obsolescence and environmental degradation—especially compared to suburban imagery that rarely depicted a factory. These vacant and underutilized industrial structures, while still functional, have become symbols of undesirable conditions and blight.

Milwaukee's central business district (CBD) also declined in the 1980s. Major retailers left for suburban malls. High-rise offices remained, but there was little or no street life to be seen after hours. On weekends, downtown streets were relatively empty. Downtown was not seen as a location of choice for new business although many financial services remained. Similarly downtown residential uses—and the accompanying economic benefits—were not present. In sum, by 1985, Milwaukee's economy was not seen favorably and the ultimate signs of a potential urban turnaround were barely noticeable.

The City in 2015

Physical Form and Conditions

By the 1990s, city leaders began to heal the shocks to Milwaukee's urban systems by demolishing an urban freeway (Park East), along the north side of Milwaukee's downtown (see Figure 4.5). This led to a bitter ideological fight with proponents of suburban supremacy. Today, no one, regardless of ideology, has asked to put back the demolished freeway. Nonetheless, this collision of ideologies has become part of Milwaukee's tradition. These conflicts seem debilitating and symptomatic of dysfunction, but ultimately they function like a useful system of checks and balances.

Today, the misaligned street grids on each side of the river create an accidental and often picturesque asset, as well as providing unique views, additional character to the urban form, and ultimately enhancing the Riverwalk. Yet the legacy of Milwaukee's grid war, while a cause of open conflict at one time, still presents an unhealed division in the downtown. Other anomalies in Milwaukee's streets and blocks fit variations in topography, environmental features, and local development history. The unique form of Milwaukee's urban pattern, especially the tight-knit fabric of smaller lots and walkable streets, influences the way development occurs and the structure of future opportunities.

As the urban economy re-emerges, debate continues about policies, infrastructure needs, and land use. Discussions often embody older, anti-urban prejudice about crime, density, mixed-use, walkability, and public transit. When positive analyses occur, they often reflect superficial concepts borrowed from other cities. Milwaukee needs in-depth focused actions that fit its unique combination of strong assets and overcome specific socioeconomic liabilities.

From an urban design perspective, Milwaukee rests on a superb fine-grained texture of smaller buildings, streets, and blocks with diverse social and economic activities, far beyond oversimplified labels of "mixed use." Much of this social and economic diversity has weathered the injuries of urban renewal, freeways, and suburban ideologies. For example, throughout the 1980s and 1990s, attempts to create urbanist models of residential units above retail on walkable streets were met with derision, especially from suburban critics and investors. Within twenty years, however, this model has reversed, not because

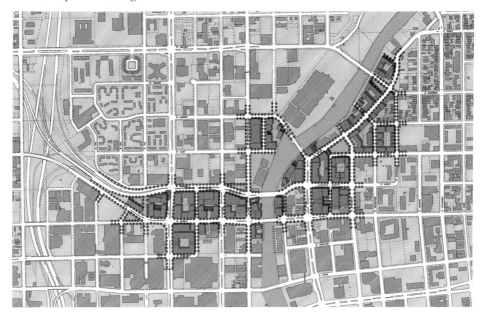

Figure 4.5 Illustration of Milwaukee's 2003 Park East redevelopment plan using a form-based code to replace the historic texture of streets and blocks that were devastated by freeway development in Milwaukee's downtown. About 60 percent of the planned development has been completed over twelve years.

Source: Drawing by GRAEF.

of enlightened thinking but due to simple changes in market preferences. Now the popularity of this approach has led some suburbs to require use of this model (albeit in areas where markets are insufficient).

Unlike many urban areas, the value of urban living in Milwaukee was intentionally suppressed through aggressive suburbanization accompanied by the political desire to shift resources away from the city. Today, however, "re-urbanism" has hit Milwaukee and has clearly impacted the economy, urban form, and infrastructure. Several factors have contributed to improved and more realistic attitudes toward Milwaukee's urban areas and the corresponding markets. For years, planning and urban design professionals have advocated higher intensity urban solutions. However, this new wave has finally taken root as many millennials have acted on their dissatisfaction with suburban lifestyles. As millennials leave home, it is fashionable for remaining suburban boomers (or empty nesters) to leave homes with too much space, higher energy costs, and demanding levels of maintenance for downtown apartments. The social attraction of higher density living, regardless of style and ideology, has grown, perhaps irrevocably, seen in Figure 4.6.

Today, Milwaukee has detailed plans for all of its neighborhoods along with effective implementation plans and ongoing action steps. The number of organizations aimed at neighborhood improvement has increased remarkably—from just a few in the late 1960s to hundreds of groups by 2010. This transition includes private sector, public sector, and non-profit organizations (Figures 4.7 and 4.8).

During the last twenty years, the nationwide shift to urbanism came to Milwaukee. The city sees itself as a high value urban form requiring a holistic and comprehensive approach. The texture of buildings, streets, blocks, and public places is returning after several new initiatives, including the demolition of an unneeded freeway, the construction of public housing using paradigms of New Urbanism, and most importantly, the recognition that a

Figure 4.6 The Milwaukee River in the Third Ward depicting older industrial waterfront buildings and recreational boating—a scene typical of many Great Lakes Cities that replaced older industrial uses with non-industrial activity

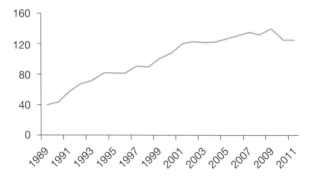

Figure 4.7 Growth in number of community improvement organizations in Greater Milwaukee, 1989–2011

Source: Derived from Laper (2014) and the National Center for Charitable Statistics.

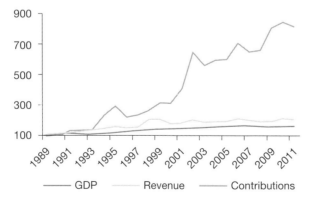

Figure 4.8 Indexed growth of GDP, revenue and contributions of community improvement organizations in Greater Milwaukee

Source: Derived from Laper (2014) and the National Center for Charitable Statistics.

city rests on its neighborhoods. The city has invested years in helping each neighborhood develop a detailed plan with local input. For the most part, these plans are in the implementation phase.

Now the question for Milwaukee is how, and in what way, will this trend impact industry? In many cities around the Great Lakes, urbanist values have been used as an excuse to diminish or discard industrial districts. This may be a hangover from the habit of yielding to suburban models (in this case the "business park"). In Milwaukee, however, there is resistance to this industrial gentrification, which may in turn become one of Milwaukee's great strengths.

Economy

In Milwaukee, the era of rejecting urban industry has closed. The question now is how industry will not only survive, but also grow. The city cannot and has little desire to recreate the 1930s. So what will urban industry in Milwaukee look like? How will it function socially and economically?

Today, Milwaukee's industrial activity might be better characterized as "reindustrialization" rather than "post-industrialization." This may seem like splitting hairs, but it reflects how Milwaukee views its urban past and future. Undoubtedly the form of factories has changed, but they still embody industrial and manufacturing activity. In many cities the preferred solution has been the conversion of older factory districts to non-industrial uses. In Milwaukee, older industrial areas (including some older buildings) are being converted to new industrial uses.

Decades earlier, Milwaukee's factories were fully integrated with neighborhoods—beer and sausage were part of the daily industrial routine at the tavern across the street from the factory. Today, the tavern and the factory are becoming reacquainted. Urban gardens, farm-to-table restaurants, and a burgeoning art scene are integrated with new industrial workplaces.

Milwaukee experienced much of its growth as a nineteenth-century industrial powerhouse. Its neighborhoods, ethnic history, social patterns, and economic conditions have been well chronicled (see References). Many challenges remain unresolved, such as insufficient funding for infrastructure, ineffective transit, poverty exacerbated by increasing social and economic inequality, a high level of racial segregation, and economic competition within the Great Lakes region. Milwaukee must respond and adapt to such realities, but also build upon its successful pre-industrial and industrial heritage.

Industrial growth depended on Milwaukee's accessible port and railroads, which, in turn dominated parts of the city's form. Moreover, many industrial areas were shaped before new streets, blocks, and utilities reached their location. In other cases industrial areas were too difficult to modify because of environmental factors. Milwaukee's industrial districts constitute a system of urban forms that abut, but rarely intertwine with residential neighborhoods.

Transformation of the City (1985–2015)

By the late 1990s, Milwaukee had begun to recover. Redevelopment of downtown, lakeshore, and riverside neighborhoods gained a foothold. Private and public leaders saw the city as an opportunity to create a new and economically sustainable community. Since 2000, and through the recession of 2008–2009, the urban renaissance spread throughout the city. Neighborhood plans were created for every part of Milwaukee. Community partnerships were formed and infrastructure expanded. Community and economic development became a central mission for many public, private, and not-for-profit organizations. Several groups took the lead, even before the Great Recession, to begin the process of reindustrialization and stabilization.

Today, however, the city's political roots—still filled with conflict—have been rekindled only to emerge with new debates over transit, employment, and social values.

What Went Right?

After 1985, five key industrial areas became the focus of major revitalization plans: *the 30th Street Corridor, Riverworks, the Menomonee Valley, the Inner Harbor District and the Aerotropolis (South Shore)*, as seen in Figure 4.2. Each district presents a unique context, historical circumstance, and opportunity. No common formula exists for revitalizing all districts. Improvements for each district must be customized to fit social, economic, physical, and political conditions—both internal within the district and external within surrounding neighborhoods. There are non-profit organizations in each district focused on this process.

Menomonee Valley: The Benchmark for Bringing Back Industry

The Menomonee Valley includes Milwaukee's historic industrial center in its 1,132 acres. Valley boundaries follow bluffs and waterways, reinforced by multiple rail lines and utilities. The Valley once contained 40,000 jobs, factories, foul aromas, and floods. The Valley—not Lake Michigan—was the most ubiquitous landmark view of the city for both residents and visitors. Today the odors are gone and waterways remediated (with trout fishing). New buildings include factories, a casino, hotel, and a museum. New infrastructure includes vehicular and pedestrian bridges, trails, and roads. Components of the Valley's industrial and natural history are back in the picture.

The Valley was targeted as an industrial park back in the 1970s but nothing happened. In the 1990s, student-based proposals at the University of Wisconsin-Milwaukee rekindled interest. Spurred further by community activists, a citywide charette and national design competition, a new Valley has emerged as a major, regional force in statewide economic development. The risks faced by early investor "pioneers" have diminished. Today the challenges concern land assembly, employee transit, reuse of older industrial buildings along the periphery, and linkages to surrounding neighborhoods.

Riverworks: A Naturally Occurring Live-Make-Work Neighborhood

The Riverworks, at 37 acres, is the smallest of the five industrial areas, tucked into a northeast corner of Milwaukee amidst distinct residential sub-areas. The north and east boundaries abut older, wealthier inner-ring suburban communities, namely Glendale (along with a successful business park) and Shorewood (along the Milwaukee River). To the south, students, artists, families, and millennials, are prevalent in the diverse Riverwest neighborhood. To the west, the primarily African-American Harambee neighborhood includes more families, but also a higher level of unemployment.

Revitalizing with little publicity, Riverworks has become an exemplar for the live-work neighborhood. It offers enormous diversity of industrial workplaces along with retail, recreational and residential uses—all integrated in a dense, compact urban pattern. Transit connections are strong. When compared to theoretical models of mixed-use neighborhoods, it exceeds expectations with "maker places," art trails, housing, shops, and cultural diversity. Most importantly, new jobs in Riverworks have benefitted the unemployed and underemployed residents of the Harambee neighborhood to the west.

Few New Urbanist neighborhoods, LEED-ND neighborhoods, or other national examples of neighborhood development intentionally include manufacturing uses as substantial as those in Riverworks. In this regard, Riverworks represents an outstanding success—something that Milwaukee should exploit. The factors that created this success need to be documented so that other urban industrial districts like Riverworks can succeed without too many "top-down" interventions.

The 30th Street Corridor: Just Started and On the Way

The 30th Street Corridor, located within the city's north side, parallels the railroad in an elongated form (a few blocks wide but over 3 miles long). The Corridor embodies the industrial impact of rail systems. Unlike Riverworks, which became a small, 37-acre, live-make-grow district, the Corridor intersects multiple neighborhoods offering 905 acres of potential. Any or all of the surrounding twelve neighborhoods can become a distinct live-make-grow sub-area.

New industry and business investment currently focuses on the approximate north–south center of the Corridor intersecting Capitol Drive, a major east–west thoroughfare. This intersection creates four quadrants, with different investment options and opportunities for driver industries. Investment planning includes both workforce development (that places unemployed and underemployed residents in new jobs) and adjacent neighborhood revitalization. Substantial industrial investments, with high visibility, have already begun—both new construction and adaptive reuse. These investments will provide the foundation for additional interventions, decrease the perceived risks, and increase the pace of redevelopment.

Inner Harbor District: The Future of a Resilient Live-Make-Grow Neighborhood

The Inner Harbor District (1,223 acres) includes an agglomeration of several sub-areas surrounding Milwaukee's inner harbor. Sub-areas include the Port of Milwaukee and the Milwaukee Metropolitan Sewerage District (MMSD) on Jones Island, open industrial land and wetlands that border Bay View, Walker's Point, the Third Ward, and the Milwaukee River. The district is overlapped by rail lines, portions of the Kinnickinnic River, major arterials, bridges, and a mixture of uses—residential, commercial, cultural, industrial, and recreational.

The Harbor District's potential for prominence, waterfront amenity, social and economic value, and adjacency to diverse populations represents an unmatched convergence of urban features. Already there are competing plans and multiple investment interests. Considerable discussion has occurred regarding land as a resource for new industry, especially for the Port of Milwaukee. At the same time, however, competing land uses offer equally valid approaches to social and economic value.

Aerotropolis in the South Shore: A New Way to Connect Industry and Urbanism

Many cities have embraced the "Aerotropolis" concept as a mega-scale development concept, usually built on greenfields, surrounding an airport, linked to major transportation arterials and regional transit systems. In Milwaukee's South Shore neighborhood however, a revised interpretation of an "Aerotropolis" is underway—that of an airport which becomes the center of context-driven development. General Mitchell International Airport

(GMIA) is the center of the Aerotropolis with 6,290 acres (most of which constitutes the GMIA). The district expands from the airport in all directions, and includes portions of four municipalities in addition to the City of Milwaukee. The context includes older urban neighborhoods as well as suburbanized areas. Decades of development (and redevelopment) include a patchwork arrangement of industry, housing, retail, parks, hotels, and pockets of open land.

The South Shore's Aerotropolis represents a logical high-target area for industry. Many jobs in the airport can be accessed through current transit service (or with moderate additions to that service), especially for residents located in the south side of Milwaukee. Also, open land near the airport, with proximity to the Inner Harbor District, can facilitate manufacturing logistics and related services for rail and water-borne transportation.

What Went Wrong?

For many decades urban industrial disinvestment has been touted as a "city" problem blamed on the innate failures of urban living. Anti-urban attitudes are a critical legacy of American history.[1] This engrained anti-urban attitude is like a virus that removes resources for urban transit, education, infrastructure and neighborhood revitalization.

While local government remained accountable for internal decisions, much of "what went wrong" was due to political rhetoric that blamed cities for their misfortunes while taking away resources unfairly. Anti-urban actions were akin to "blaming the victim." Mistakes followed two overlapping narratives—external harm caused by external authority and internal errors due to self-imposed mistakes.

Menomonee Valley: The Benchmark for Bringing Industry Back to the City

Initially, industrializing the Valley was intended to create walk-to-work jobs, reducing reliance on automobiles. In the past, walking to jobs in the Valley was commonplace. Today, walk-to-work is barely possible. Proponents of the Valley envisioned walkability but did not make it happen. Then, when bicycle movement became feasible, bicycle trails for recreation were added but real commuters were not served.

The Valley, which was never close to residential areas, is still segregated, perhaps more than before. New industries and new entertainment uses (not part of the plan for new jobs) contain enormous parking fields, consistent with a suburban, business park model. What went wrong is that the Valley became a successful suburban business park—auto-based, segregated, and focused on new construction. Fortunately the latest round of planning has started to refocus on the need for urbanization including transit, adaptive reuse and neighborhood connections.

Riverworks: A Naturally Occurring Live-Make-Work Neighborhood

Few people outside of Riverworks understand its success. Except for local government there has been little effort to promote Riverworks, largely because it lacks the suburban imagery of success. Riverworks is not a bounded "business park." Most of the buildings are old, built in diverse styles and lacking the economic "curb" appeal of new structures. Thankfully, there are no physical buffers that isolate the district. The success of the Riverworks is a story that should be told; it is compelling because it differs from the current model.

Riverworks is not "broken," nor does it require "fixing." It needs support and a strategy to resist local gentrification. The next phase for this live-make-grow neighborhood should include both more industry as well as more local employment. It also must be made visually appealing. Perhaps it could serve as a new model for other small urban industrial districts.

The 30th Street Corridor: Just Started and On the Way

The 30th Street Corridor is the opposite of the Valley with strong opportunities for neighborhood connections, but almost no new industry. Abutting neighborhoods include populations most harmed by decades of lost manufacturing jobs that began before the Great Recession. Historically, when employment was high, local problems were diminished. Yet today, the problems are blamed on the neighborhoods, not the external economic failures: unemployment due to deindustrialization; foreclosures due to housing and banking abuses; economic inequality due to shifting incomes; increasing poverty due to disinvestment; flooding due to outmoded infrastructure; defunding of social services and programs due to partisan fighting; decades of unaffordable health care; more than a century of racism; and a continuous string of failed public policies. These inequities represent external systemic abuse, not an internal failure.

Despite this overwhelming oppressiveness, many neighborhoods remain strong and poised for improvement. Local government policies have turned around. Private sector leaders have begun reinvestment. Proposed changes are now based more on the realities on the ground, not conflicting ideologies. New and reused industrial structures have emerged with more local jobs. MMSD has begun planning a greenway that mitigates flooding and provides local jobs and new public places (perhaps reflecting some of the better attributes of Milwaukee's older "sewer socialism"). The failure at this time is one of delay.

Inner Harbor District: The Future of a Resilient Live-Make-Grow Neighborhood

Not much has gone wrong in the Inner Harbor District because it is just beginning. If there is a failure it is one of omission rather than commission. There is some evidence of action with a new university campus satellite, a restored wetland, new mixed-use development to the north, and an emerging not-for-profit organization. Some see the Harbor District as the "next Valley"—a large, segregated industrial park similar to the suburbs. Others see the potential for vacant and underutilized buildings as the basis for mixed-use, live-make-grow neighborhood. Still others voice hopes for business startups, creative class jobs, and workforce training.

While some planning has begun, there is no evidence that it will effectively increase social and economic equity. Planning can cause unproductive delays and lead to more "omissions" or it can be timely, productive, and help make collaborative actions more effective. Time will tell how the Harbor District fares.

Aerotropolis in the South Shore: A New Way to Connect Industry and Urbanism

Like many mid-size airports in the United States, GMIA has experienced air service decline. While passenger facilities remain adequate, the goal is to increase ridership through joint public/private actions, increase Amtrak service (from northern Illinois), create regional transit connections, and reduce "leakage" to Chicago's O'Hare airport. None of this has yet happened. Like the Harbor District, there has been a failure to plan, act, and implement effectively.

Unrealized opportunities include larger industrial facilities to the east and south, expanded hotel/restaurant nodes, and a town center. Organized political commitment has yet to materialize. The airport itself is controlled by Milwaukee County, but development approvals are still regulated by five municipalities. Key groups have established a memorandum of understanding but work is just beginning. A private development corporation is planned but not operational. Multijurisdictional planning (coupled with tax increment financing) has been proposed. Private corporate leaders are not sufficiently involved and state support is only a future possibility.

Lessons Learned

Reindustrialization as an Attitude

A distinction for Milwaukee is the degree to which its industrial history has been, and still is, recognized as the backbone of urban vitality. Milwaukee uses its assets for reindustrialization, including its abundance of potable surface water, industrial talent, skilled workers, great buildings, and solid physical infrastructure. Other cities share these traits, but for Milwaukee they define its economic character.

Reindustrialization Coupled with Re-Cultivation

The concurrence of reindustrialization with re-cultivation of urban areas may not be coincidental. These two trends may be part of a new cycle of urbanization. Post-industrialization may not be the top mark of a linear trend line, but another curve at the end of a cycle. Cities may return to superior pre-industrial and industrial patterns as well as earlier, better patterns of agriculture and cultivation.

Post-Industrialization as the End of a Cycle

A cyclical interpretation may be a productive way to think about how we can make our cities resilient (and more equitable). Cities need to manufacture products locally as well as cultivate food for their health and well-being. Milwaukee's agricultural and industrial traditions, as well as its abundance of water, good soil, and skilled workers, make it a prime candidate to be a highly self-reliant (i.e., resilient). If valid, this hypothesis implies that reindustrialization and re-cultivation will engage each other and transform our cities yet again.

Starting a New Cycle of Resilience

One view of resilience is that the late 1700s was the last time the United States had an ecological footprint of less than one. We should not return to those days, but there may be inherent lessons that need to be rediscovered. For example, historic Williamsburg's main street includes houses with vegetable gardens and workshops in the back yard—a "live-make-grow" model of the 1700s. Riverworks in Milwaukee, within a few feet, has the same three uses. The minor difference is the land ownership pattern rather than the intent or outcome.

Planning "Live-Make-Grow" Neighborhood as the Foundation for Urban Resilience

Late twentieth-century planning viewed density as non-compatible with industry and agriculture. This view may not have been accurate and it may no longer be sustainable. A self-reliant city should integrate its needs within one cohesive urban pattern—perhaps equivalent to a contemporary city-state. A city in which land uses and infrastructure are organized as a dense, but decentralized system may be more adept in responding to change from environmental events as well as social, economic and political events. The city would be planned as a network of live-make-grow neighborhoods. Manufacturing and agricultural uses would not be isolated as an unwelcome nuisance, but integrated, just like housing, offices, retail, and recreation.

Networked Neighborhoods as the Cornerstone

Over the next twenty-five years neighborhood planning will redouble in importance. Neighborhoods represent the logical balance point between top-down city planning and bottom-up community planning. This is not a call for neighborhoods as governmental units but rather flexible, dynamic types of places. Neighborhoods can facilitate dense, but decentralized systems for energy, food, education, and other infrastructural components essential to the security and sustainability of urban areas. Networks among neighborhoods will require strengthened transit and transportation infrastructure.

Prospects for the Future

Based on the Milwaukee's reindustrialization, several speculations should be considered that could be applicable to other cities, especially those with a similar context.

Industrialization, Cultivation, and Urbanism Integrate

New integrations and divisions of industrial jobs and networks will continue, changing the industrial landscape and generating new patterns of economic behavior within the city. Urban agriculture will evolve as a key part of urban development. For industry, new ways of integrating industrial uses into urban areas will become prominent and the value of older industrial buildings—for industrial uses—will increase. The diversity of industrial activity may become a great strength, built upon the increase in unforeseen opportunities for collaboration among local businesses.

Older Conflicts Diminish

The traditional conflicts between industrial forms and the rest of the city will disappear (just like the conflict between residential and retail uses has vanished in denser urban neighborhoods). Industrial parks which lack diversity (both urban and suburban) will become less popular, especially as capital equipment investment reaches planned obsolescence and these isolated areas require untenable infrastructure reinvestment. A comparable trend in land has begun with reduced prohibitions against urban agriculture, viewing it as an asset not a nuisance.

New Conflicts Emerge

New conflicts will emerge as unexpected problems develop, such as conflicts among neighborhoods that embrace different views of their future. Planners will need to accept greater variation in patterns of form and infrastructure and, at the same time, find new ways of integrating such patterns within coherent communities. For example, Milwaukee's Oak Leaf Trail is a "low line" rail cut exposing layers of Milwaukee's industrial history (Figure 4.9), connecting neighborhoods and attracting new uses. Today these uses are simply accepted, but as they grow they may be the source of conflict.

Figure 4.9 Milwaukee's Oak Leaf Trail—an old rail cut through multiple neighborhoods—the equivalent of a "low line," where century-old stone walls reveal the layers of industrial history (palimpsest). Today residents and neighbors are modifying this rail cut as a seam uniting housing and industry within live-work-grow districts.

Formulaic Standards are Replaced by Customization to Context and Performance

As urban patterns change, new patterns will emerge that combine industry, agriculture and buildings. Plans that adopt standards-based solutions may fail—as the planning equivalent of commodity-based solutions. As the cost of customized plans increases, planners will need to do a better job of confirming payoffs for contextualized planning as well as the negative consequence of less expensive commodity planning.

Long-Term Risk Reward Becomes the Key Calculus

Models of risk and reward will need to refocus on long-term outcomes. Private and public sector demands for short-term rewards should be subordinated to long-term, consensus-based solutions. Tax Increment Financing (TIF) districts, for example, may need to pay off at the end, not the beginning. Tax codes can be revised to give developers a much better return after twenty years, but little return at the front end. The reward for sustainability must be linked to back-end performance (perhaps with back-end tax credits), not with front-end rewards.

Note

1   Morton White, and Lucia White, *Intellectual Versus the City: From Thomas Jefferson to Frank Lloyd Wright* (Literary Licensing LLC, June 2012).

References

Gurda, John, *The Making of Milwaukee*. Madison, WI: University of Wisconsin Press, 1999.

Laper, Phillip M. "Give and you will receive: An analysis of nonprofit revenue trends and charitable giving in Greater Milwaukee." Public Policy Forum, Milwaukee, July 2014.

Levine, Marc V. "Perspectives on the Current State of the Milwaukee Economy." University of Wisconsin—Milwaukee Center for Economic Development, July 2013.

"The Book of Milwaukee," *Evening Wisconsin*, 1901.

University of Wisconsin—Extension, Center for Community and Economic Development, Transform Milwaukee Research; 2014. Available at: http://cced.ces.uwex.edu/community-preparedness-resiliency/transform-milwaukee-research/

US Bureau of the Census, Economic Census, American Community Survey.

US Bureau of the Census, Economic Census, and Longitudinal Employer-Household Dynamics

Wisconsin Housing and Economic Development Authority, "Transform Milwaukee Strategic Action Plan" (draft released April 30, 2015). Available at: www.transformmilwaukee.com

5 New Orleans Case Study

Maurice Cox and Jacqueline Taylor

Introduction

New Orleans owes its physical existence and character to one of the world's largest, most habitat-diverse, and biologically productive rivers, the Mississippi, which flows 2,350 miles along the length of North America from Lake Itasca in north central Minnesota to the Gulf of Mexico.[1] The site of New Orleans was recognized early on as a valuable gateway with strategic connections along the Mississippi River's natural highways accessing the rich interior of North America. Unlike any other North American river, however, the Mississippi has a delta, is characterized by several mouths, and is flanked by very low-lying land, mudflats, sandbars, and bayous—local patois for a stream or small river (Figure 5.1).[2]

Due to the specific and highly complex geologic history of the Mississippi delta, no part of New Orleans is more than 15 feet above sea level. Naturally occurring high levels of land resulted from deposits created by the ebb and flow of the river, and successive overflowing of its banks. These were known by the French term *levée*, and originally provided the only well-drained land suitable for settlement; the back swamp areas, breeding ground for malaria and yellow fever, became suitable for building only when innovations in technology produced large-scale pumps. Moreover, the idiosyncratic nature of the Mississippi to change its course and flood parts of the city, proved a constant concern and threat to settlement, alleviated only through various man-made control devices. Together with threats posed by extreme climate and the prevalence of hurricanes and tropical rains, the Mississippi River and its geologic history have thus defined New Orleans' human history, patterns of growth and physical development. Today, much of the city of New Orleans is built on land that is sinking, some of it rapidly.[3]

New Orleans may owe its physical existence and character to the river but its cultural character and contemporary reputation derive from its foreign origins. Locals call it the Crescent City because development follows the wide crescent-shaped bend in the river; others know it as the Big Easy, the birthplace of Jazz, and as embracing a French *laissez-faire* attitude to life.[4] No matter its nomenclature, New Orleans is a very different kind of American city.

Advantageous trade connections to North America through the Mississippi, and to the Caribbean, Europe and the southern hemisphere through the Gulf of Mexico, rendered New Orleans a prime tourist destination from the start. Oil and gas resources drove the region's economy between the 1960s and mid-1980s, until the worldwide oil crash returned the city to depend on tourism and the service industry in the 1990s.[5] All of these industries have influenced the development of the city in positive and negative ways.

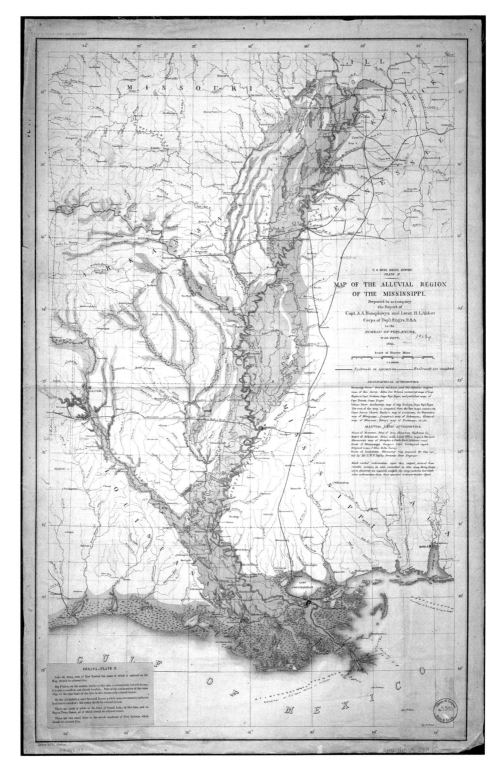

Figure 5.1 Map of the alluvial region of the Mississippi Delta, 1861
Source: Drawn by Charles Mahon, provided by Library of Congress, Geography and Map Division.

On August 29, 2005, this vibrantly colorful and cultural city, which harbors a special place in the hearts of many American and international visitors, suffered the worst environmental disaster to hit American shores. Hurricane Katrina struck, causing federally constructed levees and floodwalls to rupture, leading to flooding of 80 percent of the city's East Bank. Over 1,500 people perished, the government's response to New Orleans' human, environmental, and economic fate proved incompetent, and the world watched with horror the unprecedented virtual collapse of a modern US city.[6]

Even before Hurricane Katrina hit, New Orleans and its environs were in decline, with population figures falling from a peak of 627,525 in 1960 to 484,674 in 2000. After Katrina, numbers dropped dramatically as the majority of the population was displaced.[7] Despite various modes of outsider assistance, much remains to be done to return the city to its historic splendor, and in particular, to accommodate the needs of those most affected by the devastation. Recent revelations demonstrate that human neglect and the deliberate diversion of funds towards lucrative investment projects proposed by those with the loudest voices, have left large portions of the city and its population with inadequate resources. A more detailed account of the city's urban development history can shed light on successes and failures, while suggesting new paths for progress.

Brief History of the City

Indigenous peoples historically occupied the Mississippi deltaic plain, identifying shortcuts and portages between the Gulf of Mexico and the Mississippi River. Spanish explorers had visited the lower Mississippi Region by 1519, adding to European knowledge of the Gulf Coast area, but it was the French who settled on the banks of the Mississippi River. The site was selected because the ground was relatively high amid low-lying swampland, and it was in close proximity to Lake Pontchartrain, which, via Bayou St. John, was thought to provide a safer shortcut than the Mississippi for shipping.[8] French military engineer, Pierre Leblond de la Tour, Louisiana-appointed engineer-in-chief to the Company of the Indies, designed the city plan, envisioned as a typical French fortified town in the manner of Louis XIV's great military engineer, Sebastien le Prestre (Figure 5.2).[9]

Under charter to the Company of the Indies, land grants were measured according to the French *arpent* system, the equivalent of 192 feet. This created long lots, measuring approximately 2–4 *arpents* wide by 40–60 *arpents* deep, that took advantage of high ground beside the river. By 1718, land had been cleared on which major administrative buildings and smaller homes would be built, becoming what today is known as the French Quarter (Vieux Carrée). The city was named *Nouvelle Orléans* in tribute to Philippe II, Duc d'Orléans (1674–1723) and Regent of France. Settlers were recruited from France, Germany, and Switzerland and in 1719 shiploads of enslaved Africans arrived, subjugated by the *code noir*, to commence 170 years of slavery in the region. Disease and the first natural disaster—a hurricane in 1722—did little to thwart developers who responded by creating levees intended to control the Mississippi. After twenty years of private development by the Company of the Indies, and with a population of 7,000, New Orleans was ceded to the French government in 1731.

Significant political changes affected the city during the period from 1762 to 1803. As a result of the French and Indian Wars from 1754 to 1785, France ceded control of Louisiana east of the Mississippi to England, and areas west of the Mississippi to Spain under King Carlos III, Louis XV's cousin. French exiles from Acadia, in modern-day Canada, settled in western Louisiana where they established agricultural communities distinct from but important to the economic development of New Orleans. Known as Cajuns, this ethnic group retained aspects of their French Canadian culture, continuing to remain somewhat separate today.[10] During the forty-year Spanish occupation, after fire ravaged the

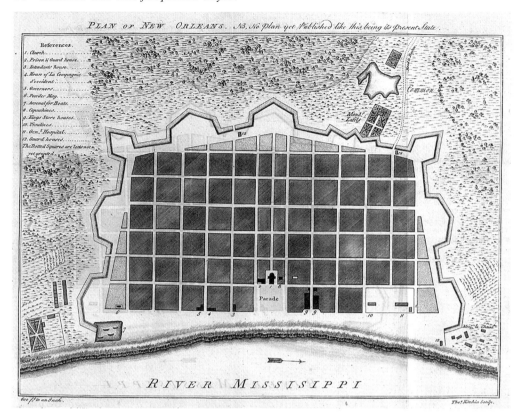

Figure 5.2 City plan, 1770
Source: Drawn by Philip Pittman, image provided by Library of Congress, Maps and Geography Division).

first-generation wooden frame buildings, stringent new regulations replaced much of the urban fabric with brick, including a cathedral still standing today. A market was established on the lower riverfront, becoming the birthplace of the tropical fruit industry and now an anchor for tourism. In 1803, Louisiana reverted to France, who then sold it to the United States in what is known as the Louisiana Purchase.[11]

The demographics of the city changed dramatically at this time as a result of a slave rebellion in Haiti and the arrival of 10,000 refugees, including French Colonists, former slaves, and free people of color. Their arrival consolidated the city's tripartite racial order; census records indicate the population was one-third white, one-third free people of color, and one-third enslaved Africans in 1830.[12] As importation of slaves ceased in 1808, immigrants from Ireland and Germany nevertheless swelled population numbers by 366 percent between 1830 and 1860. Building of the city occurred through the enforced labor of African slaves, Irish immigrants, and finally convicts, who worked under dire conditions, digging ditches and constructing levees necessary to keep a saturated city dry.[13] Only in 1882 was the US Army Corps of Engineers assigned responsibility for such construction, which continues today.[14] Migration of Irish laborers north to the industrial cities made way for Sicilian immigrants who took over their jobs, forming 39 percent of the city's population in 1910.

Throughout its history, the significance of New Orleans has fluctuated as a major port and center of international trade, with high points in the early nineteenth century, dipping to lower levels in the late nineteenth and early twentieth. Attempts to boost recognition of the city as an important center of trade occurred with the staging of the World's Industrial and Cotton Centennial Exposition in 1884, named to commemorate the 100th anniversary of the first shipment of United States cotton to Europe in 1784. Optimistic promotion of the potential of New Orleans unfortunately toppled under the weight of poor planning, overspending, lack of infrastructure and uncontrollable bad weather, causing the exposition to flop, and leaving Northerners with a highly negative impression of the city.[15]

Physical growth of the city originally spilled out from the French Quarter onto the long dry plantation lands facing the river and defining streets not according to cardinal directions, as was typical in other American cities, but in response to the river and the original city plan, that is, as riverside, lakeside, uptown, downtown (Figure 5.3). Growth upstream occurred after New Orleans was ceded to the American government and marked a division, later physically reinforced by the commercial corridor of Canal Street, between French, Spanish, Creole, and American residential space. Major flooding in 1927 prompted construction of increased drainage and levees, which led to further geographic expansion of the city's limits. Such complex drainage systems meant that increasing numbers of residents began living on low levels of land, formerly too wet to develop. Connections between the Mississippi River and Lake Pontchartrain were facilitated through the construction of an industrial canal in 1923, and more efficient access to the Gulf of Mexico was enabled through creation of the Mississippi River Gulf Outlet in 1965.

These major transportation networks spawned new residential neighborhoods so that, in 1919, 90 percent of city residents lived above sea level, but by 1960 only 48 percent lived above sea level. Irish, Italian, German, and later African-American laborers settled an area known as "back of town" because the New Basin Canal allowed access through the back of the city.[16] Later known as Central City, this area operated from the 1830s to its peak in the 1950s as a racially mixed commercial and residential community. It was one

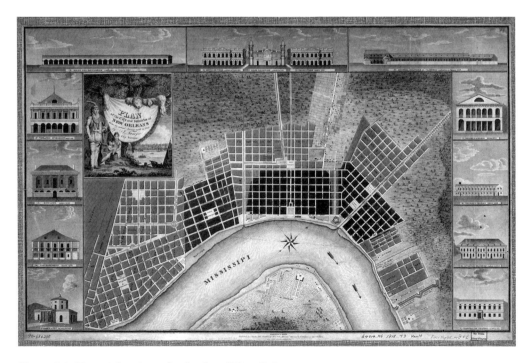

Figure 5.3 Plan of the city and suburbs of New Orleans
Source: Drawn by I. Tanesse, ca.1817, image provided by Library of Congress, Maps and Geography Division.

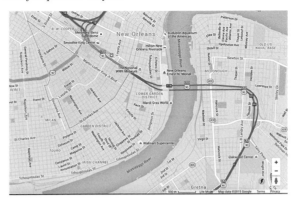

Figure 5.4 Map showing Central City in relation to the French Quarter
Source: Provided by Mapdata@Google (2015).

of few areas in which African-Americans participated freely as consumers, established their own businesses, operated their own hospital in which doctors and medical staff functioned free of racial discrimination, and developed support societies, many of which became key sites of Civil Rights activism. Older inhabitants of the city's downtown areas whose descendants identified as Creole saw the African-Americans in the Central City neighborhood as distinct from themselves, suggesting they were also of a different class; such narratives continue to define the racial character of the city, although they are often audible only to a minority audience (Figure 5.4).[17] Running parallel to the river, St Charles became a boundary between the American-developed Garden District, so-named because of its beautiful mansions and lush gardens, and the less stable and unhealthy back of town areas.[18] In the 1950s, the New Basin Canal was filled in to create the Pontchartrain Expressway and West End Boulevard, forming a transportation spine along the edge of Central City to the airport and suburbs.

During the early twentieth century, when commercial port activity flagged, profit-hungry entrepreneurs promoted tourism, making the industry a truly viable source of revenue in the 1920s. Careful cultivation of a culturally vibrant and metropolitan city with luxury hotels, nightclubs, and organized cultural events such as Mardi Gras parades, offered a Euro-centric narrative of New Orleans heritage that simultaneously celebrated a distilled black history and culture focused on Jazz music and Creole cuisine. Perpetuating a sentimentalized antebellum story, the New Orleans tourism industry provided a singular positive perspective of race relations, interracial unions, and the large free black population, while erasing the more negative aspects of local black history such as enslavement, discrimination, and even Civil Rights activism.[19]

The City in 1985

Physical Form and Conditions

In the 1970s, the embargo on oil exports by the Organization of Petroleum Exporting Companies (OPEC), which forced crude oil prices to unprecedented levels, left the coffers of oil- and gas-rich states like Oklahoma, Texas, and Louisiana brimming with possibilities for new business opportunities. Production in Louisiana of 1 million barrels a day in 1973 led to the employment of 50,000 people in exploration and production, which increased to 95,300 by 1982. High tax revenues from oil production, unknown since the city's commercial heyday of the 1850s, infused officials with optimism and led to plans for hosting the World's Exposition in 1984. This would affect two key areas of the city: an 82-acre site along the Mississippi River managed by the Public Port Authority, or Dock Board, and the area around Canal Street, which became the central business district (CBD). Canal Street received new office buildings, under-utilized downtown riverfront wharves were repurposed into new non-maritime uses, and new hotels were built to keep apace with annual visitor numbers, which had grown from 4,750 in 1960 to 10,686 in 1975. By 1985, prioritized development of tourism facilities increased New Orleans' hotel capacity to 19,500 rooms.[20]

The World's Exposition plans also saw a coalition of city officials and business interests focus on city planning, resulting in the construction of the $164 million Superdome at public expense. One building of the World's Exposition, the Louisiana Pavilion, was repurposed as the 350,000 square foot New Orleans Convention Center. Like the 1884 Fair before it, the 1984 World's Exposition was a financial failure, but nevertheless increased further small-scale development and adaptive reuse of buildings in areas such as Skid Row, a former warehouse and port-service related area. These buildings now form part of an arts district, with galleries, nightclubs, restaurants, and residential space for young professionals working in the CBD.[21] By the mid-1980s tourism was a $2.5 billion business, conventions rose in number from 764 in 1976 with 481,000 delegates to 1,092 conventions by 1985, with over 1 million delegates. Physical development of tourism-related industries occurred downtown on the edge of the historic French Quarter, but such urban improvements intensified the city's environmental vulnerability. Moreover, dredging of Louisiana's coastal marshes negatively affected wetlands, lessening their capacity to naturally dampen storm surge waves, increasing erosion, and cutting the coastline dangerously close to the city.[22]

Demographics

Transportation initiatives and racial fears sent two-thirds of the white population of New Orleans to the suburbs, reducing the city's population from a high of 628,000 in 1960 to 485,000 in 2000, the lowest it has been since the 1940s. So transformed were the city's demographics by the 1970s, it was possible to elect the first non-white Mayor, a dramatic turn of events. White flight to the suburbs left behind fragmented black ghettoes, in many cases containing segregated public housing, that over time merged to form "superghettoes" riddled with poverty, drug, and crime issues, earning the city the moniker of "murder capital of the United States."[23] Although Cubans, Hondurans, Mexicans, Nicaraguans, and Vietnamese migrants arrived in the 1970s, this did little to change the predominantly biracial demographic of the city.[24] The oil economy bust in the late 1980s heavily influenced the new demographic as the greater metropolitan area of New Orleans lost 9,434 jobs, or 2 percent of all jobs.[25]

Economy

By 1986, over-speculation by investors had led to a massive drop in oil prices and the loss of 40,000 jobs. Meanwhile, city officials had grown complacent, believing the economy could ride along without investment in areas such as education and infrastructure.[26] The 1980s in New Orleans were further characterized by quasi-public economic development corporations, known as non-elected decision-making agencies, typically with their own revenue sources, negotiation practices, and strategies that obscured decisions from public scrutiny. These public-private business organizations worked with government authorities to develop business districts and surrounding areas, typically at the expense of poorer residential neighborhoods.[27] Unchecked physical development focused on attracting tourists inspired by *The Big Easy,* a Hollywood movie released in 1987, which identified the city as an eccentric Cajun outpost obsessed with hedonistic celebration through food and festivals. Increasing numbers of tourists seeking the good life heeded the call.

The City in 2015

Physical Form and Conditions

New Orleans in 2015 was a city suffering from a series of major natural and man-made disasters: the devastating 2005 Hurricane Katrina and the BP oil spill of 2010 perhaps the most notable. For a city built on waterlogged ground, much of it below sea level, such disasters were catastrophic. Yet in the wake of both disasters, government agencies from the city to the White House responded ineptly, their work hampered by damage caused through earlier neglect, discrimination, lack of transparency, and uneven development. Proposals for rebuilding public and private facilities post-Katrina were not simply intended to address storm damage, but also to redress earlier deficits in planning and development. It is telling that on his reinstatement to the Mayoral Office in 2006 Ray Nagin exhorted the people of New Orleans to take the future into their own hands.[28] This statement rings ironic today; in 2014, Nagin was sentenced to ten years imprisonment for taking bribes and committing fraud while in public office.[29]

Demographics

New Orleans' population in 2015 is 343,829, of which 60 percent are African-American, 32 percent White, 5 percent Hispanic or Latinos, and 2 percent Asians. Home to one of the largest multi-generational populations in the nation, New Orleans is also witnessing an influx of new residents from across the country, who both invigorate and complicate the dynamic of renewal. The city's challenge during re-development is to respect and conserve traditional neighborhoods, but also to promote those aspects that have attracted newcomers to this unique place.

Economy

Public housing in New Orleans has needed attention since the 1990s, but after Katrina it became imperative. In 1993, faced with 6 percent of its public housing units labeled as severely distressed (86,000), the city embraced the federal HOPE VI program, with funding to demolish or rehabilitate units, and relocate residents. Additional funding was directed towards improving residents' living environments, revitalizing sites of public housing property, decreasing poverty concentration, and building sustainable communities. Public concerns regarding the unnecessary demolition of viable units, and prevention of returns to revitalized communities due to overly rigid screening practices, prompted the introduction of new criteria. High quality construction and the integration of sites into surrounding neighborhood fabric were given priority. The long-term viability of these new communities seemed to be secure, as they were built by private developers and maintained by property managers, much of which was completed prior to 2005. As a result of extreme post-Katrina renovation estimates, the federal Housing and Urban Development (HUD) agency authorized the total demolition and recreation of Lafitte, St. Bernard, B.W. Cooper and C.J. Peete, "the Big Four" public housing projects. HUD also authorized funds to continue previously initiated redevelopment activities at the Desire, Fischer, St. Thomas and Guste housing projects. Private development companies have taken responsibility for the work, including Columbia Residential at St. Bernard, Providence Enterprise and McCormack Baron Salazar at Lafitte, KBK Enterprises at B.W. Cooper, and Central City at C.J. Peete. Another HUD initiative, the Housing Choice Voucher Program (HCVP), currently administers more than 17,000 vouchers, and oversees 2,987 tenant-protection vouchers for Section 8 eligible families affected by the demolition of the "Big Four."[30]

Private housing rehabilitation and restoration projects have been completed, including Hollywood star Brad Pitt's Make It Right Program, providing LEED-certified, high performance, sustainable homes and communities in the Ninth Ward, a low-income and predominantly African-American neighborhood devastated by Hurricane Katrina.

In 2004, further development and capital investment infused a master plan developed by the University of Louisiana and the City of New Orleans to revitalize medical facilities. Replacing the University of Louisiana and Charity hospitals, a new 78-acre downtown site is currently under construction. An updated plan increased the site to accommodate a 1.6 million square foot complex, making it the largest health care site in the country.

Needless to say, such broad-brush projects have not been without controversy and detractors. According to *Times-Picayune* reports, private management of voucher distribution and background checks have led to individual profiteering, and conflicts of interests have been found among those receiving contracts to manage HUD funding who have also contributed to local political campaigns.[31] Incompetence and inefficiency have hampered the progress of creating better living conditions for those in public housing. In some cases, those responsible have been relieved of their duties, but the problem of accountability and transparency in the process remains, with too many private agencies interested in making financial profit at the expense of the underprivileged.[32] However, a new Housing Authority (HANO) Executive Director brings fresh hope for greater transparency and community involvement in future decisions.[33]

Currently, the New Orleans economy can be divided into four major sectors: (1) oil/gas and related activities; (2) port and ship/boat building; (3) aerospace manufacturing; and (4) tourism. Attempts are underway to harness technology ideas brought by start-ups, and to expand the knowledge sector based on medical research institutions.[34] Nevertheless, the tourism industry continues to dominate the economy.[35]

Tracking data for the New Orleans area since 2007, Greater New Orleans Community Data Center, in partnership with the Brookings Institution, positioned the city within a set of fifty-seven US metropolitan areas classified as "weak" that includes sixty-five older industrial cities in long-term economic decline. Nevertheless, New Orleans today has a more robust urban economic and social environment than it did pre-Katrina, with wages that have improved to levels closer to national figures, increased numbers of middle-income households, and greater numbers of children attending schools that meet state standards—68 percent compared to pre-Katrina levels of 24 percent. In the metropolitan area, population numbers have returned to figures close to those in 2000, but the City of New Orleans remains at 74 percent of its 2000 population. The greater metropolitan area has also increased in diversity, but the City of New Orleans' former African-American majority remains depleted. Child poverty rates are 20 percent higher than the national average, and violent crime continues to occur at twice the national rate.[36]

Transformation of the City (1985–2015)

What Went Right?

The year 1985 marked a decisive moment for New Orleans, changing the physical and social face of the city with a modicum of controversy or protest from neighborhood groups.

Large-scale projects intended to bolster tourism, such as the $40 million Aquarium of the Americas and Woldenberg Park, brought increased employment and appealed to the broader public. Investment in high-end retail brought national chain stores to the area, and a thriving system of local and internationally directed facilities invigorated the economy around the Central Business District and on the uptown side of lower Canal Street, providing 25,000 jobs. Such urban growth was directed by coalitions of business leaders and city officials, but nevertheless rallied private interest groups to protest for the protection of the city's historic character, particularly in the French Quarter and the Lower Garden District, thus sowing the seeds for future grassroots activism.[37]

What Went Wrong?

Much of the planning and development of the city since the 1970s and 1980s focused on big business, large-scale tourism and visitor amenities. In the 1990s, city officials professed interest in preserving historic walkable neighborhoods and improving quality of life by expanding park and open space. Revitalization of commercial areas, such as along Canal Street with a new medical center and a theater district, failed to respect the diverse surrounding communities, and ignored recommendations made by the Urban Land Institute to stabilize the 3,000-resident public housing community of Iberville, a vital source for retail activity located at one end of Canal Street.[38] Such decisions echoed discrimination practices remembered from the 1930s through the 1960s, when white business owners refused to cater to black consumers, prompting boycotting and protests.

Focusing on high-end retail in the CBD forced smaller mom-and-pop stores and lower-income business owners out of the competitive mix, resulting in more vacant properties and blight.[39] In the 1990s, the ratio of neighborhood to non-neighborhood projects was 1 to 4, and 88 percent of funds spent on non-neighborhood projects occurred in the CBD.[40]

Despite the protests of concerned citizens, city government forged ahead with large-scale projects, such as those described above, to the detriment of historic neighborhoods. Housing in poor black neighborhoods continued to deteriorate, leading to increased blight, social and economic demoralization, and crime.

Lessons Learned

Throughout New Orleans' development history, local government and private interests have come together to direct change, typically at the larger scale. Hurricane Katrina, and the devastation left in its wake, have provided an opportunity to rethink possibilities for the city. One month after Hurricane Katrina, Mayor Nagin established Bring New Orleans Back (BNOB) a citywide planning effort, launched with unprecedented transparency through a public conference held in collaboration with the Urban Land Institute. Neighborhood organizations formed in response to the widespread destruction of residential districts, the ineptitude of the government's ability to ensure the safety and basic needs of the citizens of New Orleans, and from outrage at the Mayor's planning proposals to effectively depopulate the city of working-class poor in favor of supporting growth in more affluent neighborhoods. Grassroots organizations successfully brought the issues of poverty and race to the table.[41]

The magnitude of the natural and man-made disaster inflicted on New Orleans by Hurricane Katrina drew international attention. Foreign groups overwhelmed the city, inspired to seek long-term environmental solutions, and transform neglected low-income communities in order to restore New Orleans to a viable, safe, and vibrant metropolis. While such attention was gratefully received, nonetheless it was not without problems. In the early days post-Katrina, the efforts suffered from a lack of organization, lack of consensus within and among other groups, and a lack of conscientious approaches.

Government agencies found partnership among specialists from countries with similar natural ecologies such as the Netherlands. The "Dutch Dialogues" model places an appropriate emphasis on fixing ecological issues first. As such, specialists have considered the integration of wildlife habitat, water storage, and flood management, as well as the development of improved pumping stations to carry storm water runoff from specific areas. Documents, such as the "Comprehensive, Sustainable Integrated Water Management Strategy" by Waggonner & Ball Architects will go a long way towards facilitating safe, healthy communities through rebuilding and revitalizing wetlands that lie at the heart of the Gulf Coast.[42]

Further government projects supported by a combination of city, state, and federal funds include a $4 billion investment in transit potential along a corridor traversing New Orleans' Central Business and Medical Districts, and the nexus of Claiborne Avenue with parallel corridors typical of an array of mixed-use neighborhoods. Mostly low-to-moderate-income historic minority communities, which since Hurricane Katrina have become recognizable household names, such as the Seventh Ward, Tremé, Central City, and Broadmoor, are central to these projects. The corridor is furthermore home to specific landmarks of the city and several places that constitute truly sacred ground. Designated funding for this area includes $2.2 billion in upcoming hospital and health care developments, $45 million in streetcar extensions and hundreds of millions of dollars in new and renovated schools, as well as over half a billion dollars in recent and ongoing affordable housing investments, such as a HUD Choice Neighborhood Implementation grant.

The city appears to have learned lessons from the past, leveraging inter-agency partnerships at the federal, state, and local level with strong community guidance and the goal of bringing equitable access to all members of the community. Post-Katrina efforts to redevelop the city using a more holistic approach have their problems as well. Large-scale infrastructure developments, such as those supported through the Dutch Dialogues and other large scale projects intended to address the city's natural and physical challenges, can often obscure the need to preserve remaining fragments of New Orleans' urban culture and traditional neighborhoods. It is these fragments that constitute the character of place. The New Orleans HUD Community Challenge and DOT TIGER II planning grant, given for fulfillment of a Sustainable Communities objective for the Claiborne Corridor Plan, did attempt to engage communities and learned some important lessons about the value of public participation, including the importance of:

- participating in and benefitting from economic investment;
- staying in communities and fighting gentrification;
- continuing cultural expression and passing it on from one generation to the next.

In New Orleans, these three concerns exemplify some of the greatest challenges facing other cities with significant investment in traditional urban neighborhoods, however, in New Orleans, history forces a more critical look. Such challenges provide New Orleans with an opportunity to approach development by envisioning the city as a place-based cultural text to be read through the form of the city.

Prospects for the Future

As described above, the Central City district, established in the 1930s concurrent with the Garden District, was a racially and ethnically mixed residential and commercial neighborhood of Jewish, Irish, Italian, and African-Americans who lived, worked and conducted business along Dryades Street (renamed Oretha Castle Haley Boulevard in the 1980s in recognition of a prominent young Civil Rights activist). It was in 1957, during a visit by Dr. Martin Luther King to Central City, that the Southern Christian Leadership Council refined its mission, shortened its name, and established its Executive Board with Dr. King at the helm. This interracial, interfaith organization would lead many Civil Rights protests and preside over many meetings, one of which, the first Voter Rights Meeting, occurred in A. L. Davis Park, named after a local Civil Rights leader.[43] Such historic significance is little known outside Central City, except among some Civil Rights scholars. This neighborhood is also home to the Mardi Gras Indians. Drawing on late nineteenth-century customs influenced by Africa and the Caribbean, these twentieth-century groups or tribes formed secret societies as part of the Social Aid and Pleasure Clubs established to support blacks during the Jim Crow era of discrimination and segregation. The Mardi Gras Indians began masking and creating elaborate suits in which they parade today in public festivals, most significantly during Mardi Gras (Figure 5.5).[44] While the public rituals enacted during Mardi Gras suggest connections with Christian, specifically Catholic feast days, the elaborate sequined and feathered costumes and ceremonial flags, second line dance moves, and accompanying jazz music underscore the spiritual philosophy and performance strategies of African-Amerindian communities of eighteenth- and nineteenth-century Louisiana.[45]

Figure 5.5 Mardi Gras Indians
Source: Photo by Keeley Rizzato, courtesy of Tulane City Center.

Neighborhood connections figure prominently in Mardi Gras Indian celebrations and daily activities. Particular streets reflect the routes and paths of second lines and marches, and are sites on which design and fabrication of the feathered and beaded costumes occur (Figure 5.6). Dispersed within this urban fabric are the purveyors of music that complement the art of the Mardi Gras Indians and underscore the activities and presence of Social Aid and Pleasure Clubs.

Taking the Mardi Gras Indian project as a case study, the Tulane City Center and Louisiana State University's Robert Reich School of Landscape Architecture work collaboratively to improve the future development of the city (Figure 5.7). Employing community and place-based strategies, which argue that people and their traditions anchor

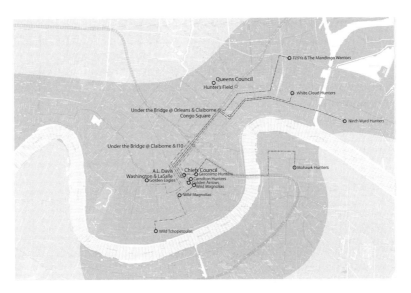

Figure 5.6 Mardi Gras Indian sites of significance, Central City, New Orleans
Source: Map provided by Tulane City Center.

Figure 5.7 Bird's-eye view of proposed development plan
Source: Drawing by Kossen Miller, courtesy of Tulane City Center.

neighborhoods, they propose focusing on the LaSalle Street Corridor, which cuts through Central City, and carries a network of landmarks bearing witness to the realities of post-Reconstruction, Civil Rights and post-Katrina life for African-Americans in New Orleans. The LaSalle Street Corridor is located only a few blocks from other significant streets such as Oretha Castle Haley Boulevard, and its significance is consistently reinforced through annual Mardi Gras Indian parades, particularly those occurring on Super Sunday and St. Joseph's Night. In addition, throughout the year, the Mardi Gras Indians meet and practice in A.L. Davis Park, located along LaSalle Street.

The Mardi Gras Indians' heritage is a palimpsest of French, Spanish, American, Native American, and African influences and it exemplifies the city's intangible heritage, renewed annually through the enactment of specific secret rituals and public performances. Yet while this rich history is deeply embedded in the city, the physical environment in which their culture unfolds is often geographically diffused, lacking in financial resources and support, and occurs without city-wide recognition or understanding.

The Mardi Gras Indian project focuses on built sites specific to the community, such as corner stores, social clubs, and homes of significant leaders, as well as green space in which spiritual, cultural, and seemingly quotidian activities occur (Figures 5.8a and 5.8b). Such an approach can support richer, more socially and economically equitable development. It functions from the premise that everyone has a right to the city and that growth and redevelopment should occur without displacement.

Figure 5.8a and 5.8b Shotgun Houses and Proposed Adaptive Reuse Connector
Source: Drawing by Jenny Renn Key, courtesy of Tulane City Center.

Employing a place-based approach empowers the Mardi Gras Indians to function as the "Eyes on the Park," a kind of unofficial deterrent against crime, which has been historically prevalent in this impoverished and underfinanced district (Figure 5.9). With funding from the Foundation for Louisiana, a proposal for preserving the culture and activities of the Mardi Gras Indians within the LaSalle Corridor includes a series of strategies as follows:

- leading a process of civic engagement to establish priorities;
- fighting gentrification of the neighborhood through renovating existing structures;
- promoting positive attention to this important cultural phenomenon;
- rehabilitating part of one traditional Shotgun home and a neighboring vacant lot to create a so-called campus in which the Mardi Gras Indians can meet, plan, raise funds and preserve their costumes and culture;
- identifying further opportunities for design intervention and community empowerment.

Any plan for the city's sustainability or resilience must acknowledge the value this culture brings and address a means of supporting it within the physical, social, and economic framework of a revitalized New Orleans. Methods for addressing this issue must by multifaceted. They must be place-based in terms of identifying and conserving sacred space and providing affordable housing. They must be economic in terms of looking at non-traditional organizing for business-like cooperatives and identifying a means of forming clusters around supply and demand. Finally, they must be social in terms of respecting the traditions of this art and how it is generated, and looking at how this culture can be passed on through generations.

While the specific case of the Mardi Gras Indians as a model for employing a place-based approach may appear unique to New Orleans, it reflects challenges facing many American cities. Traditional communities have often suffered displacement as urban reinvestment is directed elsewhere. The *Times-Picayune* recently drew attention to the squalid and debauched nature tourism has taken on in the French Quarter, noting that the problem for New Orleans remains one of perception. The newspaper reported, "The sum of life in New Orleans isn't Bourbon Street." In directing attention to development potential in areas such as the LaSalle Street Corridor and of the Mardi Gras Indian sites specifically, New Orleans can demonstrate that holding on to the cultural anchors that distinguish its uniqueness are vital as the foundation of the city's cultural economy.

Figure 5.9 Eyes on the Park Concept, LaSalle Street Community in Central City, New Orleans
Source: Drawing by Kossen Miller, courtesy of Tulane City Center.

100 *Maurice Cox and Jacqueline Taylor*

Notes

1 National Park Service, Mississippi River Facts. Available at: www.nps.gov/miss/riverfacts.htm (accessed January 26, 2015).
2 Peirce F. Lewis, *New Orleans: The Making of an Urban Landscape* (Santa Fe, NM: Center for American Places, 2003), 19.
3 Ibid., 25–7.
4 Deirdre Clemente, "Review of 'Creating the Big Easy: New Orleans and the Emergence of Modern Tourism 1918–1945' by Anthony J. Stanonis and *New Orleans on Parade: Tourism and the Transformation of the Crescent City* by J. Mark Souther," *Journal of Social History* 41(4) (2008), 1077–81.
5 Richard Campanella, *Geographies of New Orleans: Urban Fabrics Before the Storm* (Lafayette, LA: Center for Louisiana Studies, 2006), 24.
6 Robert B. Olshansky and Laurie A. Johnson, *Clear As Mud: Planning for the Rebuilding of New Orleans* (Washington, DC: American Planning Association, Planners Press, 2010), 5.
7 Ibid., 11; Richard Campanella, "New Orleans: A Timeline of Economic History." New Orleans Business Alliance, 2012.
8 Campanella, *Geographies of New Orleans*, 5.
9 Mary Christovich and Sally Evans, *New Orleans Architecture: The Creole Faubourgs* (Gretna, LA: Pelican, 1995), 3–5.
10 Louis McKinney, *New Orleans, A Cultural History* (New York: Oxford University Press, 2006), 18–19; Lewis, *New Orleans*, 30.
11 Campanella, "New Orleans: A Timeline."
12 Paul Lachance, "The 1809 Immigration of Saint-Domingue Refugees to New Orleans: Reception, Integration, and Impact," *Louisiana History*, 29 (1988), 109–41; Campanella, *Geographies of New Orleans*, 194–5.
13 Daniel H. Usner, Jr. "From African Captivity to American Slavery: The Introduction of Black Laborers to Colonial Louisiana," *Louisiana History*, 20 (Winter), (1979), 25; Elizabeth Fussell, "Constructing New Orleans, Constructing Race: A Population History of New Orleans," *Journal of American History*, 94 (Dec. 2007), 848.
14 Fussell, "Constructing New Orleans," 849.
15 Samuel Shepherd Jr., "A Glimmer of Hope: The World's Industrial and Cotton Centennial Exposition, New Orleans, 1884–1885," *Louisiana History: The Journal of Louisiana Historical Association* (Summer), 271–90.
16 Lewis, *New Orleans*, 46–7.
17 Oral History Interview in Arthe-Agnes Anthony, "The Negro Creole Community in New Orleans, 1880–1920: An Oral History," PhD dissertation, University of California at Irvine, 1978.
18 Lewis, *New Orleans*, 1, 47.
19 Lynell L. Thomas, " 'Roots Run Deep Here': The Construction of Black New Orleans in Post-Katrina Tourism Narratives," *American Quarterly* 61(3); *In the Wake of Katrina: New Paradigms and Social Visions* (Sept. 2007), pp. 749–52.
20 Downtown Development District Report on Downtown New Orleans, (DDD) 1987.
21 Brooks and Young, "Revitalizing the Central Business District in the Face of Decline: The Case of New Orleans, 1973–1993" *The Town Planning Review* 64(3) (1993), 251–71.
22 Olshansky and Johnson, *Clear As Mud*, 11.
23 Lewis, *New Orleans*, 125–8.
24 Fussell, "Constructing New Orleans," 851.
25 Alison Plyer and Elaine Ortiz, "Fewer Jobs Mean Fewer People and More Vacant Housing," Greater New Orleans Community Data Center. Available at: www.datacenterresearch.org/reports_analysis/jobs-population-and-housing/(accessed March 16, 2015).
26 John Biers, "Oil Lesson Learned in Embargo." *Times-Picayune*, October 18, 1998.
27 Brooks and Young, "Revitalizing the Central Business District," 253.
28 Lee Zurik, "Nagin's Second Inauguration," *CBS News*, June 2, 2006.
29 Andy Grimm, "Ray Nagin, once New Orleans' mayor, now federal inmate No. 32751-034," *Times-Picayune*, September 8, 2014.
30 HANO (Housing Authority of New Orleans). Available at: www.hano.org/our_story.aspx (accessed May 28, 2015).
31 Richard Rainey, "Housing Agency Under Scrutiny: Councilman Calls Expense Outrageous," *Times-Picayune*, Dec. 8, 2010.

32 Juliet Linderman, "Audit of St. John Housing Authority Reveals Negligence, Mismanagement: Agency Fails to Comply with HUD Standards," *Times-Picayune*, July 30, 2013.

33 Richard A. Webster, "New HANO Chief Focuses On Residents' Needs: 'We're Going to be Transparent,'" *Times-Picayune*, July 25, 2014.

34 Adam B. Kuschner, "How New Orleans Pulled Off an Economic Miracle," *National Journal*, April 18, 2013. Available at: www.nationaljournal.com/next-economy/america-360/how-new-orleans-pulled-off-an-economic-miracle-20130408 (accessed May 29, 2015).

35 See the City Data website at www.city-data.com/us-cities/The-South/New-Orleans-Economy.html (accessed March 16, 2015).

36 "Facts for Features: Hurricane Katrina Recovery," Greater New Orleans Community Data Center August 27, 2012, cited in Carol McMichael Reese, Michael Sorkin, and Anthony Fontenot, eds., *New Orleans Under Reconstruction: The Crisis of Planning* (London: Verso, 2014), xxvii.

37 Lewis, *New Orleans*, 113.

38 Wallace, David, Ian McHarg, Bill Roberts, and Tom Todd, *The Central Area New Orleans Growth Management Program Technical Report* (Philadelphia, PA: MRT, 1975), 40.

39 Bruce Eggler, "Merchants Brainstorm to Stem Customer Loss," *Times-Picayune*, March 19, 1991.

40 Brooks and Young, "Revitalizing the Central Business District," 268.

41 Kate Randall, "City Residents Denounce 'Bring New Orleans Back' Rebuilding Plan," World Socialist Website. Available at: www.wsws.org/en/articles/2006/01/newo-j14.html (accessed May 29, 2015). For a balanced perspective, see also Melissa Harris-Perry and William M. Harris Sr., "Ethical Dilemmas in Post-Katrina New Orleans Planning," in Reese, Sorkin, and Fontenay, eds., *New Orleans Under Reconstruction*, 158–9.

42 Lisa P. Jackson, "Environmental Protection Agency Administrator, Lisa Jackson on Gulf Coast Wetland Restoration," 2010. Available at: Dutchdialogues.com (accessed February 2, 2015).

43 See the Healing Histories website at www.healinghistories.org (accessed April 9, 2015).

44 Mardi Gras Indian Council, Available at: www.mardigrasindiancouncil.org/history/ (accessed January 19, 2015).

45 Richard Brent, ed., *Jazz Religion, the Second Line and Black New Orleans* (Bloomington: Indiana University Press, 2009), 54–5.

References

Biers, John (1998) "Oil Lesson Learned in Embargo," *Times-Picayune,* October 18.

Brooks and Young (1993) "Revitalizing the Central Business District in the Face of Decline: The Case of New Orleans, 1973–1993," *The Town Planning Review*, 64(3) (July).

Campanella, Richard (2006) *Geographies of New Orleans: Urban Fabrics Before the Storm.* Lafayette, LA: Center for Louisiana Studies.

Campanella, Richard (2012) "New Orleans: A Timeline of Economic History." New Orleans Business Alliance.

Christovich, Mary and Sally Evans (1995) *New Orleans Architecture: The Creole Faubourgs.* Gretna, LA: Pelican.

Clemente, Deirdre (2008) "Review of 'Creating the Big Easy: New Orleans and the Emergence of Modern Tourism 1918–1945' by Anthony J. Stanonis and *New Orleans on Parade: Tourism and the Transformation of the Crescent City* by J. Mark Souther," *Journal of Social History* 41(4): 1077–81.

Eaker, Jennifer, and Lee Zurik (2006) "Nagin's Second Inauguration: Ray Nagin Given a Second Chance to Lead Rebuild in New Orleans as Mayor." CBS News, June 2, 2006. Available at: www.cbsnews.com/videos/nagins-second-inauguration/

Eggler, Bruce (1991) "Merchants Brainstorm to Stem Customer Loss," *Times-Picayune*, March 19.

Fussell, Elizabeth (2007) "Constructing New Orleans, Constructing Race: A Population History of New Orleans," *Journal of American History*, 94(Dec.), 846–55.

Goldsmith, William, Edward Blakely, and Bill Clinton (2010) *Separate Societies*. Philadelphia. PA: Temple University Press.

Greater New Orleans Community Data Center. Available at: www.gnocdc.org

HANO (Housing Authority of New Orleans). Available at: www.hano.org/our_story.aspx

Jackson, Lisa P. (2010) "Environmental Protection Agency Administrator, Lisa Jackson on Gulf Coast Wetland Restoration." Available at: Dutchdialogues.com

Kellogg, W.K. Healing Histories website. Available at: www.healinghistories.org (accessed March 19, 2015).

Lewis, Peirce F. (2003) *New Orleans: The Making of an Urban Landscape*. Santa Fe, NM: Center for American Places.

Lynnell L. Thomas (2009) "'Roots Run Deep Here': The Construction of Black New Orleans in Post-Katrina Tourism Narratives, In the Wake of Katrina: New Paradigms and Social Visions," *American Quarterly*, 61(3), 749–68.

McKinney, Louis (2006) *New Orleans, A Cultural History*. New York: Oxford University Press.

Olshansky, Robert B. and Laurie A. Johnson (2010) *Clear As Mud: Planning for the Rebuilding of New Orleans*. Washington, DC: American Planning Association, Planners Press.

Plyer, Alison and Elaine Ortiz (2011) "Fewer Jobs Mean Fewer People and More Vacant Housing." Greater New Orleans Community Data Center.

Reese, Carol McMichael, Michael Sorkin and Anthony Fontenot, eds. (2014) *New Orleans Under Reconstruction: The Crisis of Planning*. London: Verso.

Shepherd, Samuel Jr. (1985) "A Glimmer of Hope: The World's Industrial and Cotton Centennial Exposition, New Orleans, 1884–1885," *Louisiana History: The Journal of Louisiana Historical Association* (summer), 271–90.

Turner, Richard Brent, ed. (2009) *Jazz Religion, the Second Line and Black New Orleans*. Bloomington: Indiana University Press.

Usner, Daniel H. Jr. (1979) "From African Captivity to American Slavery: The Introduction of Black Laborers to Colonial Louisiana," *Louisiana History*, 20 (Winter), 25–48.

Wallace, David, Ian McHarg, Bill Roberts, and Tom Todd (1975) *The Central Area New Orleans Growth Management Program Technical Report*. Philadelphia, PA: MRT.

World Port Source (2005–2015). Accessed at: http://www.worldportsource.com/ports/review/USA_LA_Port_of_New_Orleans_254.php

6 Pittsburgh Case Study

Donald K. Carter

Introduction

In 1985, at the nadir of the collapse of the steel industry in Pittsburgh, Rand McNally's *Places Rated Almanac* surprisingly crowned industrial Pittsburgh the "Most Livable City" in the US. The city received high marks for climate and terrain, housing, health care, transportation, education, the arts, and recreation. The Most Livable City designation was and is a measure of quality of life. The *Places Rated Almanac* named Pittsburgh "Most Livable City" again in 2007. In 2009, *Forbes Magazine* named metropolitan Pittsburgh the "Most Livable City" in the country. In 2005, 2009, and 2014 the British magazine, *The Economist* rated Pittsburgh the "Most Livable US City."

However, it was clear in 1985 that an economy based on heavy manufacturing was over. Unemployment was at Great Depression levels, rising to 18 percent in 1983. The departure of heavy industry and implementation of smoke control ordinances left Pittsburgh's skies clear but well-paying jobs disappeared. Something had to be done. Between 1985 and 1995, a regional economic agenda for the next thirty years was set, involving high-level leaders in the public, private, and philanthropic sectors, as well as community-based organizations and concerned citizens. Charting the transformation of Pittsburgh from 1985, when all seemed lost, to 2015 is a remarkable story.

History of the City

Beginnings

The City of Pittsburgh is located at one of the great geographic sites in North America at the confluence of the Allegheny and Monongahela Rivers. The two rivers meet to form the Ohio River that flows west and south to the Mississippi River to St. Louis and New Orleans, emptying into the Gulf of Mexico. The confluence of the three major rivers has always been a strategic location (Figure 6.1).

Native Americans inhabited the region for at least 16,000 years.[1] The dominant Native American tribe was the Iroquois. Europeans first discovered the forks of the Ohio in the early eighteenth century and established trading posts along the rivers. French and English traders and settlers vied for control of the region. George Washington traveled north from Virginia to the area in 1753 to survey the situation. The English began to build a fort at the forks of the Ohio in 1754, but were overrun by the French, who built Fort Duquesne on the site. English soldiers, including 22-year-old Major George Washington,

Figure 6.1 Pittsburgh's downtown "Golden Triangle," where the Allegheny River (left) and the Monongahela River (right) meet to form the Ohio River, July 2015
Source: Photo by Pradipta Banerjee, courtesy of the Remaking Cities Institute.

returned in the summer of 1754 to take back the region but were defeated by the French at Fort Necessity before they reached the confluence.

Thus began the Seven Years War between France and England, also known as the French and Indian War because of the alliance of France with Native American tribes. Washington returned a third time to the region in 1755 with General Braddock's army, but the English were again defeated before reaching the Ohio River. Finally, in 1758 English General John Forbes marched toward Fort Duquesne, but the French abandoned and burned the fort before his army arrived. Forbes ordered the construction of a new and larger fort, Fort Pitt, named after William Pitt, Prime Minister of England. The English thereafter remained in control of the fort. Five years later, the Treaty of Paris in 1763 ended the Seven Years War, ceding control of much of North America to England. Settlements had grown up around the fort. General Forbes named the emerging village Pittsborough.

Soon, thousands of settlers, mainly English and Scots-Irish, began to populate the area as farmers, tradesmen, and craftsmen. The village of Pittsborough, now known as Pittsburgh, grew in population and commerce. Settlers heading further west began their journeys at the head of the Ohio River in Pittsburgh, the Gateway to the West.

In 1776, the American colonies, including Pennsylvania, declared their independence from England, precipitating the Revolutionary War. Pittsburgh was not a battleground in the war but supplied soldiers and provisions to the revolutionary colonists for the epic battles in the east and south between the English Army and the Continental Army. When the war ended in 1783, Pittsburgh was poised for prosperity as settlers moved into the territories to the west. Boat building became a primary industry. By the early nineteenth century, Pittsburgh had also become a major center for iron and glass manufacturing because of the abundance of coal in the region and commerce on the rivers. In 1816, Pittsburgh was officially incorporated as a city. In the 1850s, railroads arrived in Pittsburgh. When the American Civil War began in 1860, Pittsburgh, with a population of 49,000, was the seventeenth largest city in the United States, and an emerging industrial powerhouse.[2]

Industrial Powerhouse (1865–1945)

By the end of the Civil War in 1865, Pittsburgh was producing 50 percent of the iron and glass in the United States and much of the oil.[3] The Industrial Revolution that began in England in the 1760 was now firmly ensconced in Pittsburgh. Along with industry came banking, retail, and housing. Pittsburgh entrepreneurs like Andrew Carnegie, Henry Clay Frick, Thomas Mellon, H. J. Heinz, and George Westinghouse led the way. Pittsburgh was truly a boomtown, but very polluted. James Parton in 1868 called Pittsburgh, "Hell with the lid off."[4]

In the late nineteenth century and early twentieth century, the population in Pittsburgh grew exponentially with immigrants from Eastern and Southern Europe flooding in for industrial jobs in the mills, factories, and mines. From 1870 to 1910, Pittsburgh's population grew from 86,076 to 533,905 with approximately 29 percent of the population classified as foreign born. In 1910, Pittsburgh was the eighth largest city in the United States.[5] The mills of Pittsburgh were a major destination for many of the five million African-Americans who migrated north in the first third of the twentieth century.[6]

Then came the Great Depression of the 1930s. Pittsburgh suffered high unemployment along with the rest of the country, but it was still the leading industrial city in the world. The need for ships, tanks, airplanes, and armaments for World War II returned Pittsburgh to full employment as new factories were built overnight as pollution poured out of the smokestacks and into the rivers. Pollution also meant prosperity (Figures 6.2a and 6.2b).

Figures 6.2a and 6.2b Pittsburgh steel mill, 1906 (left); and downtown Pittsburgh (right) at 10:35 am, circa 1940

Source: Provided by Corbis Bettmann (left); image from the Smoke Control Lantern Slide Collection, ca. 1940–1950, AIS.1978.22, Archives Service Center, University of Pittsburgh (right).

Renaissance (1945–1985)

In 1943, two leaders of Pittsburgh, David L. Lawrence, Democratic Mayor of Pittsburgh, and Richard King Mellon, Republican businessman, improbably got together to tackle the polluted reality and dirty reputation of Pittsburgh. What followed was "Renaissance I" that included: a smoke control ordinance; dams on the rivers to prevent flooding; creation of the nation's first Urban Redevelopment Authority; and new urban highways (Figure 6.3). Major development projects included: Gateway Center and Point State Park at the confluence of the rivers where factories and warehouses once stood; four neighborhood redevelopment projects; and new corporate headquarters buildings (US Steel, Alcoa, Westinghouse, and Mellon Bank).

Mayor Richard Caliguiri took office in 1977 and kept the momentum going with "Renaissance II" that included: six office buildings and a new hotel downtown; a light rail transit system and dedicated busway; and neighborhood revitalization projects. Unfortunately by the early 1980s, it was clear that basic manufacturing in Pittsburgh was failing fast. As the result of foreign competition, outmoded facilities, and expensive labor contracts, the steel, aluminum, and glass industries had all but disappeared. Over the span of eight years in the 1980s, 133,000 high-paying industrial jobs were lost as well as jobs in the service, wholesale, and retail companies that relied on the sub-contracting and payrolls of the big manufacturing enterprises.[7] Unemployment for the Pittsburgh MSA reached 18.2 percent, comparable to national unemployment rates during the Great Depression fifty years earlier.[8] The Renaissance was over. Gloom and despair prevailed as skilled workers and whole families left the region for jobs in other, more prosperous and growing parts of the country, primarily to the South, Southwest, and Far Western US.

Figure 6.3 Planners in Renaissance I with model of Point State Park in the foreground, 1950s
Source: Courtesy of the Allegheny Conference on Community Development.

The City in 1985

Physical Form and Conditions

The overriding physical image of Pittsburgh is a positive one of river valleys, wooded hillsides, historic neighborhoods, and a compact downtown (Figure 6.4). In many ways Pittsburgh is the most European-feeling of American cities. That inherited physical environment was one of the few bright spots in 1985.

But in 1985 not only did the region experience massive unemployment and outmigration, but also the physical infrastructure of streets, bridges, and sewers was declining, even failing. Many neighborhoods and river towns, now bereft of jobs and taxes, were deteriorating with vacant and poorly maintained housing. Abandoned factory buildings and polluted brownfield sites lined the rivers. Once vibrant and busy retail streets were now characterized by vacancies and underperforming businesses. Tax revenues plummeted in Pittsburgh and in the valley towns as factories and stores closed. Even though the regional population was not growing, suburban sprawl continued, leading to more vacancies and abandonment in the city and mill towns.

Governmental fragmentation characterized the geo-political scene. The Pittsburgh metro region currently has seven counties, 455 municipalities, 110 school boards, and 333 authorities, which made it difficult to forge a regional strategy.[9] Allegheny County, the central and most urban county with a 2010 population of 1,223,338 has 130 municipalities (Pittsburgh being just one), each with a mayor, council, and police department.[10] Cooperation on economic development, zoning, and transportation priorities was difficult to achieve.

Figure 6.4 Liverpool Street, Manchester neighborhood, 2015
Source: Photo by Pradipta Banerjee, courtesy of the Remaking Cities Institute.

Demographics

Like most cities in the so-called Rust Belt in the upper Midwest, the City of Pittsburgh lost population along with jobs. The Pittsburgh region remained stagnant with some decline in population. But adding to the woes of the City of Pittsburgh was the continued migration of the middle class (white and black) from the city to the suburban towns, leaving behind a poorer and more elderly population. From 1960 to 1990, the Pittsburgh region's population remained fairly stable at approximately 2.4 million while the City of Pittsburgh's population decreased from 604,332 to 369,879.[11] The exodus of talented and trained workers continued. Young high school and college graduates left the region for sunnier prospects, leaving behind middle-aged and older adults who were less willing or able to relocate. In addition, Pittsburgh, which was once one of the "melting pots" of America in the early twentieth century, was now the region with the lowest percentage of foreign-born residents. In 1870, almost one third of Pittsburgh's population was foreign born, but by 2000 it had declined to 2.6 percent.[12]

Economy

Disinvestment and high unemployment characterized Pittsburgh in 1985. The economy was undiversified, relying heavily on large manufacturing enterprises in basic metals industries. Entrepreneurship was not common due to the prevailing paternalistic culture of big industry providing job security and community stability, generation after generation. It was assumed that good paying jobs would always be there, as was the case for the previous one hundred years. No one was looking to change the successful status quo. No one expected a sudden collapse. Prosperity and full employment would continue. But like the turkey in Nicholas Taleb's book, *The Black Swan*, one day the feeding stopped, and the end came. Taleb writes, "Something has worked in the past, until -- well, it unexpectedly no longer does."[13]

   Within just a few years in the early 1980s, the economy turned upside down and declined across the board, except for the universities and hospitals. With no economic plan in place to deal with the situation, the region's downward slide intensified as hopelessness spread, even in the prosperous suburbs. The consequences were dire. Not only was there high unemployment and outmigration, but the public school systems in the City of Pittsburgh and the mill towns saw rapidly decreasing student enrollment and tax resources, just when retraining and education were most needed. From 1980 to 1988, 112,000 people left Allegheny County. Approximately 3,400 dislocated workers were retrained under publicly funded programs from 1985–1993 in the Pittsburgh region, ranging in age from 25–55; 1,100 were displaced steel workers.[14] The economic depression was paralleled by human depression leading to despair, hopelessness, family stress, divorce, health decline, and increased suicide rates. For example, the 1984 suicide rate in the industrial Mon Valley was double the national rate.[15]

The City in 2015

Physical Form and Conditions

The river valleys and hillsides of Pittsburgh remain the assets they always have been, but many vacant brownfields have been redeveloped in the last thirty years with technology buildings, offices, housing, and retail.[16] Struggling neighborhoods and retail districts have been revitalized. Twenty-four miles of trails and bike paths line the banks of the three rivers once dominated by railroads and factories (Figure 6.5).[17] A new bus-only roadway

Figure 6.5 Kayakers on the Allegheny River with downtown Pittsburgh skyline, July 2015
Source: Photo by Pradipta Banerjee, courtesy of the Remaking Cities Institute.

was built to the west suburbs and the light rail system was extended to the North Shore for $523.4 million.[18] Four major public buildings were constructed in or near downtown: the David L. Lawrence Convention Center, the Pittsburgh Pirates baseball park, the Pittsburgh Steelers football stadium, and the Consol Energy Center, a multi-purpose performance and Pittsburgh Penguins hockey arena at a total cost of $885 million.[19]

Air and water pollution improved. Deteriorated public housing was demolished and replaced by mixed-income housing under the federal Hope VI (now Choice Neighborhoods) and Low Income Tax Credit programs in the Hill District, Manchester, and Larimer neighborhoods. Approximately $200 million was invested to build 2,190 units of mixed-income housing, thus decreasing the concentration of poverty in those three historically impoverished communities.[20] Nevertheless, decline continued in the river mill towns, rural towns, and in many urban neighborhoods across the region. Only one Hope VI grant was awarded to a river town in the Pittsburgh region (McKees Rocks Terrace, $15.8 million for 167 units).[21] Clearly not everyone is participating in the new economy.

Governmental fragmentation remains, but there are a few bright spots, including better cooperation between Allegheny County and the City of Pittsburgh. Some local municipalities formed Councils of Governments (COGs) to jointly purchase supplies and services as well as to cooperate across borders on funding and regulation of development and transportation projects.

Demographics

By 2015, the population drain had stopped, with positive migration nearly offsetting the disparity from births and deaths in the City of Pittsburgh and the region in the past five years.[22] Young adults are not only staying in the region, but many are now migrating into the region. The 20–34-year-old age cohort increased by 7 percent from 2005 to 2010, and it is expected to grow another 8 percent by 2020.[23]

However, the Pittsburgh region, along with South Florida, has the highest percentage of people over 65 years old.[24] The poverty rate in the Pittsburgh region of 12.8 percent is lower than the national average of 15 percent, but the poverty rate for African-Americans in Pittsburgh at 30 percent is higher than the national average of 25.8 percent.[25]

The Pittsburgh region has the lowest minority population percentage of any major metropolitan region in the country (8.3 percent African-American, 2 percent Asian, 1.9 percent multi-racial, 1.5 percent Hispanic, and 86.4 percent Caucasian). Foreign immigration has not changed much since 1985, with the Pittsburgh MSA recording only 3.8 percent foreign-born residents in 2013, the lowest percentage of the top thirty metropolitan regions in the US. Some coastal gateway cities have in excess of 30 percent foreign-born residents. But even in the Midwest every other major city has a higher percentage of foreign-born residents than Pittsburgh (e.g., Chicago, 21.7 percent, Detroit 9.3 percent, and Milwaukee, 7 percent).[26]

Pittsburgh excels in educational attainment by comparison with fifteen US peer regions with 92.5 percent of adults having a high school degree or higher, exceeding Boston, Philadelphia, and Charlotte. Only Minneapolis (93%) has a higher percentage. Pittsburgh also has a high proportion of college graduates, ranking fifth among the forty largest US metropolitan areas.[27]

Economy

Unemployment in 2015 in the Pittsburgh region at 5.9 percent was only slightly higher than the national average of 5.7 percent[28] and ranked seventeenth of the thirty largest US metropolitan regions.[29] Total jobs shrank slightly from 1,114,718 in 1985 to 1,114,300 in 2015.[30] Vigorous entrepreneurship returned after a century of big company job security blankets, now mostly gone. Spinoffs from university and medical research and other startups enlivened the economy, producing well-paying jobs and local wealth building.

In the twenty-five years since 1985, manufacturing jobs decreased by 45 percent but total employment in the Pittsburgh region grew by 26 percent. In 2001, the US Census Bureau changed from the SIC to NAICS classification system. While this change presents a challenge when comparing employment data from 1985 to today, it is clear that since 1985 the Pittsburgh MSA has seen growth in the Services (which includes health care, education, and some university-based research employment), Finance, and Non-Farm Proprietorship sectors, as well as in total regional employment. When the NAICS classification system was implemented in 2001, greater detail became available about the Services sector, showing regional growth specifically in the Professional, Scientific and Technical, Health Care, Education Services, Management of Companies, and Finance sectors.[31]

While manufacturing declined steadily in the Pittsburgh MSA, the manufacturing that has remained is fueled by research and development from Carnegie Mellon University and the University of Pittsburgh. In 2014, manufacturing led all other sectors with sixty-eight major business investment deals announced out of 274 in the region. Despite those indications that manufacturing may experience resurgence, the largest employer in the region today is the UPMC Health System with approximately 62,000 employees in 2015.[32] The recently announced Pittsburgh Health Data Alliance promises to continue UPMC's forward momentum with innovation that will enable them to leverage big data in the health care industry.

A recent positive influence on the economy of the Pittsburgh region has been the rapid development of the shale gas industry in the last ten years. The Marcellus Shale formation in the region is the largest repository of shale gas in the US. Until 2005 when a new technique for horizontal drilling was developed in Texas; it was uneconomical to drill for shale gas. Since then, major energy companies have come in force to Southwestern Pennsylvania to purchase drilling rights and to set up operations. With 729 wells drilled and 1,517 permits issued in the Pittsburgh MSA from 2007–2011, the industry is still in its infancy locally. According to the Pennsylvania Department of Labor and Industry, energy-related employment in the shale gas industry increased by 97 percent from 2007 to 2011, while core extraction and ancillary industries reported 72,000 new hires. Jobs have been created for engineering, legal, construction, trucking, and service jobs, primarily in Washington and Westmoreland counties.[33] When the national economy collapsed in 2008, the Pittsburgh region was spared much of the downward affect of the Great Recession because of the infusion of those shale gas investments and jobs.

Pittsburgh also was not adversely affected by the sub-prime mortgage collapse in the US that began in 2007. First, there had not been a superheated boom in new housing construction in Pittsburgh, such as had occurred in Florida, Arizona, Nevada, and California. Second, Pittsburghers tend to be frugal and cautious homebuyers. They did not participate widely in the sub-prime variable-rate, low down payment mortgages that were being promoted by banks and mortgage lenders. Instead, most Pittsburghers opted for larger down payments and fixed rate mortgages.

Income disparity and lack of opportunity continued for the working poor. This was especially true for poor African-Americans who continue to be concentrated in a handful of census tracks, whereas poor whites are dispersed throughout the region. The poverty rate in the Pittsburgh region was 12.8 percent in 2013, rising slightly since 2010, when it was 12.1 percent. Approximately 10 percent of Caucasians live in poverty, while the African-American poverty rate has persisted at 30 percent for more than a decade. The poverty rate among Hispanics and Asians rose to 23 percent after the 2007 Recession.[34] This class and race inequality problem is not unique to Pittsburgh. It is a national issue of equitable access to education, training, and jobs for disadvantaged persons of all races. The American Dream proves elusive for generations of families caught in the cycle and culture of poverty.

Transformation of the City (1985–2015)

What Went Right?

The first important transformative effort after the collapse of Big Steel was the formation in 1985 of Strategy 21, a consortium of the City of Pittsburgh, County of Allegheny, Carnegie Mellon University, and the University of Pittsburgh that developed a strategy "to transform the economy of the Pittsburgh/Allegheny region as it enters the twenty-first century."[35] Strong emphasis was placed on creating a diversified economy to take "maximum advantage of emerging economic trends toward advanced technology and international marketing and communications systems."[36] The Allegheny Conference on Community Development and local foundations were silent partners and major funders of the effort. Strategy 21 projects included the Software Engineering Institute (1986), the Pittsburgh Super Computing Center (1986), a new international airport terminal (1992) and major infrastructure improvements and brownfield reclamation projects throughout the region.

Following Strategy 21 in 1985, a second regional visioning effort was initiated in 1993, with the publication of a white paper by Dr. Robert Mehrabian, then President of Carnegie Mellon University. Commissioned by the Allegheny Conference, the study compared the Pittsburgh region's economic indicators to those of the twenty-four largest regions in the

Figure 6.6 Oakland neighborhood with Carnegie Mellon University in the foreground, University of
       Pittsburgh and UPMC (five hospitals) in the middle ground, and downtown Pittsburgh
       in the background
Source: Courtesy of Carnegie Mellon University.

country. The comparison was sobering. From 1970 to 1990, the Pittsburgh region had the
largest decline in manufacturing jobs, the slowest growth in service jobs, and the greatest
loss of population. On the other hand, the report identified inherent strengths on which to
base an economic recovery: strong downtown; concentration of university and corporate
research; dedicated and trained workforce; growing core of high-value, high-technology
manufacturing and specialty companies; and an extraordinary range of high quality
recreational and cultural amenities (Figure 6.6). The report proposed a nine-month public
engagement process to develop a consensus vision for the region. That process involved
over 5,000 people and resulted in a report, *The Greater Pittsburgh Region: Working
Together to Compete Globally*, published the following year.[37] The Working Together
Consortium, comprised of representatives from government, business, labor, education,
community and religious organizations, and county governments throughout the region,
was subsequently formed to implement the plan.

Private corporations and foundations established the Strategic Investment Fund in 1996 to complement and support public sector investments in economic development. Originally endowed with $40 million, it received a second round of capitalization of $30 million in 2002. The Fund provides gap-financing loans from $500,000 to $4 million for two categories of development: regional core investments and industrial site reuse for technology development.

One of the most important actions of the Working Together Consortium affecting quality of life was the enactment of State Law 77, which enabled the adoption of a 1 percent added sales tax in Allegheny County in 1994. The tax was split three ways: 0.25 percent to municipalities for tax relief; 0.25 percent to Allegheny County for tax relief; and 0.5 percent to the newly created Regional Asset District (RAD). The portion of the tax designated for the RAD provides operating support to the Pittsburgh Zoo, the National Aviary, the Phipps Conservatory, Carnegie Museums, Carnegie Libraries, County Parks, the Convention Center, stadiums, and many smaller cultural organizations. From 1995 to 2014, RAD has provided $1.5 billion to these regional assets, leading to a cumulative investment of $3.2 billion in culture and quality of life.[38]

New research institutes were created, including the Thomas E. Starzl Transplantation Institute, the National Robotics Center, and the Gates Center for Computer Science. Scores of new non-governmental organizations emerged, including Leadership Pittsburgh, the Green Building Alliance, Pittsburgh Downtown Partnership, Sustainable Pittsburgh, Riverlife, and Bike Pittsburgh.

New cultural organizations joined the four established world-class institutions (Pittsburgh Symphony, Pittsburgh Opera, Pittsburgh Ballet, and the Carnegie Museum), including the Pittsburgh Cultural Trust (with four downtown theaters), the Andy Warhol Museum, the Senator John Heinz History Center, and the August Wilson Center for African American Culture. Art galleries, live music venues, performance groups, and neighborhood arts initiatives emerged and were accompanied by new coffee shops and restaurants. Four large public buildings were built downtown: the convention center, the baseball park, the football stadium, and a multi-purpose hockey arena.

The most recent transformative project is the Pittsburgh Promise. Based on the highly successful 2005 Kalamazoo Promise, the Pittsburgh Promise provides college scholarships for graduates of the Pittsburgh Public Schools or one of its charter high schools who have maintained a 2.5 grade point average and a 90 percent attendance record from the ninth grade. The Pittsburgh Promise was jump-started in 2009 with a $100 million grant and pledge from UPMC (University of Pittsburgh Medical Center), with substantial additional funding and matching contributions anticipated from businesses, foundations, and individuals over the next nine years to reach the goal of $250 million.[39]

Several demographic trends are promising. In the last twenty-five years, regional population loss has slowed each decade to the point that the population has now stabilized at about 2.4 million, with slight growth occurring in the last five years. While more people are now moving to the region than leaving, very few of them are international immigrants. Pittsburgh currently has 3.8 percent foreign-born residents, the lowest percentage among fifteen benchmark regions tracked by Pittsburgh Today. The Pittsburgh region is also disproportionately older. Nearly 18 percent of residents are aged 65 or older, which gives Pittsburgh the highest percentage of seniors and the lowest percentage of residents aged 18 and younger (19.4 percent) when compared with its benchmark regions.[40]

What Went Wrong?

Despite all that success since 1985, thorny issues remain for the Pittsburgh region, including: a surplus of vacant land and buildings (Figure 6.7); declining neighborhoods;

Figure 6.7 Vacant house on Rebecca Street, Borough of Wilkinsburg, July 2015
Source: Photo by author.

racial and socioeconomic inequities; aging infrastructure, such as combined sewer overflows and bridge maintenance; stressed municipal finances; fragmented government; and an underfunded public transit system. These problems are shared with most of the de-industrialized cities in the Northeast and Midwest as they struggle to make a comeback. Philadelphia, Youngstown, Cleveland, and Detroit are exploring innovative approaches to the vacant land problem, including urban agriculture, return of nature to the city, densifying some neighborhoods, and de-densifying others.

Attempts at government consolidation in the region have for the most part failed, leaving a large number of mill towns struggling on their own with little prospect for recovery. No regional strategy has emerged for these communities. Will they become the ghost towns of the future as they continue to depopulate, leaving behind only the poor and the elderly?

US Airways, the targeted beneficiary of the acclaimed new international terminal at the Pittsburgh International Airport (one of the key projects of Strategy 21 in 1985), pulled its hub out of Pittsburgh in 2004. At its peak in 2000, US Airways had more than 500 flights per day and more than 12,000 local employees. Following a merger with American Airlines and the resultant closure of their flight operations control center in 2014, there are now only 150 flights per day and approximately 1,200 American Airlines employees in Pittsburgh. This drastic reduction in airline service has adversely affected Pittsburgh companies that operate nationally and internationally.[41]

The public transit system remains underfunded, resulting in annual cutbacks in service, including cancellation of routes, lower frequency of trips, and older vehicles. This has a negative impact on transit-dependent persons, including the working poor, the elderly, and the disabled. Until recently, the transit system was funded only by fare revenue and annual subsidies from local and state government. There was no long-term dedicated stream of financial support. Each year the transit authority had to make its case (beg) for help from county and state officials. Fortunately, in 2013, new state legislation passed that allocated annual funding from a variety of existing user taxes and fees to the state's transit authorities. In 2014, transit agencies across the state shared an estimated $49–60 million in new revenue. According to analysis by the legislation's sponsor, Rep. Joseph Markosek, transit agencies across the state are expected to share $476–$497 million annually by 2019.[42] This has to some extent stabilized the transit system financially, but more needs to done. Pittsburgh's Port Authority is planning to use the additional funding to upgrade its vehicles, develop a bus rapid transit line, provide better fare collection and real-time vehicle arrival information, and encourage high-density transit oriented development.

The presence of large areas of vacant and abandoned land and buildings is another problem shared with other post-industrial cities. Most of these properties are tax delinquent and controlled by absentee owners. Antiquated laws and prolonged court procedures often hamper attempts by local governments to foreclose on and acquire parcels for new development. In 2014, the City of Pittsburgh passed progressive legislation setting up a land bank program that streamlines the acquisition process while at the same time protecting individual property rights. There has been some concern expressed by low income housing advocates that land banking will lead to gentrification and displacement of poor families. Other communities in the region, including some mill towns, are looking at similar land bank legislation.

Problems have begun to emerge in the first ring suburbs around Pittsburgh, many of which were developed after World War II, fueled by the GI Bill, new road construction, and middle-class flight from the central city. As the population in these modest suburbs aged, more affluent families, looking for newer and larger houses, moved to the next outer ring of suburbs. The inner ring suburbs they left now began to see an in-migration of poor working-class whites and African-Americans. Poverty rates have increased nationally outside of central cities. Approximately 79 percent of people living in poverty in Pittsburgh's metro area are not living within the City of Pittsburgh.[43] Property values in the inner ring decreased, school quality declined, crime increased, and businesses closed. Furthermore, suburbs that developed on an auto-dependent model, with cul-de-sac street layouts and no sidewalks, are poorly designed for transit-dependent persons who need convenient public transportation to get to jobs, training, and health care.

Environmental issues remain, beginning with particulate air pollution from coal-burning power plants, coke oven factories, and vehicle emissions, both locally generated and windborne from eastern Ohio. The county remains under a federal consent degree from the US Environmental Protection Agency (US EPA) to separate its combined sewer system that currently merges the flows of sanitary waste and storm water when it rains, potentially a $2 billion effort. The US EPA labeled the plan submitted by ALCOSAN as "deficient" in January 2014. Negotiations continue over what infrastructure improvements will be required to meet the goals of the 2008 consent decree.[44]

The recent emergence of shale gas, a major provider of jobs and economic development, has brought with it problems of ground water pollution, air pollution, road deterioration, and disruption of the ecosystem. There is also the prospect of a "boom and bust" cycle when the labor-intensive drilling phase ends with only monitoring of the wells and pipelines left to do. The drilling has occurred primarily in rural counties and near small isolated towns, all of which are currently experiencing new-found economic prosperity with good paying jobs, rising rents, new home construction, and increased retail sales.

When the extraction jobs depart, decline will be left behind in drilling areas. The impact may be similar to that of the collapse of the steel industry in Pittsburgh in the 1980s. Although there is a state-mandated impact fee attached to the right to drill in Pennsylvania, nearly all those fees go to repair roads damaged by the large water trucks and drilling rigs, and to a lesser extent to mitigate water and air pollution. Very little of the impact fee is being spent in these small towns for non-extraction economic development, affordable housing, or main street revitalization. There has been criticism of the state for having a one-time impact fee rather than an extraction tax that would be ongoing until the wells are exhausted. Pennsylvania is the only state in the US without an extraction tax.

Lessons Learned

Dynamic Leadership Is Essential

Pittsburgh was fortunate to have Mayor David Lawrence and banker/industrialist Richard King Mellon step forward at the end of World War II to take decisive action and to assemble a highly qualified team to implement the plans for Renaissance I. This was classic top-down planning that was fortunately led by two benevolent and altruistic men. Subsequent economic revitalization efforts by Mayor Richard Caliguiri (1977–1988) and Mayor Tom Murphy (1994–2006) were more collaborative and inclusive with the community, but also led to good results. There is no substitute for visionary and dynamic leadership.

Public/Private Partnerships Are Key

From World War II to today, Pittsburgh has been exemplary in bringing together the public and private sectors for the greater good of the region, including government (local, state, and federal), private corporations, and private philanthropies. Pittsburgh is particularly blessed with foundations set up by the industrial families of the industrial powerhouse era. New entities were created, such as the first Urban Redevelopment Authority in the US in 1946 and the Pittsburgh Cultural Trust in 1985. Strategy 21 in 1985 would not have happened without such a public/private partnership climate.

Have a Regional Strategy to Diversify

Clearly, Strategy 21 was a key turning point for Pittsburgh when large industry collapsed almost overnight. The City of Pittsburgh, the County of Allegheny, Carnegie Mellon University, and the University of Pittsburgh formed a united coalition to lobby for state and federal support for projects that would become the basis for the diversification of the region into computer software, robotics, medical research, and higher education. The strategy continues to be adjusted and recalibrated every five or ten years involving the same public/private partners as in previous iterations but also enriched by new community partners.

Bottom Up Is Also Important

Starting in the 1990s, something else was happening – an unprecedented bubbling up of entrepreneurial and quality of life initiatives from individuals, volunteer groups, and non-governmental organizations. There was receptivity to new things and willingness to take risks. This bottom-up energy was especially exhibited by young adults in their twenties and thirties who began populating older neighborhoods, renovating houses, creating art, and starting new businesses. In 1996, several young professionals formed the Pittsburgh Urban Magnet Project (PUMP) "to make a Pittsburgh where young people have an active role in advocating and caring for our city, making Pittsburgh the first choice for everyone to live, work, and play."[45] Today PUMP has 6,000 members under the age of 40 with over 25,000 participants annually in their programs.

Strengthen the Core

Pittsburgh has been fortunate that its downtown has remained relatively vibrant, compared to those in other mid-sized American cities. Too many post-industrial cities in the US, most notably Detroit, have ended up with an emptied out downtown—the so-called "hole in the donut." Multinational Fortune 500 corporations like US Steel, Alcoa, Heinz, PPG, and PNC Bank continue to have their headquarters downtown. Very little demolition took place downtown other than the replacement of warehouses and factories with the mixed use Gateway Center in the 1950s and 1960s. Continued investment strengthened the core, including new corporate headquarter buildings, hotels, and public facilities (convention center and sports stadiums). The creation of the Cultural District became the focal point of four theaters and numerous restaurants and art galleries, like a mini Times Square or London's West End. Market Square, a once derelict public square, has been redeveloped as a European-style piazza surrounded by numerous restaurants with outdoor dining (Figure 6.8). Strengthening the core also meant stabilizing and revitalizing the neighborhoods of the City of Pittsburgh—the central city of the region, and investing in public transportation that connects the jobs in the central city to the surrounding suburbs and small towns.

Figure 6.8 Market Square in downtown Pittsburgh on Farmer's Market Day, July 2015
Source: Photo by author.

Invest in Education

Essential to the economic health of any region is having an educated and trained workforce, both in breadth and depth. The demand of industry for technically proficient employees has never been higher, but the public education systems in all US post-industrial cities are chronically underfunded, leading to declines in student enrollment, performance, and graduation rates. The community investment in the Pittsburgh Promise described above has begun to show success. Since 2008, more than 5,584 graduating students in the Pittsburgh Public School System have received up to $40,000 each in scholarships; a total of $64.3 million has been given to date. The graduation rate has increased from 63 percent to 71 percent in 2014.[46] In addition, most of the local universities have established outreach and mentoring programs in the public schools.

Invest in Quality of Life

This chapter began with reference to Pittsburgh being consistently voted "The Most Livable City" by numerous rating groups and publications. It was and is well deserved, but not without the region having committed substantial resources since 1985 to parks, trails, cultural amenities, and sport facilities. Pittsburgh is a city of festivals (Three Rivers Arts Festival, Three Rivers Regatta/July Fourth, Children's Festival, First Night, and annual festivals in almost every neighborhood, such as "Art All Night" in Lawrenceville) as well as large-scale sporting events (three major league professional sports teams, Pittsburgh Marathon, the 10 kilometer Great Race, and Head of the Ohio Rowing Regatta). Urban economist Richard Florida completed his research in Pittsburgh at Carnegie Mellon University in the 1990s that led to his 2002 best-selling book, *The Rise of the Creative Class*. His book makes the case that creative and entrepreneurial people, especially young people, gravitate to cities that have talent, technology, tolerance, and territorial assets (meaning places of authenticity with walkable neighborhoods, recreational amenities, and diversity). Pittsburgh is such a place in 2015. Quality of life also means a commitment to sustainable development in all its manifestations: physical, economic, and social.

Prospects for the Future

What about the Pittsburgh of 2045, another thirty years ahead? Pittsburgh has engaged in a "big vision" process twice since the economic downturn in the 1980s: Strategy 21 in 1985; and the Working Together Consortium in 1994. Both were effective in pointing the way to investments in research, technology, education, medical, and high value manufacturing, and away from basic industry; and to investing in the regional core and in quality of life. Those leaders and efforts produced the Pittsburgh of 2015. What are today's strengths to build on this time around?

New Leadership

Pittsburgh is poised to take its transformation to a new level. New and younger leadership has emerged in the past two years. A progressive new mayor, William Peduto, and county executive, Rich Fitzgerald, were elected. Carnegie Mellon University and the University of Pittsburgh chose new leaders. Several major private foundations brought on new executive directors. All are committed to working together and with the community at large on an agenda of innovation, technology, sustainability, and equity.

Research Universities and a Research-Based Medical Center

The future is clearly about technology and innovation. Start with Pittsburgh having two major research universities, the only second-tier city in the US that can make that claim. Carnegie Mellon University conducted $3.7 billion in federal research and contract work in the last ten years, much of it for the US Department of Defense and the National Science Foundation.[47] The University of Pittsburgh School of Medicine is among the top five US medical research centers in federal research dollars, with more than $400 million in each of the last ten years.[48] Since 2007, Carnegie Mellon University has ranked first in the country among universities without medical schools in the number of startup companies per research dollar spent. Since 2000, Carnegie Mellon University faculty and graduates have launched more than 300 startup companies creating approximately 9,000 new jobs in Pennsylvania.[49]

One concerning downside is the lack of a vigorous venture capital network in Pittsburgh. In 2014, $338 million was invested in the Pittsburgh MSA by venture capital firms, slightly less than Philadelphia and Minneapolis, two of the benchmark regions tracked by *Pittsburgh Today*. When compared to Boston and New York City, regions known for tech investment activity, Pittsburgh's venture capital falls far short of their respective $4.7 and $4.5 billion.[50] This financing deficiency causes local startup companies that require venture funding to scale up their enterprises to move their operations to richer regions.

Talent Attraction

More than 95,000 undergraduate and graduate students annually attend the twenty-five colleges and universities in the Pittsburgh region. More and more of these students are pursuing careers in Pittsburgh. The age cohort of 20–34 years olds grew by 7 percent from 2005–2010, with a gain of an additional 8 percent by 2020. This cohort is also well educated with 48.1 percent of workers aged 24–34 with at least a bachelor's degree. This puts Pittsburgh in fifth place nationally after Boston, San Francisco, Washington, D.C., and Austin for educational attainment.[51] The investment in quality of life over the past thirty years has clearly paid off in attracting and retaining talent.

Stable Economy

In relation to its peer cities in the US, Pittsburgh consistently ranks near the top in low unemployment, low cost of living, and wealth building. This creates a solid and stable economic base. The shale gas boom has made up for the less than robust activity in other economic sectors since 2007. One of the issues for the region going forward will be how it will fare when the shale gas extraction boom is over in five or ten years. There is a growing interest in rebuilding a manufacturing base, especially in high-value goods for export. Additional industrial jobs would help to diversify the economy that is now heavily weighted to education, research, medical, and banking jobs.

Two Priority Initiatives

Not only does Pittsburgh have deficiencies in venture capital and enterprises and in K-12 public education, but also there are geographic, racial, and class disparities in participation and opportunity in the knowledge economy. Those regions that have a strong local investment climate for innovation and entrepreneurship combined with a rich local pool of talent will outperform those regions that do not, and as a consequence, will attract the best and brightest from less endowed regions. Below are two priority initiatives.

Invigorate Venture Capital

The region must develop a robust regional financial strategy with public and private money not only for investing in startup businesses, but even more importantly for the expansion of startups and existing businesses. A number of organizations were established for just this purpose: Pittsburgh Technology Council; Ben Franklin Technology Partners (known locally as Innovation Works); Pittsburgh Life Sciences Greenhouse; AlphaLab Gear; Thrill Mill; University of Pittsburgh Institute for Entrepreneurial Excellence; and Project Olympus of Carnegie Mellon University.

Develop Technological Skills for All

There are geographic, racial, and class disparities in participation and opportunity in the knowledge economy, both in Pittsburgh and across the United States. National economists are concerned that the future American workforce will not have appropriate and adequate skills. Those regions that develop their own pool of talent will outperform those regions that do not, and as a consequence, will attract the best and brightest from the less endowed regions. The Pittsburgh region must invest in K-12 education, community colleges, and training schools, especially in teaching technical and digital skills. The new buzzword in education is STEAM (science, technology, engineering, art, and math). Those skills lead to higher-paying jobs for high school and technical school graduates and to higher education for those who want to pursue it. An advanced workforce development program must reach out especially to under-served children and families in poor urban neighborhoods and declining mill towns.

Notes

1   J.M. Adavasio and Jake Page, *The First Americans: In Pursuit of Archaeology's Greatest Mystery* (New York: Modern Library, 2003).
2   US Census, Population of the 100 largest urban places: 1860.
3   David Lowry, James Mills, and E. A. Myers. *Pittsburgh, its Industry and Commerce: Embracing Statistics of the Coal, Iron, Glass, Steel, Copper, Petroleum and Other Manufacturing Interests of Pittsburgh.* (Pittsburgh: Barr, Myers, 1870).
4   James Parton, "Pittsburg." *The Atlantic Monthly* 21(123) (Jan. 1868): 17–36.
5   J. Gibson Campbell and Emily Lennon, "Historical Census Statistics on the Foreign Born Population of the United States: 1850–1990" (Working Paper 29, US Bureau of the Census, Population Division, Washington, DC, February 1999).
6   Joe W. Trotter and Jared N. Day, *Race and Renaissance: African Americans in Pittsburgh since World War II* (Pittsburgh: University of Pittsburgh Press, 2010), 1–43.
7   Singh Giarratani, and Christopher Briem. "Dynamics of Growth and Restructuring in the Pittsburgh Metropolitan Region," in Ulrich Hilpert (ed.) *Regionalisation of Globalised Innovation: Locations for Advanced Industrial Development and Disparities in Participation* (New York: Routledge, 2003), 136–52.
8   Bill Toland, "In desperate 1983, there was nowhere for Pittsburgh's economy to go but up," *Pittsburgh Post-Gazette*, December 23, 2012.
9   Christopher Briem, "A Primer on Local Government Fragmentation and Regionalism in the Pittsburgh Region." Available at: www.briem.com/frag/PittsburghIndex.htm (accessed March 19, 2015).
10   US Census Bureau, State and County QuickFacts.
11   US Census Bureau, State and Metropolitan Area Book, 1979 and 1991.
12   Gibson and Young, "Historical Census Statistics on the Foreign Born Population of the United States: 1850 to 2000." (US Census Population Division: Working Paper no. 81, Feb. 2006)
13   Nicolas Taleb, *The Black Swan.* (New York: Random House, 2007), 41.
14   Robert Bednarzik and Joseph Szalanski, "Examination of the Work History of Pittsburgh Steelworkers, Who Were Displaced and Received Publicly-Funded Retraining in the Early

1980's."(IZA Discussion Paper No. 6429, Institute for the Study of Labor (IZA), Bonn, Germany, March 2012).

15 J. Corbett, *A Study of Unemployment in the Mon-Yough Valley and Its Impact on Social and Psychological Functioning*, Mon-Yough Community Mental Health and Mental Retardation Center (McKeesport, PA: July 1985).

16 Andrew Moore, "EPA funds brownfield development in McKees Rocks," *Pop City Media*, June 29, 2011.

17 Friends of the Riverfront, "About Us."

18 Jon Schmitz, "Trains ready to roll under the river to the North Shore," *Pittsburgh Post-Gazette*, March 13, 2012.

19 David Lawrence Convention Center, Building Overview; Zuang, Zhe, Steinbrenner Institute Brownfields Center, PNC Park Case Study, and Heinz Field Case Study, June 2010; and Pittsburgh Sports and Exhibition Authority website, "North Shore Development by Continental."

20 Mindy Turbov and Valerie Piper, "Hope VI and Mixed-Finance Redevelopments: A Catalyst for Neighborhood Renewal – Pittsburgh Case Study: Manchester," Washington, DC: Brookings Institution Metropolitan Program, September 2005.

21 Rhae Parkes and Heather Wood, "Successful Transitions: Sustaining Support Services beyond Hope VI," US Department of Housing and Urban Development, December 2001.

22 Jason Cato, "Census shows slow PA population gains," *Pittsburgh Tribune-Review*, January 4, 2014.

23 *Pittsburgh Today*. "Young Adults Report," October 2012.

24 Rotstein, "New trends in aging demographics hit Allegheny County," *Pittsburgh Post-Gazette*, December 1, 2014.

25 Suzanne Macartney, Bishaw, Alemayehu, and Fontenot, Kayla, "Poverty Rates for Selected Detailed Race and Hispanic Groups by State and Place: 2007–2011." US Census Bureau, American Community Survey Briefs, February 2013.

26 *Pittsburgh Today*, "Behind the Times: The Limited Role of Minorities in the Greater Pittsburgh Workforce," March 2015.

27 US Census Bureau, interpreted by *Pittsburgh Today*, accessed on March 26, 2015.

28 US Department of Labor Local Area Unemployment Statistics, released January 2015, interpreted by *Pittsburgh Today*, accessed March 26, 2015.

29 US Census Bureau, Population Division, Annual Estimates of the Resident Population, April 1, 2010 to July 1, 2014. US Department of Labor, Local Area Unemployment Statistics, "Unemployment Rates for Large Metropolitan Areas," released January 2015.

30 US Department of Commerce, Bureau of Economic Analysis, Total Full Time and Part Time Employment by SIC/NAICS Industry, 1985 and 2013, table CA25N, Pittsburgh MSA.

31 Ibid.

32 Bill Toland and Born. "UPMC employees protest job, wage cuts," *Pittsburgh Post-Gazette*, July 30, 2014.

33 Frank Gamrat and Jake Haulk. *Gauging the Economic Impact of Marcellus Shale Drilling in the Pittsburgh Region*, July 2011.

34 Carol DeVita and Maura Farrell, "Poverty and Income Insecurity in the Pittsburgh Metropolitan Area," November 2014.

35 "Strategy 21 Proposal to the Commonwealth of Pennsylvania," (June 1985)

36 Ibid.

37 R. Mehrabian and T. O'Brien, *The Greater Pittsburgh Region: Working Together to Compete Globally*. (November 1994).

38 Allegheny Regional Asset District website, "What is RAD?" page.

39 Pittsburgh Promise website, "About Us – Our Impact Dashboard" page.

40 *Pittsburgh Today*, "Pittsburgh Today and Tomorrow: Regional Annual Report," 2014.

41 Allegheny Institute for Public Policy website. Available at: www.alleghenyinstitute.org/tag/usairways/. Centre for Aviation website, http://centreforaviation.com/analysis/pittsburgh-international-airport-works-to-reduce-costs-to-attract-airlines-post-consolidation-204365. Belko and Smydo. "US Airways to close Moon flight operations center, affecting 600 jobs" *Pittsburgh Post-Gazette*, January 24, 2014.

42 Jon Schmitz and J. Giammarise. "Governor Corbett signs transportation funding bill." *Pittsburgh Post-Gazette*, November 24, 2013.

43 Niederberger, "Pittsburgh suburbs suffering poverty at high rate," *Pittsburgh Post-Gazette*, November 17, 2013.

44   Clean Rivers Campaign website, "About – FAQ" page.
45   Pittsburgh Urban Magnet Project website, "Home" page.
46   Pittsburgh Promise website, "About Us – Our Impact Dashboard" page.
47   Carnegie Mellon Institutional Research and Analysis. "Factbook 2014–2015, volume 29," page 199 and "Factbook 2009–2010, volume 24," page 6.9 and "Factbook 2005–2006, volume 20," page 6.9.
48   University of Pittsburgh School of Medicine website, "Fast Facts," 2013.
49   Pittsburgh Council on Higher Education website.
50   *Pittsburgh Today* website. "Key Indicators for Understanding our Region: Economy/Venture Capital" page.
51   *Pittsburgh Today*. "Young Adults Report."

References

Adavasio, J.M. and Jake Page (2003) *The First Americans: In Pursuit of Archaeology's Greatest Mystery*. New York: Modern Library.

Allegheny Regional Asset District, "What is RAD?" Available at: www.radworkshere.org/pages/what-is-rad (accessed March 28, 2015).

Bednarzik, Robert and Szalanski, Joseph (2012) "Examination of the Work History of Pittsburgh Steelworkers, Who Were Displaced and Received Publicly-Funded Retraining in the Early 1980's." IZA Discussion Paper No. 6429, Institute for the Study of Labor (IZA), Bonn, Germany, March.

Briem, Christopher, "A Primer on Local Government Fragmentation and Regionalism in the Pittsburgh Region." Available at: www.briem.com/frag/PittsburghIndex.htm (accessed March 19, 2015).

Campbell, J. Gibson and Emily Lennon (1999) "Historical Census Statistics on the Foreign Born Population of the United States: 1850–1990," Working Paper 29, US Bureau of the Census, Population Division, Washington, DC, February.

Carnegie Mellon Institutional Research and Analysis. "Factbook 2014–2015, Volume 29," page 199; "Factbook 2009–2010, volume 24," page 6.9; "Factbook 2005–2006, volume 20," page 6.9.

Corbett, J. (1985) *A Study of Unemployment in the Mon-Yough Valley and Its Impact on Social and Psychological Functioning*. McKeesport, PA: Mon-Yough Community Mental Health and Mental Retardation Center.

DeVita, Carol and Maura Farrell (2014) *Poverty and Income Insecurity in the Pittsburgh Metropolitan Area*. The Urban Institute, November.

Florida, Richard (2002) *The Rise of the Creative Class*. New York: Basic Books.

Gamrat, Frank and Jake Haulk (2011) *Gauging the Economic Impact of Marcellus Shale Drilling in the Pittsburgh Region*. Allegheny Institute for Public Policy, Report #11-05, July 2011.

Giarratani, Frank, V. P. Singh and C. Briem (2003) "Dynamics of Growth and Restructuring in the Pittsburgh Metropolitan Region," in Ulrich Hilpert (ed.) *Regionalisation of Globalised Innovation: Locations for Advanced Industrial Development and Disparities in Participation*. New York: Routledge, 136–52.

Hardin, Paul Kapp and Paul J. Armstrong, eds. (2012) *Synergicity: Reinventing the Post-Industrial City*. Urbana, IL: University of Illinois Press.

Kalson, Sally (2010) "Pittsburgh named Most Livable City again." *Pittsburgh Post-Gazette*, May 4.

Lowry, David, James Mills, and E. A. Myers (1870) *Pittsburgh, its Industry and Commerce: Embracing Statistics of the Coal, Iron, Glass, Steel, Copper, Petroleum and Other Manufacturing Interests of Pittsburgh*. Pittsburgh: Barr, Myers.

Macartney, Suzanne, Alemayehu Bishaw, and Kayla Fontenot (2013) "Poverty Rates for Selected Detailed Race and Hispanic Groups by State and Place: 2007–2011." US Census Bureau, American Community Survey Briefs, February.

Mehrabian, Robert and Thomas H. O'Brien (1994) "*The Greater Pittsburgh Region: Working Together to Compete Globally*." A Report for the Regional Economic Revitalization Initiative by Carnegie Mellon University and the Allegheny Conference on Community Development.

Moore, Andrew. "EPA funds brownfield development in McKees Rocks," *Pop City Media*, June 29, 2011.

Parkes, Rhae and Heather Wood (2001) "Successful Transitions: Sustaining Support Services beyond Hope VI" for the US Department of Housing and Urban Development, December.

Parton, James (1868) "Pittsburg," *The Atlantic Monthly* 21(123) (Jan.): 17–36.

Pittsburgh Today (2012) "Young Adults Report," October.

Pittsburgh Today (2014) "Pittsburgh Today and Tomorrow: Regional Annual Report."

Pittsburgh Today (2015) "Behind the Times: The Limited Role of Minorities in the Greater Pittsburgh Workforce," March.

Pittsburgh Today website, "Key Indicators for Understanding our Region: Economy/Venture Capital" page. Available at: www.pittsburghtoday.org/view_vcinvestment.html

Rottstein, Gary (2010) "Pittsburgh's population expected to grow in a few years: Region's exodus finally slowing." *Pittsburgh Post-Gazette*, June 21.

Schmitz, Jon (2012) "Trains ready to roll under the river to the North Shore," *Pittsburgh Post-Gazette*, March 13.

Strategy 21: Pittsburgh/Allegheny Economic Development Strategy to Begin the 21st Century. 1985. A proposal to the Commonwealth of Pennsylvania by the City of Pittsburgh, Allegheny County, University of Pittsburgh and Carnegie Mellon University.

Taleb, Nicolas (2007) *The Black Swan*. New York: Random House.

Toker, Franklin (2009) *Pittsburgh: A New Portrait*. Pittsburgh: University of Pittsburgh Press.

Toland, Bill (2012) "In desperate 1983, there was nowhere for Pittsburgh's economy to go but up," *Pittsburgh Post-Gazette*, December 23.

Trotter, Joe W. and Jared N. Day (2010) *Race and Renaissance: African Americans in Pittsburgh since World War II*. Pittsburgh: University of Pittsburgh Press.

Turbov, Mindy and Valerie Piper (2005) "Hope VI and Mixed-Finance Redevelopments: A Catalyst for Neighborhood Renewal – Pittsburgh Case Study: Manchester." Washington, DC: Brookings Institution Metropolitan Program, September.

US Census Bureau. "Pennsylvania population of counties by decennial census: 1900 to 1990." Available at; http://www.census.gov/population/cencounts/pa190090.txt

US Census Bureau. "Population of the 100 largest urban places: 1860 and 1980"

US Census Bureau (1979, 1991) *State and Metro Area Book*. Washington, D.C.: US Census Bureau.

US Census Bureau. "Population Division, Annual Estimates of the Resident Population, April 1, 2010 to July 1, 2014."

US Department of Commerce, Bureau of Economic Analysis, "Total Full Time and Part Time Employment by SIC/NAICS Industry, 1985 and 2013," table CA25N, Pittsburgh MSA.

US Department of Labor (2015) Local Area Unemployment Statistics, "Unemployment Rates for Large Metropolitan Areas," released January. Available at: www.bls.gov/web/metro/laulrgma.htm (accessed March 26, 2015).

Zhe Zuang (2010) Steinbrenner Institute Brownfields Center, "PNC Park Case Study" and "Heinz Field Case Study," June.

Part II

European City
Case Studies

7   The View from Europe

Geraldine Gardner

Introduction

When the first Remaking Cities Congress convened in Pittsburgh in 1988, many Western European cities were in the midst of a period of crisis like their American counterparts. Failing economies, population and job loss, environmental degradation, protests, and political strife were all common symptoms of the European post-industrial urban malaise. The prescription for emerging from crisis varied from city to city, shaped by its unique local context, national policies, and the stepwise gaining of the influence of the European Union (EU).

The view from Europe is decidedly complex when it comes to cataloguing and commenting on the past thirty years of remaking post-industrial cities. While this chapter provides an overview of trends in the European experience using the case study cities, it does not attempt to provide a comprehensive assessment of the unique local, national, and EU level contexts that produced both the crisis and regeneration of post-industrial European cities. Rather, this chapter focuses on the experience of five Western European cities, which were the primary European case studies at the 2013 Remaking Cities Congress. There are several examples of post-industrial rebirth in cities of the formerly Communist East, principally in the East of Germany; however, the circumstances of the post-1989 period had a unique influence on the trajectory of Eastern European cities from rapid decline following the collapse of the Berlin Wall to a more moderate revival in recent years. Despite this uneven experience across the continent, many formerly industrial European cities have made significant strides along the path of regeneration.

While there may be no single European experience, cities and metropolitan regions have been and will continue to be a vital part of the economic, political, social, and cultural vibrancy of Europe. In comparison to the United States, Europe has a similar level of urbanization with more than 71 percent of the population living in urbanized areas.[1] Yet, the urban European population lives overwhelmingly in small-to-medium-sized cities of less than 250,000 inhabitants. The resulting polycentric urban form both within Europe and within most individual countries is an important factor in understanding the challenge and opportunity for post-industrial urban regeneration. Currently, 67 percent of Europe's gross domestic product (GDP) is produced in cities of 250,000 or more inhabitants, which means that less than 20 percent of Europe's cities produce a considerable portion of the GDP.[2] Therefore, activating the network of smaller European cities, many of which have an industrial legacy, is a critical challenge for both local, regional, national, and EU policy-makers.

Unlike the United States, where cities are making great strides without a robust national-level policy framework and federal assistance, European cities are connected to strong national and EU policy initiatives. This layering of policies and their attached resources have greatly influenced post-industrial European regeneration. However, in order to meet the challenges of the next twenty-five years, it will be important for European cities to adopt the entrepreneurial spirit of their American counterparts, to continue to push for open government, and to develop a more robust approach to civic engagement. Moreover, European cities are moving swiftly towards asserting their collective power across national and EU scales to push a renewed focus on urban policy.

Europe: Cradle of Industry

As the birthplace of the Industrial Revolution, perhaps it is fitting that European cities were among the first confronted with the urgent crisis of how to rebound after the collapse of industrial capitalism. In the immediate aftermath of World War II, European cities were left in various states of physical, economic, and social crisis. Devastation by German and Allied bombing raids left many cities, especially in the industrial heartlands of Europe, in rubble and ashes. Even if the historic core of some cities escaped the bombing, critical infrastructure and manufacturing centers were targeted. Rebuilding Europe, fueled in part by the European Recovery Program (or Marshall Plan), took on different strategic objectives across the continent but left a lasting impact on urban economies, city spaces, and the environment.

In terms of the economy, rapid redevelopment of the industrial machine was a primary recovery strategy for many cities in the post-war period. Cities across the continent rebuilt their economic infrastructure in key sectors of the pre-war economy with very little attention to economic diversification. For example, Italy diverted more than 30 percent of its European Recovery Program resources to rebuilding Fiat automotive plants in Turin; thus, the city's economy remained focused on one core manufacturing industry in the post-war period. The haste to return to productive activity often resulted in rebuilding industrial infrastructure and manufacturing facilities in the same physical location as the pre-war period. While this expedited the recovery, it resulted in other planning and policy choices that would shape cities for decades to come.

The rise of modernist planning also had a profound impact on post-war planning decisions at the local level. For example, Rotterdam lost almost its entire medieval-era center in the war (Figure 7.1), but instead of restoring the urban fabric, it elected to rebuild in the style of new, modernist urban planning (Figure 7.2). The steady migration of low-skilled workers to the cities to fill industrial and service sector jobs demanded quick-fix housing solutions, often proximate to the job sites. In some cases, this meant cheaply constructed housing located on the periphery of the city with little access to amenities, services, and transportation choices. In other cases, housing was quickly rebuilt in and around the city center in large housing estates. Modernist planning principles also supported the growth of automobile-oriented development in many European cities, including those not physically impacted by the war. In the 1950s, many planners and engineers from these countries traveled to the US to learn from its transportation and land use planning policies. In Sweden, for example, these lessons were captured in seminal texts that influenced a generation of planners and shaped major infrastructure and planning decisions in Stockholm and other major cities.[3] The cumulative effect of auto-oriented development, the razing of central urban neighborhoods, and the development on the periphery helped to destroy as much of the desirable urban fabric as World War II did.

Figure 7.1 German bombings in 1940 destroyed Rotterdam's medieval center
Source: Photo by US National Archives and Records Administration via Wikimedia Commons.

Figure 7.2 Modernist buildings on Rotterdam waterfront
Source: "Rotterdam-Kop van Zuid, World Portcenter, Montevideo en hotel New York foto12 2011-01-09 14.12," by Michielverbeek, Own work. Licensed under CC BY-SA 3.0 via Wikimedia Commons.

The impact on the environment of the post-war rebuilding is closely related to urban physical and economic transformation. In many areas, the economic recovery ramped up industrial production and natural resource extraction. Whether it was coal mining in the Ruhr Region in Germany or the steel industry in Bilbao, Spain, cities and metropolitan regions began to suffer an increased level of environmental consequences from hazardous industrial practices. The famous London smog of 1952, which killed over 4,000 people in less than a week, is a notorious example of the dangerous impact of the post-war industrial boom. While industrial pollution had impacted cities since the early nineteenth century, its resurgence in the post-war period coincided with the rise of the environmental movement and public consciousness in Europe. This would later influence many post-industrial cities to focus on remediation as a critical first step in the recovery. Coal and other extractive industries were already declining when the first in a series of energy crises began in the late 1960s and culminated in the 1973 oil embargo. Soaring energy prices had a devastating impact on manufacturing-based economies. The next domino to fall was the integration of European markets and their opening to global competition. As in the United States, European industrial cities suffered as production moved closer to new markets with access to cheaper labor and more efficient transportation.

The impacts of the crisis on industrialized European cities are well known and are illuminated in the case study cities that follow this chapter. Immediate consequences included job losses and unemployment that led to escalating tensions and social unrest in many cities. Cities were left with an economic, spatial, and environmental legacy of post-war policy and planning decisions, including poor-quality housing, neighborhoods of concentrated poverty, neglect of the center city, and suburbanization. It also left large swaths of brownfield sites that would require significant environmental restoration to be viable for any kind of new development.

While there are shared experiences regarding the impact of these global challenges across the continent, there were vast differences in the national policy responses to the crisis. For example, the Netherlands supported suburbanization, especially by the well educated and the elite. In contrast, Italy was so wracked with political crisis at the national level that cities and metropolitan regions were left largely on their own to manage a host of challenges and chart their own path to recovery.

In summary, the view from European cities in 1985 can be sorted into several interrelated trends:

- Collapse of manufacturing and extractive national resource industries had an acute impact on European cities with no economic "back-up plan."
- Inner city decay and population loss contrasted with growth on the periphery of wealthy enclaves, "dormitory suburban neighborhoods," and low-income housing estates.
- Large concentrations of unemployed, low-skilled workers and immigrants with few transferable skills to new industries.
- Poor environmental conditions from decades of extractive, polluting industries and large-scale contamination of now vacant industrial sites and infrastructure.

Europe's Urban Renaissance

The tipping point for positive change varied from city to city, but often occurred during a moment of crisis that prompted city and regional actors to devise more aggressive economic and social strategies that were a structural change from past efforts. While each city has its own unique transformation story that was shaped by specific context and needs, there are similarities across the case studies in the areas of physical regeneration, economic diversification, and environmental stewardship. Underlying these policy responses were new trends for European cities toward bold leadership decisions, new partnerships with the private sector, and in some cases active citizen engagement. The stories from these cities instruct us that there are rarely quick-fix solutions—significant change occurs over a long-term horizon and requires carefully constructed and disciplined commitments across government scales. However, they also illustrate the importance of shifting the mental maps for how local stakeholders understand local identity and its tie to a city's industrial legacy. Even as heavy industry began to decline across the Ruhr Region during the 1960s and 1970s, many local actors continued to believe that the industry would come back and initially reacted negatively to diversification strategies.[4]

Emphasis on the physical regeneration of the center city core is a common strategy across the case study cities, especially to enhance transportation and mobility systems and repurpose industrial spaces and infrastructure. Turin developed the city's first master plan in 1995 to lay out a vision for a revitalized historic core and for large-scale urban transformation projects, including a plan to bury the rail lines that bisect the city and cover them with a network of grand boulevards (Figure 7.3). The scale of physical change is especially remarkable in Bilbao, where an entire shipyard area was famously redeveloped and now is the site of a mixed-use urban riverfront district anchored by the iconic Guggenheim Museum, designed by Frank Gehry. In both cases, physical transformation projects were one plank in a more comprehensive revitalization approach.

Figure 7.3 Boulevard Spina in Turin
Source: Photo by FrancoFranco56 via Wikimedia Commons.

While large-scale urban regeneration projects fueled by heavy subsidies from national and regional governments as well as the European Union helped to heal the physical scars of deindustrialization, the long-term challenge was to diversify the economy.[5] One strategy was to build upon industrial legacies, historical core competencies, and cultural influences. Many post-industrial cities invested heavily in advanced manufacturing, while others have turned to business services. Bilbao, for example, is leveraging its experience with urban regeneration to promote a niche "urban solutions" cluster of companies. Through the activities of Bilbao International, the city has had success in promoting this sector and exporting Bilbao's brand of urbanism. Dortmund in Germany's Ruhr Region is leveraging its central European location to promote a logistics cluster of 640 companies that employ over 24,000 people.[6]

In other places, de-industrialization provided the opportunity to expand higher education choices and invest in knowledge institutions as key components of a new growth strategy. The first university in the Ruhr Region was established in the 1960s as part of a deliberate strategy, and today, there are more than a dozen universities and universities of applied science.[7] In other European cities this strategy meant using existing universities as knowledge hubs and reconnecting them to economic development growth strategies. In Turin, the Polytechnic University of Turin uses its network of facilities, researchers, and incubators to drive the region's economic development and international cooperation.

Similar to cities in the United States, European cities have embraced their natural assets and made commitments to cleaning up environmental degradation from industrial activities. River clean-up and restoration projects in Liverpool and Bilbao illuminate the importance of reclaiming waterfronts and opening access for active recreation and redevelopment. In the Ruhr Region, the region has taken this opportunity a step further by recognizing the importance of the Emscher River as an industrial heritage site; since the 1990s, the region has worked with the Government of North Rhine-Westphalia to clean and naturalize the river while using it as a unifying principle for an industrial heritage-themed open space network.[8]

Beyond remediation, other cities are pioneering new approaches to urban sustainability. This is an imperative for cities such as Rotterdam, which, as a port city on a low-lying delta, is uniquely vulnerable to the effects of climate change. The city, along with a large group of institutions and companies, has committed itself to reducing its carbon footprint by 50 percent. Furthermore, the city is adapting to the anticipated effects of climate change in creative and playful ways that also increase local quality of life and bring residents back to its city center, for example, through water plazas and green infrastructure. Such efforts point to the use of sustainability principles to reshape planning strategies and to add to the resiliency of city centers.

A final commonality is the role of funding from the European Union in making critical investments in infrastructure, mobility systems, and environmental remediation projects. Many of the funding mechanisms are designed to bring equity and parity to disadvantaged regions in Europe. These funding strategies have taken on particular importance through the various waves of EU enlargement.[9]

In the early period of transformation the intense focus on physical regeneration, economic diversification, and environmental stewardship was a common trend across the case study cities in this book, and follows more general parallels across a wider spectrum of European post-industrial cities. There are many differences in policy frameworks and tactical implementation strategies within these trends.

In addition, there were different approaches to regional cooperation, cross-sector partnerships, and neighborhood development. For example, in the Ruhr Region, the role of regional collaboration in driving regional and land use planning cannot be overstated.

Multiple regional organizations and major employers support local planning efforts and coordinate marketing, services, and transportation. This strong coordination creates multiple opportunities to unify efforts and jointly pursue opportunities, such as when the Ruhr Region was designated the European City of Culture for 2010. There are many lessons from the Ruhr Region's experience that are relevant in today's context for cities in Italy and the Netherlands; interestingly, both countries enacted a major policy shift in 2015 to create "Metropolitan Cities" to push for collaboration and metropolitan planning approaches. Based on empirical evidence and inspiring case studies, communities throughout Germany have begun lobbying for the creation of policies and programs deliberately designed for metropolitan regions.[10]

Exploring specific neighborhood development approaches within the context of a broader citywide revitalization strategy has also varied. During the past few decades, post-industrial cities have grappled with structural inequality. This was partly a legacy of deindustrialization, when sudden factory shutdowns forced many into long-term unemployment. More recently, and especially as EU enlargement has facilitated migration from peripheral European countries, the attention has shifted to the integration of migrants.

The Road Ahead

Post-industrial cities in the United States and Europe share much of the same DNA when it comes to the origins and responses to the crisis. In looking ahead at the challenges for the next twenty-five years, the vibrancy of European cities becomes particularly important for European integration and the "Europe project."

In response to the economic crisis, the European Commission created a ten-year jobs and growth strategy called Europe 2020 to pave the way for "smart, sustainable, and inclusive growth." It is based in part on the integrated approach to urban development, which was first formalized under the Leipzig Charter on Sustainable European Cities and adopted in 2007 by the then twenty-seven EU Member States and the European Commission. With ambitious targets in five key areas and seven flagship initiatives, Europe 2020 has the hallmark of a typical Brussels policy agenda with both EU and national level responsibilities (see Figure 7.4). The quantitative targets for action include increased employment, increased investment in research and development, stronger sustainability indicators, improved education outcomes, and decreased social exclusion and poverty (see Table 7.1).

Cities play an important role in implementing the Europe 2020 vision, yet only in the past few years have cities begun to assert a collective voice regarding their role in realizing the goals of European growth and competitiveness; moreover, there is a growing constituency advocating for a more "bottom-up" approach to establishing targets based on the realities on the ground. The drivers of this more pointed urban agenda include the EU Ministers responsible for urban development in their respective countries, the CEMR (Council of European Municipalities and Regions), the official umbrella association of over 100,000 local and regional authorities of all twenty-eight EU Member States, and the EUROCITIES advocacy and networking organization of the one hundred most populous European cities. These organizations and others have been active in pushing the European Union to recognize the critical role of cities. The incoming EUROCITIES president, Johanna Rolland, Mayor of Nantes, France, recently commented:

> [City leaders] are committed to tackling some of Europe's major challenges, many of which are the same as those we face in our cities on a daily basis, around social inclusion, climate and economic development. The solutions we are developing in cities can benefit Europe as a whole.[11]

Figure 7.4 Europe 2020 Flagship Initiatives
Source: http://ec.europa.eu/europe2020/europe-2020-in-a-nutshell/flagship-initiatives/index_en.htm

Table 7.1 Europe 2020 targets

Europe 2020 target	Quantitative target
Employment	75% of the 20–64-year-olds to be employed
Research and Development	3% of the European Union's GDP to be invested
Climate Change and Energy Sustainability	Greenhouse gas emissions 20% (or even 30%, if the conditions are right) lower than 1990 20% of energy from renewables 20% increase in energy efficiency
Education	Reduce rate of early school leaving to less than 10% Minimum 40% of 30–34-year-olds completing third level education
Fighting Poverty and Social Exclusion	Minimum 20 million fewer people in or at risk of poverty and social exclusion

Source: http://cities-today.com/2014/11/cities-key-achieving-eu-2020-goals-says-new-eurocities-president/

More closely linking this policy framework to specific funding streams for cities (as opposed to the previous focus on large regions akin to US states) has been the recent focus of policymakers in Brussels. The current EU funding period (2014–2020) requires that a minimum 5 percent of the European Structural and Investment Funds (ESIF) be spent on integrated urban development projects. In the case of Germany in the next seven years, €19.2 billion are available for urban development that aligns with the Europe 2020 areas. A recent study by the German Federal Institute for Research on Building, Urban Affairs and Spatial Development (BBSR) and BTU Cottbus revealed that this represents 14 percent of Germany's ESIF amount and an increase of 7 percent in city level investment compared to the previous funding period (2007–2013).[12] While this urban leadership from Germany is an important signal, the ability of many Southern and Eastern European countries to support integrated urban development at that scale is challenged. Post-industrial cities are not only navigating local-level complexities for regeneration, but also national policy goals, structural issues, and the Europe 2020 agenda. In terms of specific challenges for the road ahead, the top priority will be the continued goal of repositioning the post-industrial city in the global economy and strengthening its resiliency to global stresses and shocks. Many cities, including the case studies in this book, are rebuilding their brands to compete in new economic sectors that leverage historical assets or new competencies. Despite these new specializations, many post-industrial European cities still rely heavily on the service sector economy. The strategies for advancing a new economy vary and differences are particularly acute in comparing the experience of northern and southern European cities because local success also depends on the health of the national economy.

Having a vision for the post-industrial city's economic future is one thing, but having the talent and human capital to make it happen is quite another. More post-industrial European cities need to focus on connecting the sectors of their new economy to education and workforce training. The vocational education systems prevalent in northern European countries offer a promising pathway for new workers and those who can be retrained. More importantly, the strategy of aligning local economic sectors with post-secondary education and training programs provides career pathways in fields with available jobs. This alignment can happen at the policy level, but also through institutions. For example, the RDM Campus in Rotterdam is a multi-use facility that connects established companies in the maritime industry with graduate students and new start-ups.[13]

The success of economic diversification and talent development systems hinges on how Europe and European cities manage the wave of demographic change unfolding on the continent. From lower birth rates to higher life expectancy and migration, the demographic question is complex and varies greatly from country to country and from city to city. According to EU statistics, the number of persons 60 years and older is increasing at twice the rate it was three years ago.[14] By 2050, the United Nations estimates that the proportion of people aged 65 and older will be more than 30 percent in many Western European countries, including Spain, Italy, and Germany.[15] These trends pose labor market challenges, stretch the social welfare system, and impact municipal budgets in ways that are much discussed and documented.

A related demographic challenge is how cities are accommodating the needs of increasingly diverse communities. Rotterdam, for example, is bucking the trend of other European cities in becoming an increasingly younger city and is one of the most diverse in Europe with over 50 percent non-Dutch population.[16] In another case, Birmingham, UK, has increasing populations of youth, senior, and foreign-born populations—over a quarter of the city's population is foreign-born and 20 percent of the population identifies as Muslim.[17]

The increasing diversity poses challenges for post-industrial communities in particular because the initial recovery often focused heavily on physical regeneration and environmental revitalization at the expense of addressing more complex social and socio-economic issues. This has caused lingering social and economic tensions that have been compounded by the global economic recession and austerity measures that have impacted local governments. The social safety net policies are no longer enough to buoy up struggling families and there is a strong trend of increasing inequality across a range of metrics. There is also a growing concern that deepening social polarization, physical segregation, and economic isolation will have profound local impacts for European cities in the decades to come. Innovative practices such as active inclusion and comprehensive neighborhood developments are emerging in many cities, including Rotterdam and Turin.

The challenges that remain for the post-industrial European city are the development of better governance and more cross-sector partnerships. In terms of governance and fiscal management, the austerity measures put in place following the global financial crisis of 2008 are still having an impact on municipal budgets across Europe. The legacy of large public sector employment in European cities thwarts the type of innovative municipal governance tactics seen in the United States, such as performance management systems and performance-based budgeting. Applying the bold leadership decisions that turned the tide of the physical and economic trajectory of post-industrial cities to the practice of municipal governance and finance is an opportunity for local leaders to innovate.

Underlying all of the above challenges is the need for European cities to engage more strategically and ambitiously in public/private partnerships (P3). American cities have long out-performed their European counterparts on this issue; however, with shrinking national and EU budgets for major projects, more European cities are exploring the P3 model and finding opportunities to innovate.

A related issue is the need to expand efforts for community partnerships, civic engagement, and participatory budgeting, especially when channeled in support of political inclusion in local decision-making and ultimately in locally elected leadership. There is very little data available at the EU level about the level of minority participation in elected office in local governments; while the US has publicly available data through websites such as http://wholeads.us/, Europe still must make considerable progress to achieve an elected leadership that reflects the demographic composition of the US. There is an important opportunity for continued transatlantic learning at the local and national levels on this pivotal issue.

Despite this litany of issues and challenges, European post-industrial cities have made tremendous progress, with many having been held up as models of urban renaissance. Cities are constantly in flux and through the resiliency already shown by European cities, in particular those in this book, they demonstrate that they have the capacity and the tools to adapt to future demands. Encouraging a culture of city-to-city peer learning, especially across the Atlantic, will be a key principle for ensuring that all post-industrial cities continue to make progress towards change.

Notes

1   Eurostat website, http://ec.europa.eu/eurostat/documents/3217494/5786473/KS-HA-14-001-14-EN.PDF/aa72d461-8c09-4792-b62b-87b26e47e152?version=1.0
2   European Commission, *Cities of Tomorrow*. Available at: ec.europa.eu.regional … citiesoftomorrow.pdf, p. 2.
3   *Bilstaden: USA visade vägen* (Åhrén & Lundin, Stockholmia förlag, 2010).
4   Gert-Jan Hospers. "Restructuring Europe's Rustbelt." Intereconomics. (2004) Accessed at http://link.springer.com/article/10.1007%2FBF02933582
5   Examples include: Städtebauförderung or Urban Development funds in Germany and European Union Structural and Investment Funds (e.g. Cohesion Funds, Regional Development Funds).
6   City of Dortmund Economic Development Bureau website, accessed at www.logistics-dortmund.de/en/standort/
7   Ruhr-Universitat Bochum website, accessed at http://international.rub.de/mam/content/intoff/bochum_and_the_ruhr.pdf
8   *Bilstaden.*
9   A nice history of the EU Structural and Investment Funds can be found at: http://ec.europa.eu/regional_policy/en/policy/what/history/
10 Initiativkreis Europaische Metropolregionen in Deutschland website, accessed at www.deutsche-metropolregionen.org/
11 Cities Today website, accessed at http://cities-today.com/2014/11/cities-key-achieving-eu-2020-goals-says-new-eurocities-president/
12 Bundesinstitut fur Bau-, Stadt-, und Raumforschung website, accessed at www.bbsr.bund.de/BBSR/DE/FP/ReFo/Staedtebau/2008/StaedtDimensionStrukturfondsprog/StaedtDimension_Endbericht.pdf
13 RDM Centre of Expertise website, accessed at www.rdmcoe.nl/english
14 Eurostat, demographic projections, in Europop (2008).
15 Pew Research Center website, accessed at www.pewglobal.org/2014/01/30/attitudes-about-aging-a-global-perspective/
16 Cities for Active Inclusion, "Demographic Change in European Cities: city practices for active inclusion." (2012) Accessed at http://nws.eurocities.eu/MediaShell/media/Eurocities-Demchange-web_final.pdf, p. 3.
17 Ibid., 3.

Reference

Eurostat, "Focus on European Cities," in *Regional Yearbook 2014*, available at: http://ec.europa.eu/eurostat/documents/3217494/5786473/KS-HA-14-001-14-EN.PDF/aa72d461-8c09-4792-b62b-87b26e47e152?version=1.0

8 Bilbao Case Study

Juan Alayo, Garbiñe Henry, and Beatriz Plaza

Introduction

In just a few decades, Bilbao has come from being the city of iron, symbolized by large, polluting steel furnaces, to a city of titanium, with a new gleaming and iconic Guggenheim Museum Bilbao. It has been a remarkable and recognized transformation, which has put the city at the international forefront of urban transformation. This has not been just a physical change; it has also meant a significant transformation of the socio-economic fabric.

Bilbao is located in the Basque Country, one of the Spanish Autonomous Regions, on the northern edge of the Iberian Peninsula border with France. The municipality of Bilbao has a population of 350,000 and is the capital of the province of Bizkaia.[1] The metropolitan area, also known as "Gran Bilbao," comprises the City of Bilbao as well as twenty-five municipalities. It has a population of 900,000, which is 40 percent of the total population of the Basque Country.[2] The metropolitan area has no overall administrative authority but forms a nearly continuous urban footprint along 14 kilometers in the Nervion River valley that constitutes the most important economic concentration in the region.

An important characteristic of the Basque Country is that, as a result of the 1979 Statute of Autonomy negotiated at the time of the transition from Franco's dictatorship to democracy, it enjoys the highest degree of economic autonomy in Spain.[3] It has the power to collect taxes locally (VAT, corporate income tax, and personal income tax) and to keep 94 percent of the taxes in the territory, giving the Basque Parliament a high degree of self-governance.

The "Bilbao effect," also referred to as the "Guggenheim Museum effect," has been the subject of considerable analysis from a variety of perspectives, particularly its cultural, urban, and social transformations, as well as its social and economic impacts. It has been the subject of many internationally recognized case studies and has been featured in numerous publications.

Brief History of the City

Bilbao was founded in 1300 as a Villa, or a chartered town, because of its strategic location as an inland port site leading north along the Nervion River to the Bay of Biscay and the Atlantic Ocean. Other advantages include the flat topography of the river valley, nearby coal mining activity, its location along the St. James Pilgrimage Way, and a communication link to the central Spanish plateau and city of Madrid. These attributes consolidated Bilbao's commercial position as the most important economic center in the Seignory of

Biscay throughout the fifteenth and sixteenth centuries. In 1511, the Consulate of Bilbao (Consulado de Bilbao) was created to regulate trade and shipping activity. It was the most influential institution in the city for the next three centuries.

A sharp increase in population accompanied the area's commercial growth, despite the deep economic crisis affecting most of Europe in the seventeenth century. Bilbao and the region maintained their growth because of the large English and Dutch commercial shipping companies that had established major port operations along the river valley.

Demographic growth required the extension of the boundaries of the city during the eighteenth century. Many city regeneration plans were developed through public competitions by some of the most important and well-known architects of the time. These plans ensured that growth took place in an orderly fashion, providing Bilbao with a high-quality urban grid. Large mansions and major civic buildings with notable architecture were constructed at this time.

Wars set the tone for the first decades of the nineteenth century. Economically powerful and liberal Bilbao was a key target during the Carlist Wars in the Basque Country. Despite the upheaval from 1846 to 1849, Bilbao continued to develop. In 1862, the railway reached the city. By the end of the nineteenth century, Bilbao was the most important industrial city in the Iberian Peninsula.

Through two world wars and the Great Depression in the twentieth century, Bilbao continued to grow due to its strengths in heavy manufacturing and port activities. The corresponding demand for labor doubled Bilbao's population. By the 1980s, however, Bilbao's industry-based economy began to decline precipitously as part of the worldwide shift in the steel and shipbuilding industries, particularly affecting traditional industrial cities in Europe and North America. Unemployment in Bilbao reached 23 percent.[4]

Severe floods in August 1983 combined with the most active period of the Basque terrorist group ETA (Euskadi Ta Askatasuna) and the economic collapse to plunge Bilbao and the entire region into a deep crisis. Fortunately the end of the Franco dictatorship in 1975 and the subsequent arrival of democracy in Spain in 1978 brought about new governance structures along with new enthusiastic and pragmatic leaders in the Basque Country, many of who came from the business world. They recognized the need for change and initiated the Strategic Plan for the Revitalization of Bilbao, placing emphasis on economic diversification, the modernization of industry, the redevelopment of industrial properties, and the improvement of human resources. This was the beginning of the transformation of Bilbao. One crucial initiative that was central to the effort was the creation of the Basque Business Development Agency (SPRI Group) in 1981, an agency of the Basque Government set up to restructure and promote the Basque economy.[5] As a result of those efforts, Bilbao has evolved over the last thirty years from a city with severe environmental problems and a run-down industrial economy to one of the most attractive cities in Europe to live in, invest in, and visit.

The City in 1985

Physical Form and Conditions

The Bilbao Metropolitan Area (BMA) is situated on both banks of the Nervion River and occupies an area of 375 square kilometers (Figure 8.1). The physical form and environmental state of Bilbao in 1985 reflected the following negative factors:

- More than one hundred years of industrialization paired with little or no environmental standards and controls.

Figure 8.1 Map of Bilbao with elevation scale
Source: Map provided by Bilbao Ekintza E.p.e.l.

- Population growth and immigration in the twentieth century that dramatically expanded existing urban areas at a rate that local planning authorities struggled to accommodate.
- The effects of the deep socio-economic crisis that followed the industrial decline of the late 1970s and early 1980s, when a significant proportion of Bilbao's industry collapsed.

Bilbao's industrial complexes (steel factories, shipyards, chemical companies, and port facilities) were located predominantly on the flat land along the river to take advantage of the navigable character of the Nervion River. Port activities stretched 14 kilometers south from the river mouth at the Bay of Biscay to the heart of Bilbao. Because of the relatively narrow river valley, there was significant competition for the most desirable property. The result was that much of the residential and commercial growth that took place during the twentieth century was adjacent to noisy, polluting shipyards and factories. Now that these industrial uses were disappearing, contaminated and vacant properties were left behind.

The continuous footprint of industrial and port activities along the river resulted in a disconnected urban structure. This fragmentation was compounded by a lack of investment in transit and road infrastructure that could have improved connections between municipalities in the metropolitan area. For instance, a number of railway lines radiated out of central Bilbao serving separate corridors, but there was no connection between them. The rail stations in Bilbao were in different, disconnected locations. As a result, there were no railway links across the river or to areas where the majority of the population was located.

In environmental terms, air and water quality had badly deteriorated. The widespread use of coal for energy meant that air pollution was omnipresent and that the city was literally dirty. Being in a wet region, Bilbao became "a gray city," with even the finest buildings obscured by a layer of grime from polluted air and dirty rainfall. In addition, the

Nervion River was the recipient of uncontrolled domestic and industrial wastewater. Over the decades, and in spite of being affected by cleansing tides from the Atlantic Ocean, enormous unregulated waste discharges into the river generated a toxic and foul-smelling fluvial environment with very little oxygen in the water, and, therefore, no aquatic life. Devastating floods in 1983, which caused significant loss of life and property, punctuated the lowest point in Bilbao's recent history. It was also the turning point for a remarkable urban regeneration effort.

Demographics

The City of Bilbao, the Bilbao Metropolitan Area (BMA), and the Basque Country experienced exponential population growth from 1900 to the early 1980s. During the 1980s, emigration exceeded immigration and the natural growth of the population was negative as deaths outnumbered births. It was the beginning of population decline for the Bilbao region. The losses can be attributed primarily to the return of workers and their families to their home regions in other parts of Spain when jobs disappeared in Bilbao. In 1985, the population of the BMA was 43 percent of the Basque Country and 78 percent of Bizkaia Province, with a population density of 2,469 inhabitants per square kilometer (Figure 8.2).[6]

According to the 1986 census, the BMA had 926,949 inhabitants, 49 percent of whom were male and 51 percent of whom were female as shown in the population pyramid in Figure 8.3.

In 1985, the main demographics indicators in the BMA showed the population starting to decline after continuous growth since the beginning of the century. The average age was 35 years (34 for men and 37 for women). Children (0–19 years) comprised 28 percent of the total population, and the elderly (65 and older) comprised 11 percent. The region's Dependency Index in 1985 was 44, meaning that one hundred people of working age economically supported forty-four people under 15 years old and over 64 years old. The foreign population in 1985 was only 1 percent of the total population of the region.[7]

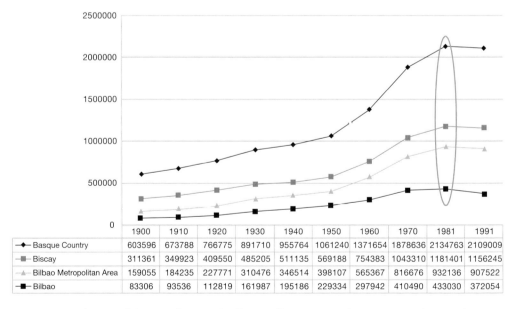

	1900	1910	1920	1930	1940	1950	1960	1970	1981	1991
Basque Country	603596	673788	766775	891710	955764	1061240	1371654	1878636	2134763	2109009
Biscay	311361	349923	409550	485205	511135	569188	754383	1043310	1181401	1156245
Bilbao Metropolitan Area	159055	184235	227771	310476	346514	398107	565367	816676	932136	907522
Bilbao	83306	93536	112819	161987	195186	229334	297942	410490	433030	372054

Figure 8.2 Evolution of the population of Bilbao, Bilbao Metropolitan Area, Bizkaia and Basque Country between 1900 and 1991
Source: Data adapted from INE. Prepared by the authors on the basis of INE.

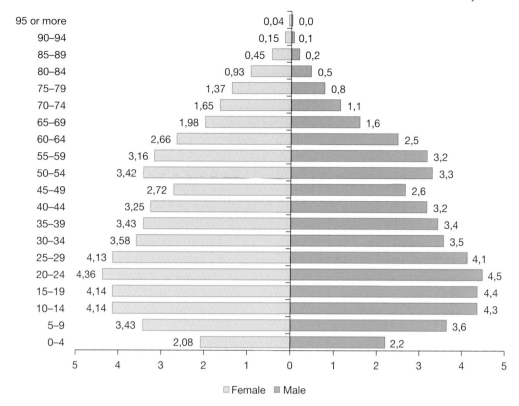

	Female	Male
95 or more	0,04	0,0
90–94	0,15	0,1
85–89	0,45	0,2
80–84	0,93	0,5
75–79	1,37	0,8
70–74	1,65	1,1
65–69	1,98	1,6
60–64	2,66	2,5
55–59	3,16	3,2
50–54	3,42	3,3
45–49	2,72	2,6
40–44	3,25	3,2
35–39	3,43	3,4
30–34	3,58	3,5
25–29	4,13	4,1
20–24	4,36	4,5
15–19	4,14	4,4
10–14	4,14	4,3
5–9	3,43	3,6
0–4	2,08	2,2

Figure 8.3 Pyramid of population of BMA in 1985 and demographics indicators and rates
Source: Prepared by the authors on the basis of EUSTAT.

Economy

The Atlantic Ocean seaport and ready access to raw materials formed the basis for Bilbao's wealth as an international commercial center throughout the sixteenth and seventeenth centuries. Bilbao developed into an early industrial city, based upon the exploitation of nearby iron ore deposits and coal. During the industrial revolution of the nineteenth century, the Basque economy grew rapidly. Industrial activities centered on steel and shipbuilding. In the 1950s and 1960s, massive industrialization processes continued to focus on heavy industries. Significant in-migration of workers from other parts of Spain and the construction of new housing complexes in the limited space of the Nervion River valley led to higher population densities.

During the 1970s and 1980s, Bilbao, like many European industrial cities, was in rapid economic decline with high unemployment and undergoing a massive urban restructuring process. Traditional industries had become obsolete, but the city center was still home to a river port plagued with severe traffic congestion. Other troubles included violence from extremist Basque separatists, urban deterioration, pollution, and a poor public transportation system.

These problems were tackled by implementing public policies targeted at productivity and economic diversity, coupled with a strong cultural component. Regional public authorities developed policies aimed at creating a competitive environment with strong innovation, technology, and entrepreneurship components.[8]

The City in 2015

Physical Form and Conditions

In the last thirty years, starting after the floods in 1983, Bilbao has undergone one of the most impressive urban transformations in the world. With the new powers and resources that the Basque administration gained during Spain's transition to a democratic government, the leaders of the region embarked on a series of initiatives to change Bilbao physically and to improve its quality of life and economic competitiveness. Many of the projects were identified in the 1992 *Strategic Plan for the Revitalization of Metropolitan Bilbao*, a study commissioned by the city and regional authorities. A new public-private agency, Bilbao Metrópoli 30, was established to produce a regeneration framework with maximum public consensus. Below is a summary of the key initiatives and interventions in the remaking of Bilbao after the economic collapse in the 1970s and 1980s.

Cleaning up the River and the Air

In 1979, the Water Authority developed a plan to intercept all domestic and industrial wastewater polluting the Nervion River. Thirty years later, after an investment of nearly €1 billion, the river has been transformed from an open sewer to a public amenity where watersports can be practiced and where marine life has returned. The most significant factor in cleaning up the air was the creation of a comprehensive natural gas network, serving domestic and industrial customers, which has supplanted coal and oil as the main source of energy, contributing to significantly better air quality in the region.

Bilbao Metro

After several false starts and numerous proposals, in 1987, the Basque Government approved a transit plan that incorporated parts of an existing suburban railway.[9] Construction began in 1988 with the inaugural service in November 1995. The system's design, with stations designed by British architect Norman Foster, included two lines threading through municipalities on either side of the river. It is one of the most widely used metro systems in Spain with 90 million passengers per year.[10] Internal connectivity within the metropolitan area was thus achieved with the development of a single Metro system of 43 kilometers, with connections on both sides of the river. Travel times from one end of the system to the other in the core area are now no more than 30 minutes. The network continues to grow with extensions at the ends and three other lines that are in the planning stages.

The Port, Highways, and the Airport

Central and regional government investments contributed to a major overhaul and upgrading of these transportation infrastructures. The Port Authority developed an "external port" closer to the Bay of Biscay with land reclamation, freeing up the banks of the Nervion River in the city for other, more appropriate urban uses. Over three decades, the Bizkaia Provincial government has developed a rebuilt and extended highway network, tackling one of the most critical shortcomings identified in the 1992 revitalization plan. Aena S.A., the national agency overseeing airports, financed a new airport terminal building designed by Spanish architect Santiago Calatrava, which opened in 2000.

Urban Regeneration

In 1992, in a joint effort by central, provincial, regional, and local governments, BILBAO Ría 2000 was set up as a limited liability company. It is entirely publicly owned, with the goal of dealing in a holistic manner with remaining sites in need of urban regeneration. In just over twenty years, the company has transformed more than 100 hectares of mainly industrial land, creating new neighborhoods and new open space, some of it next to the Nervion River. BILBAO Ría 2000 finances its investments in infrastructure through the sale of land to developers. Over €1.3 billion have been spent to create a new rail infrastructure and open space, to remediate contaminated sites, and to construct civil works for new neighborhoods (Figure 8.4).[11]

The Guggenheim Museum Bilbao

This iconic building, designed by American architect Frank Gehry, opened in 1997. It immediately put Bilbao on the international map (Figure 8.5). Although the investment in the building amounted only to a small fraction of the total public investment in the metropolitan area over the last three decades, its impact has been much greater than the expenditure. Less known, but perhaps more interesting than the visual impact, is the economic impact of the Guggenheim. The idea for the new museum was actually conceived as a business case, counting on the number of new tourists attracted and the additional

Figure 8.4 Abandoibarra waterfront, before and after the transformation
Source: Provided by Bilbao Ekintza E.p.e.l.

Figure 8.5 Guggenheim Museum Bilbao
Source: Courtesy of FMGB, Guggenheim Bilbao Museoa, 2015.

economic activity generated by them to produce increased tax revenue for the provincial government. With nearly one million visitors per year on average, the additional taxes collected have paid off the original investment.[12] Bilbao now has another sector of economic activity, tourism, accounting for 5 percent of the city's gross domestic product, unthinkable in 1985.[13]

Demographics

The Bilbao Metropolitan Area population dropped by 74,000 between 1981 and 2014, declining from 936,848 in 1981 to 862,813 in 2014, a loss of 8 percent.[14] However, Bilbao has managed to stabilize its population in recent decades, unlike most second-tier post-industrial cities (Figure 8.6).

The population structure by gender has not changed in thirty years although the population is aging, as can be seen in the population pyramid in Figure 8.7. This is a clear trend not only in Bilbao, but also across Europe.

In Bilbao, there was a decrease in the number of younger people and an increase in older people from 1985 to 2015. Bilbao's population of children (0–19 years old) fell from 28 to 17 percent, while the elderly population (65 and older) doubled from 11 to 22 percent.[15] The average age of the population has increased ten years, going from 35 in 1985 to 45 years in 2015.[16] The Dependency Index has increased from 44 in 1985 to 53 in 2015.[17] In spite of this regressive demography, there is a bright spot. The loss of endogenous population (deaths exceeding births) is being offset by an increase in international immigration to the region. The foreign population in the BMA increased from 1 percent in 1985 to 8 percent in 2015.[18]

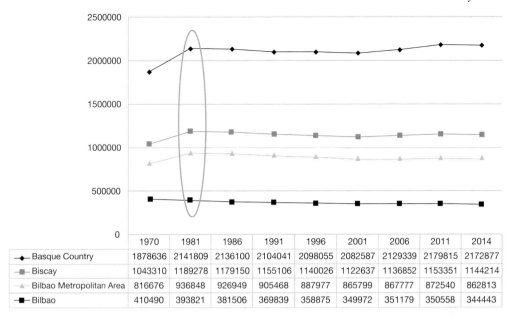

Figure 8.6 Evolution of the population of Bilbao, Bilbao Metropolitan Area, Bizkaia and Basque
Country between 1970 and 2014
Source: Prepared by the authors on the basis of INE.

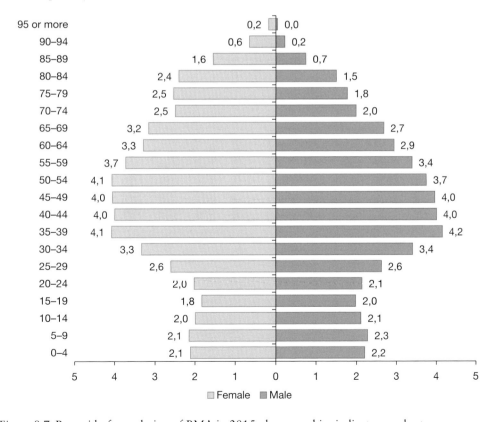

Figure 8.7 Pyramid of population of BMA in 2015, demographics indicators and rates
Source: Prepared by the authors on the basis of Eustat.

Economy

The Basque Country, together with Madrid and Navarre, is ranked highest in Spain in per capita income, with the gross domestic product (GDP) per capita for the Basque at €29,959 compared to €22,279 for Spain in 2014.[19]

Traditional industries have given way to auxiliary industrial goods, such as machinery, machine tooling, chemicals, aeronautics, as well as high value consumer goods. In recent years, as in other Western economies, services have become the main economic activity. The Service sector generated 62.6 percent of the Basque GDP, while the Manufacturing sector generated 21.3 percent, the Construction sector generated 6.5 percent, and the Agriculture and Fisheries sector accounted for only 0.8 percent in 2013.[20]

In Spain, innovation and entrepreneurship are mainly concentrated in Madrid, Barcelona, and Bilbao, which together account for 34 percent of the innovation economy.[21] Although first-tier cities such as Madrid and Barcelona generate a significant portion of these new business services, the vibrant second-tier city of Bilbao also has an important role.

Figure 8.8 illustrates the main business sectors, reflecting the change in the employment structure in Metropolitan Bilbao, where business services (NACE 72-74) ranked first in 2009.[22]

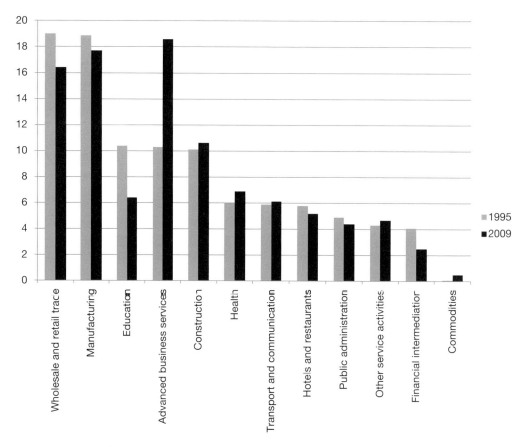

Figure 8.8 Diversification of Metropolitan Bilbao's economy in terms of employment percentage
Source: Prepared by Plaza (2008) and Authors based on EUSTAT (2014): Directorio de actividades económicas [Directory of companies and establishments]. Vitoria.

The increased number of jobs in knowledge-intensive business services is 38 percent of the overall employment growth from 2000 to 2009 in metropolitan Bilbao. The knowledge-intensive business services sector is one of the fastest growing areas of the European economy, and Bilbao is no exception (Figure 8.9).[23] The rapid growth of the ICT sector (Information and Communication Technologies), the process of internationalization and globalization, and the changes in regulatory structures by the European Union (e.g., health and safety standards, environmental regulations), are the driving forces of growth in this sector.[24] Architecture and engineering companies constitute an important subset in Bilbao as a well-established sector in the economy of the city, particularly during the last thirty years of physical transformation in the region. In addition to the general trend, the multiplier effects of the ambitious urban regeneration strategy for the region should not be underestimated. Public policy changes have driven aggregate demand for private investment. Bilbao and its region have also seen an expansion of higher-end manufacturing and knowledge-intensive activities over recent years. The higher rates of innovation are mainly related to manufacturing specialization and business services.[25]

NACE	Activities	1994		2009	
		Number of Establishments	Employment	Number of Establishments	Employment
63	Computer and related activities	277	NA	1,869	15,605
72	Research and development	41	NA	309	2,040
69–82	Other business activities	5,572	20,757	16,238	76,138
69–70	Legal and management activities	2,702	6,040	5,685	12,795
71	Architectural, engineering and technical activities	1,419	4,282	3,440	12,311
73	Advertising and market research	20	327	927	4,217
80–82	Other business support activities	320	746	3,102	38,026
	Total	5,890	NA	18,416	93,783

Figure 8.9 Business services in Metropolitan Bilbao: number of establishments and employment
Source: Prepared by Plaza et al. (2013) based on EUSTAT (2010): Directorio de actividades económicas [Directory of companies and establishments]. Vitoria.
Note: Data for the province of Biscay. Metropolitan Bilbao has over 900,000 inhabitants, which is the majority of the 1,100,000 inhabitants of the Biscay province (the city of Bilbao has over 353,000).

Transformation of the City (1985–2015)

What Went Right?

Economic Diversification and the Unique Fiscal and Political Basque Model

Several factors explain the positive results; among them, a policy to drive the economic recovery strategy that favored investment in large-scale urban infrastructure projects; a complementary policy to diversify the Basque productive model; and a regeneration model partially enabled by the fiscal and political autonomy of the Basque Provinces. Public institutions led the regeneration of Bilbao, but there was no money for public infrastructure investments. The only asset available was the free land arising from the closure of the obsolete and uncompetitive steel and shipbuilding factories. The Basque Government quickly understood that there was no better opportunity. A change in the governance structure brought fresh initiative in the creation of the SPRI Group to promote the Basque economy. It was critical to focus the whole society on a shared vision. Nevertheless, at first, there was strong distrust of any projects proposed by the public authorities that had to be overcome, based on many years of failed efforts.

Revitalization Plan: Public-Private and Public-Public Collaboration

One of the keys to Bilbao's success was the 1992 Revitalization Plan, initiated by the Basque government in collaboration with the business community, and implemented by Bilbao Metrópoli 30, a public-private entity. The plan clearly established priorities and selected key projects that developed physical infrastructure and addressed socio-economic issues in the region. The collaboration between the public and private sectors worked well, and there was a shared focus on implementation. However, achieving political consensus of more than two-thirds of the elected representatives, and being able to maintain it during multiple legislative and budgetary cycles, were significant challenges.

Local Strategic Focus on Balancing Neighborhoods

Territorial connectivity was a challenge that was overcome for all the neighborhoods, not just the city center, through the construction of bridges, tunnels, as well as new public transportation modes such as the Metro and Tramway. This brought greater social cohesion to Bilbao, mitigating the isolation of poorer areas. Neighborhood redevelopment strategies, led by local government, included programs and initiatives fostering economic, social, and cultural balance, continuous improvement for districts through civic participation, and continuous rehabilitation in all city areas.[26]

Social Decline Halted and Economic Crisis Averted

One of the main achievements of the transformation of Bilbao is that public policies and revitalization plans managed to halt social decline at a time when it seemed impossible. At the same time, Bilbao's leaders were working to strengthen the economy, which was also in crisis. While the region has been lauded for successfully managing both the social decline and economic crises, it is not well known that they were occurring concurrently.

Masterpiece of Twentieth-Century Architecture

The Guggenheim Museum Bilbao put the city on the world stage and enabled the city to attract new people and new development after the financial crisis. Fortunately for the city of Bilbao, the museum is a masterpiece of twentieth-century architecture, but it was not a sure thing. Being famous is not a sufficient condition to ensure the uniqueness of an architect's design. Even notable artists produce inconsistent pieces of art. Creativity is a highly elusive reality, for architects, as for other artists.[27] The Guggenheim Museum Bilbao opened in 1997 at the same time as the Internet boom began to have an impact on global communication and news transfer.[28] The exposure of the museum in English-speaking news outlets, especially in the US, accelerated the branding of the Guggenheim Museum Bilbao. As a result, the museum boosted the international connectivity of Bilbao, putting a second-tier city on the global map of highly specialized international art-related circuits.[29] Striking images of Gehry's masterpiece drove long-term regional branding efforts forward.

Studies have shown that the accumulation of positive images fuels increasing demand for place, which reinforces the region's brand, and ultimately attracts cultural visitors, creating new cultural tourism and related economic activity in Bilbao.[30] Major cultural infrastructure projects are expensive, have a very high operative risk, and often are unpopular among the citizens.[31] Fortunately for Bilbao, the Guggenheim Museum Bilbao is a masterpiece and is a continuing powerful global branding engine. The so-called "Bilbao effect" or "Guggenheim effect" has generated "urban policy tourism"—short trips to Bilbao by policy-makers from other cities to learn from Bilbao.[32] The project has given legitimacy to other culture-focused strategies in the Bilbao political arena, where many were quite skeptical before the opening of the Guggenheim.

Innovative Formula for Urban Regeneration

One of the main agents responsible for the physical transformation of Bilbao was BILBAO Ría 2000 (BR2000). This publicly-owned, limited liability company was set up by a collection of public institutions ranging from the central government to local authorities. It also included the railway and port authorities, which owned a significant amount of centrally located industrial lands now sitting vacant or underused. The company operates by consensus. Shareholders and board members are split evenly between the central government and the Basque authorities, striking a political balance of power. The concept was for BR2000 shareholders to transfer the vacant lands to BR2000. The company would then commission a master plan to turn the vacant lands into new urban districts, generate the planning documents, follow through with all municipal approvals, commission all projects, and manage construction of all infrastructure and civil works. The plots of land resulting from the master plan for housing, retail, office, and public uses would then be sold, and the proceeds would pay for the infrastructure. The remaining public spaces and infrastructure would then be turned over to the appropriate local authorities. In this way, brand new districts were built, like Abandoibarra where the Guggenheim Museum is located, without requiring funding from the operating and capital budgets of local and regional governments.

What Went Wrong?

Living with Terrorism

Terrorism in the Basque Region is a daily fact of life that has had a significant impact on the local economy. Apart from its painful social consequences and tragic loss of life, it has been estimated that the ETA has caused economic losses of 20 percent across the board. According to a 2003 study by Abadie and Gardeazabal, there appears to be an average 10 percent difference between the actual Basque Country's per capita GDP and the per capita GDP of a hypothetical Basque Country without terrorism. In their study, changes in the per capita GDP correlated with periods of intense terrorism.[33] Terrorism disproportionately impacted the Basque Country's entrepreneurial community, as Basque entrepreneurs were the specific targets of violence and extortion, including kidnapping for ransom, robberies and assassinations. In the early 1970s, the Basque Country was one of the richest regions of Spain, and by the late 1990s it had dropped to sixth in per capita income among Spanish regions.

Investment Effectiveness Facing Such a Broad Range of Interventions

The regeneration of Bilbao did not escape its share of poor or ineffective investments. It is unavoidable that with such a broad range of interventions, occurring over such a long timeframe, some projects would not meet expectations. Several recent additions to the highway infrastructure (e.g., Super Sur) and large civic buildings (e.g., the Bilbao Exhibition Center) are performing well below forecasts. The 2008–2009 financial crisis can be blamed in part, but probably more important is that the cost benefit analysis of these projects was less rigorous than required. This is an area where Bilbao's public sector needs to improve as municipal resources become more scarce, particularly in the context of an aging and declining population.

Private Investment Lagged

Despite facing the widespread need for public-private partnership, the urban regeneration process has mainly been the result of public intervention and investment. Private investment has been more symbolic than substantial and has not matched the public commitments.

Lessons Learned

Bilbao has been a laboratory for testing new economic development ideas and new regeneration strategies. The successful transformation of Bilbao did not consist of just several high profile architectural projects by Gehry, Foster, and Calatrava. Rather it was an integrated transformation process with many and varied inputs.

The confidence in the capacity of public institutions to perform was very important at the beginning and only got stronger as projects were executed. People could see the efficiency of public institutions. The public innovation of the leaders in local, provincial, and regional bodies of the Basque Country, supported by the central government, made this successful transformation possible, despite some harsh political controversy at the outset.

The Guggenheim Museum Bilbao's success led to the implementation of other adventurous and risky proposals that would have been impossible without the proven success of the museum. There was a sea change in valuing the arts and culture of Bilbao. It became clear that cultural infrastructure could lead the transformation process and that planning proposals had to include both local and global dimensions.

Prospects for the Future

Bilbao has not only cleaned up its image, it has also renovated its physical framework, efficiently managed its public assets, and developed a transparent and cooperative governance structure that ensures continuance of the transformation. Balanced investment in neighborhoods is essential for the prosperity of any metropolis. Bilbao has been working on this goal for the last thirty years and will continue to do so on the basis of distributing investment and diversifying sectors of activity to help the economies and living conditions in all neighborhoods.

One of the main threats to Bilbao's success continues to be demographic decline. Bilbao is one of the oldest regions in Europe with a population that continues to shrink and age. To survive, Bilbao will have to attract more and younger people (for which a beautiful and renovated city is always a plus) and improve the efficiency, productivity, and diversity of its economy. Despite having a highly qualified workforce in the past, Bilbao is now challenged to maintain and attract talent. Talent is highly mobile and moves fluidly from city to city, from country to country. The Basque Country must deal with its population decline by offering high value job opportunities not only to keep local talent in place, but also to appeal to residents of other regions in Spain and to foreigners by providing an attractive and creative city in which to live, work, and play.

It is essential to learn from and value the lessons of the last thirty years by maintaining a strategic vision for the city, integrating both short-term and long-term planning, having a transparent planning process, and fostering networking between public organizations, private stakeholders, and academic partners, such as universities and research centers.

The key factor when redesigning the economic and business climate of a city and region, as Bilbao-Bizkaia has been doing since 1983, is the successful engagement and support of both the leaders and the people themselves. The ultimate success of any urban transformation depends on value creation for all. Connectivity and relational networks are important. Living in the global economy, where ideas are accessible and shared, opens up interconnections between people, companies, and institutions, providing opportunities for both renewal of existing assets and sustained new growth.

Notes

1   EUSTAT, 2014.
2   Ibid.
3   Organic Law 3/1979.
4   Data from EPA (Labour Force Survey), for the Basque Country in 1985: 22, figure is 69 percent.
5   State Law 27/1984, declaring Urgent Reindustrialization Areas.
6   EUSTAT 1986, Population Density.
7   Ibid.
8   Plaza, B., "On Some Challenges and Conditions for the Guggenheim Museum Bilbao to Be an Effective Economic Re-Activator." *International Journal of Urban and Regional Research* 32(2), (2008): 506–17.
9   Decree 19/1987.
10   Metro Bilbao, adapted from passenger figures.
11   *Bilbao Ría 2000*, adapted from a range of publications and press notes.
12   Guggenheim Museum Bilbao, *Annual Report*. Available at: www.guggenheim-bilbao.es
13   EUSTAT, 2014.
14   INE (Spanish Statistical Office) figures.
15   EUSTAT, 2014.
16   EUSTAT/INE.
17   Ibid.
18   Ibid.
19   Ibid.

20   EUSTAT, 2014.
21   Boix, R. and Trullén, J., "Industrial Districts, Innovation and I-District Effect: Territory or Industrial Specialization?" *European Planning Studies* 18(10), (2010): 1707–29.
22   NACE, Classification of Economic Activities in the European Community.
23   The effectiveness of transferring innovation to Small and Medium Enterprises (SMEs) depends critically on the knowledge-intensive business services (KIBs), which are mainly concentrated geographically in first-tier cities (Muller and Zenker, 2001). The KIBs sector includes many R&D intensive firms that provide services to firms, such as ICTs, software development, R&D, and non-technological innovations, which contribute to the upgrading of the firms (Plaza et al., 2011). KIBS are seen to function as facilitators of innovation, and through their almost symbiotic relationship with client firms, some KIBS act as co-producers of innovation (Den Hertog et al., 2003). The high scientific and technological profile of the KIBS can help increase the economic competitiveness of a region (metropolitan). The weight of this industry related to the GPD is one of the indicators used by the European Commission to compare the national research and innovation carried out by EU member states (European Commission, 2009).
24   Plaza, "On Some Challenges and Conditions for the Guggenheim Museum," 506–17.
25   Plaza, B., Galvez-Galvez, C., and Gonzalez-Flores, A,. "Urban Regeneration and Knowledge-Intensive Services." *Proceedings of the ICE-Municipal Engineer* 166(4), (2013): 257–64.
26   Local Government Programs Period 2011–2015.
27   Plaza, B., "The Return on Investment of the Guggenheim Museum Bilbao." *International Journal of Urban and Regional Research*, 30(2), (2006): 452–67.
28   Plaza, B. and Haarich, S.N. "The Guggenheim Museum Bilbao: Between Regional Embeddedness and Global Networking." *European Planning Studies* 23(8), (2015): 1456–75.
29   Ibid.
30   Ibid.
31   Plaza, "The Return on Investment of the Guggenheim Museum Bilbao."
32   Plaza and Haarich (2015) "The Guggenheim Museum Bilbao."
33   Abadie, Alberto and Javier Gardeazabal. "The Economic Costs of Conflict: A Case Study of the Basque Country." *American Economic Review*, March 2003, 113–32.

References

Bilbao Metrópoli 30 website. Available at: www.bm30.es

Bilbao Ría 2000 website. Available at: http://bilbaoria2000.org/ria2000/ing/home/home.aspx

Boix, R. and Trullén, J. (2010) "Industrial Districts, Innovation and I-District Effect: Territory or Industrial Specialization?" *European Planning Studies* 18(10), 1707–29.

Den Hertog, P., Broersma, L. and Van Ark, B. (2003) "On the Soft Side of Innovation: Services Innovation and Its Policy Implications." *Economist* 151(4): 433–52.

European Commission (2009) *Challenges for EU Support to Innovation in Services*. PROINNO Europe Paper no. 12. Brussels: EC.

Muller, E. and Zenker, A. (2001) "Business Services as Actors of Knowledge Transformation: The Role of KIBS in Regional and National Innovation Systems." *Research Policy* 30(9). 1501–16.

Plaza, B. (2006) "The Return on Investment of the Guggenheim Museum Bilbao." *International Journal of Urban and Regional Research* 30(2): 452–67.

Plaza, B. (2008) "On Some Challenges and Conditions for the Guggenheim Museum Bilbao to Be an Effective Economic Re-Activator." *International Journal of Urban and Regional Research* 32(2): 506–17.

Plaza, B., Galvez-Galvez, C., and Gonzalez-Flores, A. (2013) "Urban Regeneration and Knowledge-Intensive Services." *Proceedings of the ICE-Municipal Engineer* 166(4): 257–64.

Plaza, B., González-Casimiro, P., Moral-Zuazo, P. and Waldron, C. (2015) "Culture-led City Brands as Economic Engines: Theory and Empirics." *The Annals of Regional Science* 54(1): 179–96.

Plaza, B. and Haarich, S.N. (2015) "The Guggenheim Museum Bilbao: Between Regional Embeddedness and Global Networking." *European Planning Studies* 23(8): 1456–75.

Strategic Plan for the Revitalization of Metropolitan Bilbao. Available at: https://app.box.com/s/rbjiz6qyr6ersbyhej39

9 Liverpool Case Study

Erik Bichard

Introduction

As evening gathers on a Friday or Saturday night, a remarkable sight rewards diners sitting at restaurant tables that fringe and overlook the pedestrianized avenues of Liverpool One, the city's new retail centre. A dozen men dressed as pirates will be negotiating around fifteen women dressed as ballerinas coming in the other direction. Further down the way there will be others who will move in and out of clubs, bars and eateries dressed as fruit, crocodiles, Sir Cliff Richard (complete with masks) and many more imaginative themes. More often than not, one of them will have a sash or T-shirt marked "bride-to-be" or "trainee groom", but there will also be parties celebrating significant birthdays and anniversaries.

These visitors might have been attracted to Liverpool because it is the home of the Beatles, or because it once was the mightiest port in the world, or because they are die-hard Liverpool FC or Everton fans, and many people do come to the city for these reasons. But this latest influx of revellers represents a turning point for the city, and a recent one at that. In 2008, Liverpool was the European Capital of Culture. This was a one-year long festival of music, fine and performing art, urban installations, and street entertainment. Hundreds of thousands of people came to the city for the first time, overcoming the negative perceptions that originated in the 1970s and 1980s and that took almost a generation to shake off.

This chapter describes the innovative way in which Liverpool has used its legacy of culture and celebration to help visitors and its own population rediscover the value of the city. It also looks critically at whether confidence and a "destination city" reputation are going to be a firm enough basis for longer-term transition from one of the most deprived cities in Europe to a successful, sustainable post-industrial city of the future.

Brief History of the City

Today the Liverpool City Region (LCR) is a predominantly urban area that covers 724 square kilometres and has a population of almost 1.5 million, giving it a population density of 2,061 inhabitants per square kilometre. There was a settlement on the current site of Liverpool as early as the first century AD. Existing as a fishing village for almost a millennium, Liverpool's fortunes changed in 1207 when the port was granted a town charter by King John who wanted his own gateway to use as an embarkation point to send his troops to Ireland. There is no definitive agreement about the origin of the city's name, but many assume it relates to the dark pool formed in the northern shore of the Mersey estuary that served as a tidal harbour. As a port, Liverpool was insignificant compared to the walled Roman city of Chester. This settlement was established on the Dee estuary south across the other side of the Wirral peninsula. However, the Dee changed course in the eighteenth century and Chester's port silted up, leaving the way clear for Liverpool to emerge alongside Bristol as England's primary west coast ports.

When maritime exploration led to the establishment of colonial trading stations in the West Indies, Brazil, and other parts of the Americas, shipping traffic increased exponentially. The first wet dock in Liverpool was built in 1715. Urban growth was rapid in the eighteenth and nineteenth centuries, and wealth accumulated from the trans-Atlantic trade. The city emerged as a global port based on international trade in salt and slaves, serving as one of the three points of the notorious trade triangle between Africa, Europe and the Americas. Later business boomed with the import and export of raw materials and manufactured goods. Cotton was a particularly significant commodity in the history of the port. The first eight bales of cotton from the Americas were unloaded in Liverpool in 1784.[1] By the middle of the nineteenth century cotton was almost half of the city's trade. Over 1.5 million bales were handled each year representing approximately 85 per cent of global trade volumes. The cotton was finished into a range of textiles and garments in the nearby Lancashire mills, and was in turn exported back through Liverpool. In 1901, cotton still made up almost half of the total exports of the port.

In the early part of the nineteenth century, Liverpool was handling almost 40 per cent of the entire world's trade and challenged London in terms of its global connections and significance in world commerce.[2] Consequently, the population grew from approximately 5,000 in 1700 to over 500,000 by 1881. City status was granted to Liverpool in 1880.

Like many ports, Liverpool was the stepping-off point for travellers and seafarers from across the globe. This accounts for the multi-ethnic flavour of its people. The city is home to the oldest Chinatown in Europe and a substantial population of people of African descent settled in the city as early as the 1730s. The 2011 census describes almost 87 per cent of the population of Liverpool as White British or Irish. But this masks the presence and influence of a wide range of peoples from across the globe, and the centuries-old mixed race population in sections of the city.

The population was also heavily influenced during the Irish potato famines of the mid-1840s, when approximately two million Irish people (one quarter of that island's population) came through Liverpool in search of a better life in the United States and Australia. Many remained in the city, swelling the ranks of port workers and bringing their own cultural influences to an already diverse society. The Irish exodus was just one of many mass movements of peoples from Europe to the New World. Between 1830 and 1930, some nine million people emigrated through Liverpool.[3] With each movement some people stayed in the city and sought to bring their culture with them, and this then had an effect on the local population. For example, Liverpool solicitor and convert to Islam, William Abdullah Quilliam, opened England's first mosque in 1889.

Conditions for those who stayed and had to start at the bottom of society were harsh, and diseases, including cholera, were common in the poorer areas of the city. This led in 1847 to the appointment of William Henry Duncan as Britain's first Medical Officer of Health. Together with James Newlands (occupying the newly created position of Borough Engineer), and Thomas Fresh (Inspector of Nuisances), Duncan started what was to become the template for urban public health across the globe.

Investment in civic architecture by those that had made their fortunes in shipping transformed the city which today is home to the highest number of "listed" buildings (protected for their heritage value) of any UK city outside of London (Figure 9.1). The neo-classical St. Georges Hall (built as a cultural forum and courts) began construction in 1938 (Figure 9.2). Building the iconic Albert Dock complex in 1846 established Liverpool as a city capable of handling large volumes of cargo and passengers.

Figure 9.1 Liverpool Town Hall
Source: Photo by Lily Bichard-Collins.

Figure 9.2 St. George's Hall
Source: Photo by Lily Bichard-Collins.

Institutions such as the University, the Walker Art Gallery, the Liverpool Philharmonic Society, and the two football clubs at Liverpool and Everton were all created in the latter part of the nineteenth century. Many large urban green spaces dotted the city. Funded by both public and private sources, many people escaped to these parts of the city from the polluted dockland streets. Joseph Paxton and his protégés designed Sefton, Birkenhead, Stanley, and Princess Park before Paxton went on to design the Crystal Palace for Queen Victoria's Great Exhibition in London. Birkenhead Park was also Olmsted's inspiration for Central Park in New York City.

Civic engineering, infrastructure and architecture flourished in Liverpool in the latter part of the nineteenth century with innovations and ideas such as orbital parkways around the city centre, inter-city rail and electric tram systems being pioneered in the city. In 1934, the first Mersey Tunnel under the estuary linked Liverpool and Birkenhead. At 2 miles it held the record for the longest underwater road tunnel for the next twenty-five years.[4] This added to the already impressive array of municipal buildings, which were crowned "the Three Graces" on the waterfront. Conceived at the dawn of the twentieth century and completed before the end of the First World War, the Liver Building, the Cunard Building, and the Port of Liverpool Building are collectively designated as a World Heritage site (Figure 9.3). They were renowned worldwide and inspired the Shanghai waterfront in the 1920s.

By the early twentieth century, Liverpool was at the height of its powers. With a population of almost 850,000 and a booming economy, it could justifiably be called one of the most important cities in the world. However, by the end of the Second World War, the outlook for Liverpool had dramatically changed. There are many explanations for the decline. Damage to trade lines and the physical fabric of the city during the war (from heavy bombing) was the most visible manifestation. In addition, the shift of the cotton

Figure 9.3 The World Heritage waterfront
Source: Photo by Lily Bichard-Collins.

trade to India weakened the core economy. Increasing air travel and a redirection of trade from the Americas to Europe diverted cargoes towards southern England. The upstream half of Liverpool's 7.5-mile dock system closed in 1971, and ocean liners ceased to dock in the city in same year.[5] The Thatcher government's pursuance of de-industrialization in the early 1980s accelerated job losses in the region. There were a number of notable regional incentives to entice industry back to Merseyside but these were short-lived as plants closed when the subsidies ran out.

Despite the economic decline, there were a number of positive developments during this time. The city's music scene was burgeoning and Liverpool became a cultural centre in the 1960s. While the Beatles became the iconic front for this movement, others such as Cilla Black, Frankie Vaughn, and Gerry and the Pacemakers also had worldwide success. A few decades later a new wave of music represented by bands like Echo and the Bunnymen and Frankie Goes to Hollywood continued to maintain Liverpool's reputation for creativity. Venues such as the Everyman and Unity Theatres and the Bluecoat Centre for Arts hosted theatre, poetry, and performance art on a regular basis and the legacy of this remains in the city today.

The City in 1985

Physical Form and Conditions

In 1985, Prime Minister Margaret Thatcher was in a one-sided battle with an ultra-left-wing Liverpool local authority that had infiltrated the Labour Party. The local leaders refused to implement the public sector cuts imposed by London by cancelling redundancy notices and freezing public housing rents. Fearing Liverpool was about to go bankrupt, the government considered appointing commissioners to run the city.[6] In a distant foretelling of the Greek bailout crisis of 2015, the Council thought it could convince their paymasters in government to make an exception for a city with unprecedented social and economic problems. They were mistaken. Some funds were awarded for short-term housing problems, but the government ran out of patience and the forty-seven rebellious councillors were surcharged over £100,000 and disqualified from office for failing to set a budget. This episode in the city's history gave credence to the public's perception of Liverpool as a dangerous and uncooperative place that was best avoided. In 1985, this feeling had reached a particular high.

The Militant Council rebellion had made the then Chancellor Geoffrey Howe sceptical about whether Liverpool was worth further investment,[7] but Michael Heseltine (Minister for the Environment at the time) convinced Margaret Thatcher that he could turn its fortunes around. When he investigated, the Minister found a city in dire need of regeneration. Between 15 and 20 per cent of the land was derelict or not in use, and many historic buildings were suffering decay. Serious economic and spatial disparities had emerged where neighbourhoods originally created to re-house working people out of slum conditions were now home to families that had two or even three generations who had never worked in the mainstream economy. These neighbourhoods, often but not exclusively located in the northern and peripheral parts of the city were characterized by low educational achievement, poor health, and high levels of crime.

Heseltine established a Merseyside Task Force to tackle some of the city's long-term land and property problems. His main tactic to achieve this was to encourage the private sector to invest, and the vehicle for this was the Merseyside Development Corporation (MDC) – one of the first two Urban Development Corporations (UDCs) in the country.[8] The government effectively appropriated a large area of derelict docklands (without the

Council's agreement) and gave the MDC the ability to ignore local planning powers.[9] Most of the physical regeneration of the city during the 1980s was carried out by the MDC. This included the regeneration of Albert Dock (the largest group of Grade 1 listed structures in Britain) (Figures 9.4a, 9.4b and 9.4c), which had been derelict and abandoned since 1972. The contaminated industrial land was remediated for the redevelopment of new industrial space. Albert Dock was the location of the 1984 International Garden Festival.

a

b

c

Figures 9.4a, 9.4b and 9.4c Images of the Albert Dock
Source: Photos by Lily Bichard-Collins.

While the Corporation ended in 1998 and was never popular in Liverpool, the rehabilitation of the Albert Dock was important for a number of reasons. It brought a symbol of the city's decline back into use. However, it also drew people back to the waterfront, which had been blocked off by fences and hoardings for so long. The Dock was not an overnight success. Inner-city living units were built into the upper floors, while the ground floor colonnade had shops selling souvenirs and low cost cafés. Later the Dock hosted an ITV television studio between 1988 and 1996, which helped to raise the profile of the Dock and the city. While Albert Dock could not be said to be a catalyst of change, it did mark a tipping point in a "gradual but sustained transformation of the city's fortunes".[10] Two rounds of European Union regional development fund grants pushed this transformation forward from 1994–1999 and 2000–2006.

Demographics

By the early 1980s, the city was suffering from high unemployment, low economic investment, a low-skilled workforce, and a depleted business sector. A national recession made matters worse and this period marked the ebb of the city's fortunes. The core of the city lost almost half of its population between 1930 and 2001. While net outmigration has recently ended, the greater Merseyside area now has a population no larger than it was in the 1880s.

Liverpool's government, dominated by the Militant Tendency in the mid-1980s (now known as the Socialist Party), clashed with the Thatcher Government over public sector cuts, leading to a financial crisis in the city. Strikes were common; in the summer of 1981, the Toxteth riots exploded across inner-city areas. The riots lasted for nine days. It resulted in hundreds of police and public injured, one man dead, 500 arrested, seventy buildings destroyed and damage estimated at £11 million. It was also the first time that CS (tear) gas had been used on the British mainland.[11] The Liverpool unrest had been preceded a few months earlier by the Brixton riots in London and could be said to have fed on the febrile atmosphere generated by an opposition to the government throughout urban Britain. The riots had a lasting negative impact on those who already thought of the city as synonymous with crime and unemployment. It also had serious policing implications for the ethnic minorities who lived in the Toxteth area of the city where some of the worst rioting took place.

Economy

From 1961 to 1985, all sectors of the economy in Liverpool, with the exception of car manufacturing, were either declining or growing more slowly than the UK average. Parkinson wrote that of the twenty largest employers in Merseyside, just one was locally controlled.[12] With no allegiance to the region, it was easy to disinvest, and this in turn affected local suppliers. Between 1979 and 1984, Liverpool lost 40,000 manufacturing jobs. The economic performance of the region had declined so much that in 1994 Merseyside qualified for European Structural Funding, which targeted the regions of member countries in the European Union that reported an average gross domestic product below 75 per cent of the EU average. In other words, Merseyside was among the poorest places in Europe.

The decline occurred between 1966 and 1977 when over 350 factories in Liverpool closed and, by 1985, the city had lost one-third of the jobs it maintained in the 1960s. The acceleration of job losses was at its most acute at the start of the Thatcher administration from 1979 to 1981 when employment fell by a further 18 per cent. However, the City Council estimated that the true number of unemployed persons by the late 1970s was over 150,000 (20–30 per cent of the working aged population) with just forty-nine jobs on offer for the 13,505 youngsters registered as unemployed in 1981.[13] The citywide unemployment figure hid an even worse situation. In 1991, inner-city electoral districts such as Liverpool Riverside had a male unemployment rate of close to 38 per cent. These figures were the worst of any parliamentary constituency in the United Kingdom.

A symbolic yet locally important landmark in Liverpool's shrinking economy was the closure of the Tate and Lyle syrup-making plant in Bootle in 1984 with the loss of 1,570 jobs. Tate's first sugar refinery was set up in 1862 within the dock area of the city, and the company made the world's first sugar cubes there in 1875. There had been a sustained but ultimately unsuccessful effort to keep the business going and many of those who lost their jobs felt that the City Council had not made a strong enough effort to keep the plant open.

The City in 2015

Physical Form and Conditions

Visitors returning to Liverpool after an absence of thirty years would be hard-pressed to recognize parts of the city. The tired and under-invested retail core of Liverpool has been transformed in the past decade. The Duke of Westminster's company, Grosvenor completed Liverpool One (L1) on a 17-hectare site with an investment valued at close to £1 billion (Figures 9.5a and 9.5b). The city was badly in need of retail revitalization In 2004, Liverpool ranked just thirteenth in the league of national retail destinations, a fall of ten places from its heyday in 1971 when it was ranked third.[14] The city centre complex was

Figures 9.5a and 9.5b Liverpool One Leisure and Retail Centre
Source: Photos by Lily Bichard-Collins.

completed in 2008 and now boasts a footfall of more than twenty-six million. The significance of a revitalized retail centre had the effect of retaining local spending by shoppers who used to travel outside the city to Manchester or Chester for quality or specialist goods. This explains why the fears that the former shopping centre, the pedestrianized Church Street and the more bohemian Bold Street would be abandoned once L1 opened were never realized. The Council had rejected an enclosed mall design in favour of a "covered street" layout, which retains the feel of the more intimate city-centre lanes. However, Grosvenor insisted on a pseudo-public space, which allowed it to control and manage entry and exit to the development. This "malls without walls" approach still rankles with some commentators.[15]

Previously under-developed land to the south of Albert Dock has similarly been transformed and the former Kings Dock now supports a new conference centre, an indoor arena and exhibition space valued at £400 million. Land between the Albert Dock and the Three Graces has also been developed. The Mann Island Scheme (£112 million) primarily consists of new modern office space but also includes a new modern Museum of Liverpool (£33 million) designed by Danish architects 3XN.

Dominating all of these achievements is the promised redevelopment of Liverpool's derelict North Docks and Birkenhead Docks, which are to be renamed Liverpool Waters and Wirral Waters. Both areas have recently been designated as Enterprise Zones, which offer planning and funding concessions. These plans represent a long-term investment in the order of £10 billion to transform 320 hectares of land owned by Peel Holdings. Peel is a major regional property developer. As owner of the Mersey Docks and Harbour Company, Liverpool Airport and the Manchester Ship Canal, the company owns much of the waterside land in Merseyside and has ambitious plans to transform the derelict and underused docks in a way that the former Development Corporation tried but failed to do thirty years previously. Peel also plans to improve the Port of Liverpool with a new "in-river terminal" capable of taking the largest new "post-Panamax" container ships and will continue to attract cruise liners, which have begun to dock again in the city.

Demographics

Given the large strides forward in the physical regeneration and appearance of the city centre of Liverpool since 2000, the social deprivation indicators are less encouraging. A 2012 study comparing the UK's sixty-four primary urban areas by the Centre for Cities ranked Liverpool among the lowest for a number of key economic, demographic and social indicators.[16] The pockets of deprivation in the city are still among the most acute in the UK. The most recently published Indices of Multiple Deprivation (IMD) ranks Liverpool as the poorest performing city in the country and an analysis of the fifty worst performing neighbourhoods in the country shows that seventeen are in Liverpool.[17] Approximately 70 per cent of Liverpool's thirty-three central, northern and peripheral residential wards are among the 10 per cent most deprived in England and Wales and there is a thirty-year difference between the city's wealthiest and poorest wards in terms of life expectancy. These statistics might suggest a city that is in terminal decline, and yet the recent change in the urban form suggests a prosperous and vibrant place with major redevelopment and a feeling that the spark has returned to the city.

Economy

By 2013, Liverpool city region had a £23.1 billion economy and, since 2000, has outperformed many other city regions in England in terms of Gross Value Added (GVA) growth rates. However, average GVA per head was £15,600, just 75 per cent of the national average. The city region suffers from an £8.2 billion output gap compared to national performance.[18] There are still deficits compared to the national average for skills, employment and enterprise, but the gap has been narrowing. Between 1998 and 2011, employment growth has been 9.9 per cent, outpacing the UK growth rate of 7.8 per cent.

The desire to perpetuate the outward rise in the fabric of the city, and the continuing struggle to improve social challenges have confronted successive Council administrations. The swagger seems to have returned to Liverpool and many point to a single reason: the 2008 Capital of Culture.

Transformation of the City (1985–2015)

What Went Right?

The Capital of Culture

In 2000, the UK government launched a competition in which English cities could bid to become the European Capital of Culture. The award was first made in 1985 when Athens became the inaugural winner. Governed by the European Commission, a winning bid needed to have strategic planning and clear objectives for cultural tourism; involvement of local people and local culture; facilities management and development of partnerships; and contributions given to the city by the development of events. The winner was given assistance to host a year-long festival of cultural events. In June 2003, Liverpool was announced as the winner for 2008, partly on the basis that the award would contribute to the regeneration of the city. Glasgow, Scotland was the last UK city to win this prize (in 1990) and it transformed perceptions of that city. Liverpool hoped for the same outcome.

Liverpool did not begin from a standing start. It already had several museums and galleries, including the Tate of the North (the James Stirling-designed interior that had been occupying a space in the Albert Dock since 1988). In addition, there was the iconic Art Deco Philharmonic Hall, four historic theatres, the Foundation for Art and Creative Technology or FACT gallery (opened in 2003) and the Biennial of Contemporary Art, famous for its massive street installations (founded in 1999). This underpinned the better-known architecture, sport, and music heritage offerings all spearheaded by the legacy of the Beatles.

The Strategic Regeneration Framework of 2000 identified the bid for the Capital of Culture as a way of "improving the regional, national and international perception of the City Centre".[19] The strategy was based on a culture-led regeneration model, which also included a new cruise liner port, the linking of canals on the waterfront, and the Lime Street Gateway, which transformed the front of the main rail station into a high quality public realm space. All of these projects were realized in time.

A study commissioned by the City Council and carried out by the Universities of Liverpool and Liverpool John Moore recorded the following outcomes that stemmed from the Liverpool 2008 Capital of Culture:

- A 50 per cent rise in visitor figures to Merseyside's seven largest attractions (from a base in 2004), peaking at 5.5 million people in 2008.
- 9.7 million additional visits to Liverpool, constituting 35 per cent of all visits to the city in 2008.
- An economic impact of £753.8 million (additional direct visitor spend) across Liverpool, Merseyside, and the wider North West region.

- 2.6 million European and global visits motivated by the event, of which 97 per cent were first-time visits to the city.
- An additional 1.14 million staying visitor nights in Liverpool hotels, 1.29 million in the rest of Merseyside and 1.7 million in the rest of the North West.
- An increase of 71 per cent in positive national media coverage that dominated over the traditional emphasis on (negative) social issues. These stories were also diversified from the traditional focus on popular music and the built heritage to the visual and performing arts, and growing references to Liverpool's creative industries.
- Surveys found that 65 per cent of UK residents were aware that Liverpool was the European Capital of Culture; 77 per cent of visitors felt the city was "safer than I expected"; and 99 per cent of visitors particularly liked the "general atmosphere".
- The event generated the highest amount of sponsorship and earned income of any European Capital of Culture, a total of £22.3 million of sponsorship (both cash and in kind) and £4.1 million in earned income.

Shaw, Sykes, and Fischer (2009) commented that while the Capital of Culture cannot be said to have kick-started many development projects (most importantly the Liverpool One retail centre), more ambitious and faster inward investment seems to have followed the news that Liverpool was going to host the event. The event also concentrated minds and helped many of the actors and agencies to recognize the role that place and historical cultural assets played in the ability to identify with Liverpool.

What Went Wrong?

Austerity

Cruelly for Liverpool, the recession, which had its roots in the liquidity crisis in the summer of 2007, started to undermine confidence in the economy (and the construction industry in particular) just as the Capital of Culture was ending. The General Election in 2010 returned a right-of-centre Coalition government determined to reduce public spending as the means to accelerate economic recovery. This was very bad news for Liverpool, which was looking for investors to capitalize on a successful year. But the city was also very vulnerable to austerity policies due to the relatively high number of people employed in the public sector. In 2012, the public sector was still responsible for 39 per cent of the city's jobs even after several rounds of redundancies.[20]

By 2015, Liverpool City Council had suffered a 58 per cent cut in funding in real terms since 2010/11, some £329 million. Local councillors believe that by the middle of 2016 the authority will have lost all of its discretionary spending powers, leaving its sole purpose as trying to fulfil its statutory duties to the young, the old, and the vulnerable. Most of the other Merseyside authorities suffered similar reductions.

This triggered an older fault-line in the Council between the few councillors who thought that the private sector could help to invest the city out of trouble, and the social justice politicians who were focused on alleviating poverty. This argument had governance ramifications. Should the city be driven by top-down policies that would be open to commercial decisions that could boost job creation and inward investment (improving infrastructure and central business district modernization, for example) or should the city be driven by bottom-up ward-level decisions that improved social conditions such as better housing, parks and gardens, education and health care provision?

Housebuilding Stalls

At a national level, Britain has not built enough housing for several decades and is now paying the price with long waiting lists for public housing, high private rents, and runaway house prices in many areas. Liverpool benefitted from the 1997–2010 Labour administration's Housing Market Renewal Pathfinder programme, which was designed to address the imbalance between a large number of small two-bedroom terraced housing that had become undesirable and larger, more modern dwellings with gardens. The programme targeted over 18,000 properties for clearance, and streets and neighbourhoods became blighted as they were progressively acquired for demolition. The reluctance of private house builders to construct cheaper homes on brownfield sites was compounded by the recession and led to years of delay before some (but not all) of these deserted and derelict residential areas were finally regenerated.

Brown (2009) wrote that one of the greatest ironies of the Capital of Culture promotional narrative was that Liverpool's built heritage (predominantly seen as being located in the city centre) was lauded as a distinctive jewel of the cultural city, while away from the sightlines of millions of visitors, many of the city's inner Victorian suburbs continued to suffer from under-investment and decay.

The Governance Question

While a Combined Authority for the Liverpool City Region has been formed, consensus on how this should be governed has been more difficult to find. One example of this was the failure to agree on a site for the disposal of the city-region's waste within Merseyside in 2013, leading to an expensive solution to export all of this material to the North East of England. If this continuing trend towards parochial power retention persists, many think it is likely to hold back the entire region. Most British core cities are economically weaker in comparison to their European counterparts. A reversal of centralized policies that have stifled the potential for local decision-making may reverse this under-performance.

Governance of the city-region has been ebbing and flowing in England since the mid-1970s. Various regional and sub-regional arrangements have come and gone since then. The last two national governments (since 2010) have pushed city regions to break down local authority decision-making boundaries and to form combined authorities. In exchange, London would cede responsibility and budgets for issues such as health, transport, regeneration, skills, and training and, in time, local tax-raising powers. In Liverpool's case this requires six local authorities surrounding the Mersey estuary (with Liverpool City Council at its geographical core) to agree on common policies. On 1 April 2014, the six municipalities, the Local Economic Partnership (a grouping of business, public and third sector representatives) and Merseytravel (the regional public transport body) agreed to work together and formed the Liverpool City Region Combined Authority.

The offer from London is not universally welcomed, with some worrying that the devolution of powers to city regions like Liverpool is an easy way for central government to shift the blame for austerity cuts away from the Treasury. However, just thirty miles to the east, Manchester's ten local authorities have negotiated a package that includes £300 million over ten years to support delivery of at least 10,000–15,000 new houses; more funds and greater control over public transport; funding to promote the city-region's businesses in international markets; and funds and control over further education and other skills programmes such as the apprenticeship scheme.

The new Authority is likely to be able to agree to pool certain functions in return for extra powers, but the question of holding an election for a mayor for the city-region is proving divisive. There is a concern that power and influence would push resources away from the peripheral authorities and towards the economically dominant Liverpool City if a single mayor were elected. The debate is framed by two opposing views. Councillor Phil Davies, leader of Wirral Council, was elected chair of the Combined Authority in 2014 rather than Joe Anderson (Mayor of Liverpool City). Davies said: "The focus should be on using existing structures if there is greater devolution of powers from Westminster." Anderson disagreed, stating: "A 'Metro Mayor' presiding over a single city-regional authority is the way forward for Merseyside."[21] The "Metro Mayor" approach is preferred by the central government as well. While this problem remains unresolved, the city-region will not be able to capitalize on the promise of extra funding.

Lessons Learned

The Realization of the "Destination City" Model

Malcolm Kennedy, Labour councillor and Cabinet Member for regeneration at Liverpool City Council, believes that the good-time city reputation is a double-edged sword.[22] He says that greater visitor numbers are good for the retailers, restaurants and hotels, but if allowed to get out of hand, it can put off many visitors who want a more sedate experience. There is further evidence that local disaffection can build up over high numbers of over-exuberant visitors at popular European city-break destinations like Barcelona and Venice.[23] The CEO of Sefton's Chamber of Commerce (one of the six Combined Authority Councils), Jenny Stewart, also worries about a one-track economy saying: "Greater devolution must help Liverpool become a more attractive destination for business and investment, not just tourists and students."[24]

Kennedy would also like people to come to the city for a wide variety of reasons, not just to party. For him, the main benefit of the Capital of Culture for Liverpool was the removal of its bad reputation. Visitors no longer worry about their personal safety and instead come to rely on the warm welcome the city offers. Politicians and businesses previously put off by the suspicious or adversarial treatment of outsiders now view the city as a cooperative and innovative place.

The academic community is also burgeoning. The three universities (Liverpool, Liverpool John Moore, and Liverpool Hope) have all enhanced their campuses and built extensively within the city. Liverpool has opened a new campus in China, leading to a rapid increase of Chinese students visiting Liverpool for some or all of the academic year. This revives and reinforces the city's multicultural credentials and may boost investment in Chinatown, a district disadvantaged by the absence of casual footfall, as it is situated on the periphery of the city centre and surrounded by underinvested property.

The architectural additions to the cityscape have replaced many of the blighted areas, particularly on the waterfront, and the historical structures make the city look the part for all types of visitors. However, there is still an imbalance of outdated commercial space in historic buildings. If Liverpool Waters is ever built, this may worsen the situation. The Council's recent occupation of the old Cunard Building shows how historic buildings can be rehabilitated. A number of listed buildings, including the Bank of England (occupied in 2015 by a movement supporting the homeless) and the Martins Bank Buildings, just two of the many historic buildings, could further enhance the architectural reputation of the city with innovative re-purposing.

Finally, the city's gateway routes (both rail and road) are still a work in progress, and the airport, still small by nearby Manchester standards, has the potential to attract more direct access from abroad but suffers from a lack of connectivity to the city centre. The cruise port will also bring in another influx of visitors, but could be improved by a reception terminal similar to the Zaha Hadid structure recently commissioned by Salerno in Italy. In this sense the city represents more opportunity than delivery.

Confidence Matters

Liverpool can still suffer from self-inflicted wounds that stem from the same source as many of its strengths. Bianchini and Bloomfield (2008) write that port cities, particularly those that are situated on the edge of their countries like Liverpool, often have an "exceptionally strong sense of their own cultural identity, shaped by influences such as immigration and emigration, and by distinctive religions and political traditions". This singular self-regard fosters a self-reliant attitude, which is an asset when things are going well, but can be counter-productive when times are hard. Boland (2008) thinks that throughout the last century, the continued decline of Liverpool impacted on the self-confidence of its inhabitants and external perceptions of the city. The Capital of Culture award has gone a long way to rediscover the belief that imbued the city a century ago. Ultimately, politicians like Malcolm Kennedy think that this will remain fragile until Liverpool's economy is based on the creation of stable, sustainable jobs.

The national government is now interested in trying to rebalance the economic gravitational pull of London. An example of this is a report of the government's plans (dubbed "The Northern Powerhouse") to improve the North of England's economic prospects.[25] After an analysis of the vision, the authors advise northern cities to do the following:

* Seize new opportunities for further devolution deals with a sense of urgency and fresh resolve, setting aside parochialism in the interests of the greater good and developing plans for city governance with ingenuity and openness.
* Extend the opportunities for business involvement in all aspects of economic development and strategic planning, and not exclusively through Local Economic Partnerships, especially in the areas of skills, infrastructure and business rates.
* Continue to develop creative and resourceful approaches to collaboration both locally and between areas, thereby enhancing strategic planning.

If it is strong enough, confidence and civic pride should transcend local interest and enable the kind of cooperation that is being suggested. Perhaps this is not quite at levels that would allow local leaders to let go of some powers for the greater good, but if Manchester proves to be a successful model, then eventually Merseyside is likely to follow suit.

Prospects for the Future

Plans to invest £10 billion in a modern city on either bank of the Mersey have dominated discussions about Liverpool's future. The architectural additions in the past ten years show that a degree of prosperity has already returned to Liverpool city centre. Under Mayor Anderson, this push to modernize the built environment shows no sign of abating. However, some have their doubts about this approach. Crouch (2003) says that there was a "lack of a unified approach in the past when development sometimes disintegrated into a series of localised projects that were lacking in strategic context and focused only on short-term goals". He is concerned that the lack of public money, and the desire to continue to modernize the city centre may result in ill-advised and destructive additions to the built environment. UNESCO, the body that awards (and can take away) World Heritage status, voiced warnings that the planned Liverpool Waters development as currently conceived would undermine the integrity of the waterfront.[26]

Couch and Cocks (2012) write that a long period of sustained decline is now being replaced with modest, but significant growth. However, they are cautious and say work remains to be done. This is particularly true for the decades-long erosion of social and economic conditions that significant parts of the population still suffer today. The grandeur of the cityscape still masks many sites of physical dilapidation and vacancy in many city centre buildings. The current budgetary "austerity" imposed by London on the public sector is hurting those cities that have ingrained social problems and a high dependency on public sector jobs.

Sykes et al. (2013) feel that the European Capital of Culture year in 2008 has helped the outside world to notice Liverpool, and those inside the city to appreciate its assets for their intrinsic value rather than viewing them as a burden and a barrier to shaping a modern city. They point to two challenges that lie ahead. First, there is a need to try to maintain the momentum of the past decade. Second, to ensure that future prosperity is accessible to the whole population.

This is a tall order in the face of crippling public spending cuts. There is likely to be an understandable tendency for the Council to revert to its focus on mitigating poverty and fighting injustices. Governance is likely to play an important role in any attempt to mount a more progressive strategy for the city region. This means finding a way to co-operate and earn the government's trust and investment, in the first instance by conceding defeat and electing a "Metro Mayor".

Whatever the future, it is undeniable that Liverpool is emerging from a long night of economic gloom. If the profusion of hen and stag groups on the walkways of Liverpool One is anything to go by, the "shrinking city" moniker of this iconic post-industrial city is certainly a fading memory.

Notes

1   S. Wilks-Hegg, "From World City to Pariah City? Liverpool and the Global Economy, 1850–2000". In R. Munck, ed., *Reinventing the City: Liverpool in Comparative Perspective* (Liverpool: Liverpool University Press, 2004).

2   J. Brown, "Liverpool Betrayed: From Post-War To Pathfinder". In *Triumph, Disaster and Decay in the SAVE Survey of Liverpool's Heritage* (London: SAVE Britain's Heritage, 2009), 23–7.

3   O. Sykes, J. Brown, M. Cocks, D. Shaw, and C. Couch, "A City Profile of Liverpool". *Cities* 35 (2013): 299–319.

4   Ibid.

5   C. Couch, *City of Change and Challenge: Urban Planning and Regeneration in Liverpool* (Aldershot: Ashgate, 2003).

6   H. Grady, "The English City that Wanted to 'Break Away' from the UK". *BBC Magazine* (2014). Available at: www.bbc.co.uk/news/magazine-29953611

7   P. Burnell, "Why Liverpool Never Loved Margaret Thatcher". *BBC News* (2013). Available at: www.bbc.co.uk/news/uk-england-merseyside-22073199 (accessed 20 July 2015).

8   M. Heseltine and T. Leahy, *Rebalancing Britain: Policy or Slogan? Liverpool City Region – Building on its Strengths: An Independent Report*. Department for Business, Innovation and Skills, Oct. 2011. Available at: www.bis.gov.uk/assets/biscore/economic-development/docs/r/11-1338-rebalancing-britain-liverpool-city-region

9   J. Murden, "City of Change and Challenge: Liverpool since 1945". In J. Belchem, ed., *Liverpool 800; Culture, Character and History* (Liverpool: Liverpool University Press, 2006), 393–485.

10 D. Shaw, O. Sykes, and T. Fischer, "Regeneration and Urban Renaissance in Liverpool". *RaumPlanung* 143 (2009): 122–7.

11 *Liverpool Echo*, "Toxteth Riots, 1981 Background – And How It All Began". 2011. Available at: www.liverpoolecho.co.uk/news/liverpool-news/toxteth-riots-1981-background-3369242 (accessed 16 July 2015).

12 M. Parkinson, *City on the Brink: One City's Struggle Against Government Cuts* (Hermitage, Berks: Policy Journals, 1985).

13 Murden, "City of Change and Challenge".

14 A. Daramola-Martin, "Liverpool One and the Transformation of a City: Place Branding, Marketing and the Catalytic Effects of Regeneration and Culture on Repositioning Liverpool". *Place Branding and Public Diplomacy* 5, (2009) 301–11.

15 A. Minton, *Ground Control: Fear and Happiness in the 21st Century* (Harmondsworth: Penguin, 2012).

16 *Cities Outlook* (London: Centre for Cities, 2012).

17 Sykes et al., "A City Profile of Liverpool".

18 N. Christie, Liverpool City Region Evidence Report. Report produced by the Liverpool Local Economic Partnership" (2013). Available at www.liverpoollep.org/wp-content/uploads/2015/06/wpid-liverpool-city-region-evidence-report-09-2013.pdf (accessed 18 July 2015).

19 Liverpool Vision, City Centre Strategic Regeneration Framework (SRF), Liverpool City Council, July 2000.

20 A. Chape and A. Wray, "Better Together – The Way Ahead for Liverpool and Manchester". *Town and Country Planning*, February 2012: 77–83.

21 L. Murphy, "City Region Leader Says 'No' to a Mayor for Merseyside". *Liverpool Echo*, 28 September 2014. Available at: www.liverpoolecho.co.uk/news/liverpool-news/liverpool-city-region-leaders-very-9597759 (accessed 15 July 2015).

22 Malcolm Kennedy, personal communication, 2015.

23 C. Matlack, "Barcelona's Mayor to Tourists: Go Away". Bloomberg.com, June 5, 2015. Available at: www.bloomberg.com/news/articles/2015-06-05/barcelona-s-mayor-to-tourists-go-away (accessed 20 July 2015).

24 L. Murphy, "Liverpool City Region Leaders Have 'Very Constructive' Meeting with Communities Secretary". *Liverpool Echo*, 6 July 2015, Available at: www.liverpoolecho.co.uk/news/liverpool-news/liverpool-city-region-leaders-very-9597759 (accessed 15 July 2015).

25 E. Cox and J. Hunter, "Full Steam Ahead: Business Attitudes Towards the Northern Powerhouse". *IPPR North* (2015). Available at: www.ippr.org/publications/full-steam-ahead-business-attitudes-towards-the-northern-powerhouse (accessed 15 July 2015).

26 H. Carter, "UNESCO Meets to Discuss Liverpool's World Heritage Status". *The Guardian*, 20 June 2012. Available at: www.theguardian.com/uk/the-northerner/2012/jun/20/liverpool-unesco-heritage-risk (accessed 18 July 2015).

References

Bianchini, F. and Bloomfield, J. (2008) "Informality and Social Creativity in Four Port Cities". ed. Guidi, E., *Urban Makers* (Berlin: b-books, 2008).

Boland, P. (2008) "The Construction of Images of People and Place: Labelling Liverpool and Stereotyping Scousers". *Cities*, 25(6): 355–69.

Brown, J. (2009) "Liverpool Betrayed: From Post-War To Pathfinder". In *Triumph, Disaster and Decay in the SAVE Survey of Liverpool's Heritage*. London: SAVE Britain's Heritage, 23–7.

Burnell, P. (2013) "Why Liverpool Never Loved Margaret Thatcher". *BBC News*, Available at; www.bbc.co.uk/news/uk-england-merseyside-22073199 (accessed 20 July 2015).

Carter, H. (2012) "UNESCO Meets to Discuss Liverpool's World Heritage Status". *The Guardian*, 20 June 2012. Available at: www.theguardian.com/uk/the-northerner/2012/jun/20/liverpool-unesco-heritage-risk (accessed 18 July 2015).

Chape, A. and Wray, A. (2012) "Better Together – The Way Ahead for Liverpool and Manchester". *Town and Country Planning* February: 77–83.

Christie, N. (2013) "Liverpool City Region Evidence Report. Report produced by the Liverpool Local Economic Partnership". Available at: www.liverpoollep.org/wp-content/uploads/2015/06/wpid-liverpool-city-region-evidence-report-09-2013.pdf (accessed 18 July 2015).

Couch, C. (2003) *City of Change and Challenge: Urban Planning and Regeneration in Liverpool*. Aldershot: Ashgate.

Couch, C. and Cocks, M. (2012) "From Long-Term Shrinkage to Re-Growth? The Urban Development Trajectories of Liverpool and Leipzig". *Built Environment* 38(2): 162–78.

Cox, E. and Hunter, J. (2015) "Full Steam Ahead: Business Attitudes Towards the Northern Powerhouse". *IPPR North*. Available at: www.ippr.org/publications/full-steam-ahead-business-attitudes-towards-the-northern-powerhouse (accessed 15 July 2015).

Daramola-Martin, A. (2009) "Liverpool One and the Transformation of a City: Place Branding, Marketing and the Catalytic Effects of Regeneration and Culture on Repositioning Liverpool". *Place Branding and Public Diplomacy* 5: 301–11.

ERM Economics (2002) *European Capital of Culture: Socio-Economic assessment of Liverpool's Bid*, Manchester: ERM Economics.

Garcia, B. (2006) "Press Impact Analysis (96, 03, 05) – A Retrospective Study: UK National Press Coverage on Liverpool Before, During and After Bidding for European Capital of Culture Status". *Impacts 08*, Liverpool.

Garcia, B., Melville, R. and Cox, T. (2010) "Creating an Impact: Liverpool's Experience as European Capital of Culture, European Capital of Culture Research Programme, University of Liverpool. Available at: www.liv.ac.uk/impacts08/publications/ (accessed 28 June 2015).

Grady, H. (2014) "The English City that Wanted to 'Break Away' from the UK". *BBC Magazine* (2014). Available at: www.bbc.co.uk/news/magazine-29953611

Heseltine, M. and Leahy, T. (2011) *Rebalancing Britain: Policy or Slogan? Liverpool City Region – Building on its Strengths: An Independent Report*. Department for Business, Innovation and Skills, Oct. 2011. Available at: www.bis.gov.uk/assets/biscore/economic-development/docs/r/11-1338-rebalancing-britain-liverpool-city-region

Liverpool Echo (2011) "Toxteth Riots 1981 Background – And How It All Began". Available at: www.liverpoolecho.co.uk/news/liverpool-news/toxteth-riots-1981-background--3369242 (accessed 16 July 2015).

Liverpool Vision (2000) *City Centre Strategic Regeneration Framework (SRF)*, Liverpool City Council, July.

Matlack, C. (2015) "Barcelona's Mayor to Tourists: Go Away". Bloomberg.com, 5 June 2015 Available at: www.bloomberg.com/news/articles/2015-06-05/barcelona-s-mayor-to-tourists-go-away (accessed 20 July 2015).

Minton, A. (2012) *Ground Control: Fear and Happiness in the 21st Century*. Harmondsworth: Penguin.

Murden, J., "City of Change and Challenge: Liverpool since 1945". In J. Belchem, ed., *Liverpool 800; Culture, Character and History*. Liverpool: Liverpool University Press, 393–485.

Murphy, L. (2014) "City Region Leader Says 'No' to a Mayor for Merseyside". *Liverpool Echo*, 28 September. Available at: www.liverpoolecho.co.uk/news/liverpool-news/liverpool-city-region-leaders-very-9597759 (accessed 15 July 2015).

Murphy, L. (2015) "Liverpool City Region Leaders Have 'Very Constructive' Meeting With Communities Secretary". *Liverpool Echo* 6 July. Available at: www.liverpoolecho.co.uk/news/liverpool-news/liverpool-city-region-leaders-very-9597759 (accessed 15 July 2015).

Parkinson, M. (1985) *City on the Brink: One City's Struggle Against Government Cuts*. Hermitage, Berks: Policy Journals.

PWC (2015) *Delivering the Decentralisation Dividend: A Whole System Approach*. PWC.

Shaw, D., Sykes, O. and Fischer, T. (2009) "Regeneration and Urban Renaissance in Liverpool". *RaumPlanung* 143: 122–7.

Sheard, S. (2014) "James Newlands and the Origins of the Municipal Engineer". *Proceedings of the ICE: Engineering History and Heritage* 168 (2014): 83–9.

Sykes, O. Brown, J., Cocks, M., Shaw, D. and Couch, C. (2013) "A City Profile of Liverpool". *Cities*, 35: 299–319.

Wilks-Hegg, S. (2004) "From World City to Pariah City? Liverpool and the Global Economy, 1850–2000". In R. Munck, ed., *Reinventing the City: Liverpool in Comparative Perspective*. Liverpool: Liverpool University Press.

10 Rotterdam Case Study

Nico Tillie, Iris Dudok, Peter M.J. Pol, Luc Boot, and Roland van der Heijden

Introduction

Rotterdam is the second largest city of the Netherlands and one of the major cities in Northwest Europe. The city, situated at the Rhine–Meuse Delta in the province of Zuid Holland, has always been part of a dynamic delta where sea, land, rivers, and urban areas come together. This can be seen in many aspects of the city. Water is an integral part of Rotterdam.

In 2015, Rotterdam's population was more than 624,000 and comprised 173 nationalities. It is one of the youngest cities in Europe with 30 percent of the population younger than 25 and only 15 percent older than 65. The annual population increase in the past five years has averaged 5 percent. Approximately 50 percent of Rotterdam residents (or their parents) are foreign born. On January 5, 2009, the first mayor in the Netherlands of Moroccan ethnicity, Mayor Ahmed Aboutaleb, took office. The City covers an area of 213 square kilometers, including the port area (Figure 10.1).

Rotterdam is Europe's largest port city with a varied history in shipping and logistics. The port facility along the riverfront is 40 kilometers long and stretches between the city and North Sea. Rotterdam hosts one of the largest refining and chemical clusters in the world. Due to energy and resource constraints, many companies are slowly shifting towards cleantech, one of the major focal points in the port's development master plan. Although the port industrial complex is still a big driver for the city's economy, since the 1980s other economic clusters have emerged in the city.

Important metropolitan regions close to Rotterdam are Amsterdam (55 kilometers), the Ruhr Valley (125 kilometers), Antwerp (60 kilometers), and Brussels (125 kilometers). Air connectivity is excellent with four airports nearby, including Schiphol-Amsterdam (25 minutes) and Brussels (1 hour and 25 minutes).[1] The city is part of the Rotterdam–The Hague metropolitan region with 2.5 million inhabitants. During the past two decades Rotterdam and The Hague have expanded and grown together as a result of large housing developments in the previously undeveloped areas between them. Rotterdam and The Hague are becoming 'twin cities' with the medieval city of Delft in between.

The city of Rotterdam is also classified within the Randstad conurbation, a geographically defined area where cities and populated areas have expanded to such extent that they form a continuously developed urban area. The Randstad conurbation includes the Netherlands' four largest cities (Amsterdam, Rotterdam, The Hague and Utrecht), and it is home to 7.1 million people, comparable to the San Francisco Bay Area in the United States. It is considered one of the most important economic regions in Northwest Europe.

Figure 10.1 Port expansions over time. The port is moving westward towards the sea.
Source: Drawing by Hans van der Boor, courtesy of the City of Rotterdam.

Brief History of the City

In the thirteenth century a dam was constructed at the confluence of the small River Rotte and the River Meuse to prevent tidal water from traveling upstream in the River Rotte. Merchants and businesses located along the dam were soon flourishing. Tradespeople, fishermen, and sailors thus created a new settlement. The city grew as more ports were built, including Delfshaven, where in 1620 the Pilgrims left for the United States. After the opening of the New Waterway (Nieuwe Waterweg) in 1872, created from the canalization of the main river and a direct connection to the North Sea, the port economy of Rotterdam grew rapidly. Workers from beyond Rotterdam came to work in the port and the city. In a period of few decades the large harbor inlets of the Rijnhaven, Maashaven, and Waalhaven were constructed on the south bank of the river. In the 1900s, the city continued to grow with additional port expansions. The rapidly growing economy attracted workers to relocate to the city from the countryside in the Netherlands and Belgium. Residential areas were rapidly developed with primarily small and inexpensive housing units. Between 1880 and 1900, the population increased from 148,000 to 318,000. By 1920, Rotterdam had more than half a million inhabitants. Before World War II, Rotterdam had become a dynamic internationally oriented metropolis with large investments in port expansion and infrastructure. The image of the city was of an industrial metropolis with modern European qualities, including boulevards (Coolsingel) (Figure 10.2), passages, urban streets, squares, modern buildings, entertainment, and culture; it was a city with a global orientation. There were movie theaters, dance halls, and stages for performance art, especially as jazz music became popular. Rotterdam was on the world stage.

Figure 10.2 Large new boulevards, 1928, the Coolsingel with City Hall and busy street life
Source: Photo by L. van Leer, courtesy of the City of Rotterdam.

Everything changed during World War II. In May 1940, the port and the city were bombed with devastating effect. The firestorm that followed destroyed 25,000 houses, leaving 900 people dead and 80,000 people homeless. The heart of the city was in ashes. Rubble was used to fill up the waterways near the center. After the war ended, the port was the first area to be restored. Over time, new ports were created west and south of the river such as Botlek, Europoort and Maasvlakte, which included large crude oil storage tanks and major oil refineries. As the war ended, there was an urgent need for new housing. Some housing was built in the suburban areas north of the city but new housing was mainly built on the south bank in the neighborhoods of Pendrecht, Zuidwijk, Lombardijen and IJsselmonde. By the 1960s and early 1970s, the economy was booming. In 1962, Rotterdam became the number one port in the world, a position it held until 2004. In 1968, the first metro system in the Netherlands opened in Rotterdam. In the 1960s, many immigrant workers came from Italy and Spain, and later, from Turkey and Morocco. These "guest workers" mostly settled in Rotterdam South.

However, economic prosperity came to an end with the oil crises of 1973 and 1979. Port activities had begun steadily shifting westward to bigger and newer locations that accommodated larger ships. This resulted in reduced employment by the early 1980s in the ports of Rotterdam South. In addition, the national government designated several municipalities around Rotterdam as "centers for population growth" (*groeikernen*), with funding for new housing. For many, especially middle-class families, this was an ideal alternative to living in the city. People who could afford it left the city.

The City in 1985

Economy

The 1973 oil crisis, combined with the availability of cheap labor and new ship building industries in Asian countries, caused traditional shipyards and related industries to decline in Europe. As a result, in the late 1970s and early 1980s, many industrial workers in Rotterdam were laid off, creating an economic crisis. It was clear that the city needed a more diverse economy.

By 1985, the economy in the Rijnmond (Rotterdam) region showed signs of recovery that corresponded with national and international economic development efforts. Growth in the services sector drove the relocation of economic activities from the "wet" areas to the "dry" areas of the city (Figure 10.3). Rotterdam now was not only a world port of stature, but also began to develop its distribution function and thereby position itself as an economically competitive global center.

The area of Bospolder-Tussendijken (BoTu) is exemplary of what happened in other neighborhoods connected to the port that were built before 1940. Many people from those neighborhoods once worked in the nearby port areas. The harbor area thus contributed to local purchasing power and local amenities. By 1985, the relationship between the port and the city with respect to local labor had passed its peak. In addition to foreign competition and outsourcing of jobs, automation resulted in the loss of more port jobs. Housing in BoTu was primarily worker housing in small units. As port unemployment grew, immigrants moved into BoTu. Local purchasing power decreased, and with it the viability of neighborhood retail and offices, which led to more local unemployment.

Figure 10.3 Port activities continue to move westward out of the city
Source: Photo by Claire Droppert, courtesy of the City of Rotterdam.

Demographics

In the 1970s and 1980s, those people who were able to left the city, leaving behind people who could not relocate as easily. This led to the rapid deterioration of parts of Rotterdam, especially the older districts. The housing stock no longer met the requirements of modern times. Immigrants and guest workers moved to these less expensive neighborhoods, creating a multicultural community of Dutch and non-Dutch born residents. In addition to the guest workers from the Mediterranean, new immigrants arrived from China, Cape Verde, Indonesia, Surinam, and the Dutch Antilles. In 1985, for the first time in twenty years, the population of the city grew. The people who came to the city were young, between 18 and 30 years old primarily. They were students and starters and they seemed to bring a new vitality and a different atmosphere in the city.[2] In 1985, Rotterdam had a population of 571,116.

Physical Form and Conditions

City Center

Until 1940, the inner city of Rotterdam was a bustling and prosperous traditional European city center. However, after World War II its character changed. The bombing of May 1940 unwittingly led to the fulfillment of a civic yearning to become a modern city. A new city center with modern architecture developed upon the ashes of destruction. Unfortunately, as in many post-war cities, the redevelopment was driven by new Modernist anti-urban planning theory that separated the functions of the city. As a result, new housing was not part of the rebuilding of the city center. Instead it was located outside the city in new suburban neighborhoods. The vibrant cultural life of pre World War II Rotterdam was gone. In 1970s and 1980s, the initial gloss of the new modernity was also gone. The modern Lijnbaan shopping mall in the center of the city had become outdated. The Cubic Houses (*Kubuswoningen*) of Piet Blom were built (Figure 10.4). There were large vacant areas in the city center and the streets were deserted in the evening.

Rotterdam Zuid (South)

Rotterdam is a city on two banks. Rotterdam South is relatively young. In 1880, the area was largely open grassland. It was developed in several stages, beginning with the development of worker housing in conjunction with new port developments. Each port inlet has a rail yard at the end of its basin, which is surrounded by industrial property and warehouses. Behind the basin, and along the river and port inlets, dikes protect and separate these areas from the residential neighborhoods. As a result, most of the waterfront has been used for port activities and industry, with the dikes leaving little access for the public.

In the 1970s and 1980s, improvement of living conditions in Rotterdam South's pre-1940 housing developments became urgent. The urban renewal approach that followed was very physically oriented. Important principles were to bring more light, air and space into the property and to guarantee the affordability of housing for its residents.

The District of Bospolder-Tussendijken (BoTu)

BoTu is located on the north bank of the river adjacent to Merwehaven/Vierhavens Port, which has been transforming over time. In 1985 the BoTu neighborhood was separated

Figure 10.4 The famous Cubic Houses (*Kubuswoningen*) by architect Piet Blom, built in the 1980s
Source: Photo by Jan van der Ploeg, courtesy of the City of Rotterdam.

from the port by a large rail yard. Port workers living in BoTu reached their jobs via an aerial walkway, which was the only commuter connection between the BoTu neighborhood and the greater harbor area.

The City in 2015

Economy

The Rotterdam economy has always been tied to the port. However, the port currently has a strong focus on sectors that have an uncertain future (cargo and oil refineries, for example). The port continues to embrace new technologies, including automation. As a result, port jobs continue to decline. From the 1980s onward, there has been a decrease in employment at the port industrial complex of approximately 2 percent per year.[3] The port must be innovative, sustainable, and competitive to keep its position in the global economy. As a result, Rotterdam has had to look at other economic clusters to provide new jobs. Over the years the economy has diversified. For instance, industrial jobs declined 11 percent in the last fifteen years, whereas health care jobs increased by 37 percent. In 2015, the number of health care jobs (68,000) surpassed that of port-related jobs (65,000). Other important clusters are consumer services (91,000) and knowledge and education (47,000).[4] The economic output of Rotterdam in 2015 was €36 billion, of which the port contributed €15 billion, approximately 42 percent.

During the Great Recession of 2008, unemployment rose from 7 percent to 15 percent, but now is slowly dropping. There are two major universities in the Rotterdam region: Erasmus University Rotterdam and the Delft University of Technology. In addition, Rotterdam Hoge School is an applied sciences university. In total, there are 80,000 students in the region. As a port city, Rotterdam has not historically had large numbers of workers with higher education degrees. In recent years these numbers have risen due to a more diverse economy, investments in better housing, and increased cultural amenities. The number of higher education degrees attained in 2001 was 70,000, which increased to 110,000 in 2015. The well-regarded university teaching hospital, along with other hospitals in the city are now key economic drivers of the city. Due to the availability of relatively cheap space in the former port areas, the cultural sector has grown, providing 10,000 jobs, in fields such as art, film, and architecture. In recent years the city has completed long-term infrastructure and quality of life projects such as the central train station, the Market Hall (Figure 10.5), new and upgraded public spaces, and new quality housing. The city was awarded European City of the Year in 2015 by the Academy of Urbanism. Tourists are discovering the city; in 2014 there was a 13 percent increase in tourism.

Demographics

Between 1985 and 1995, the population increased slowly to 598,000, followed by years of alternating decline and growth. Since 2008 the population has risen annually to reach 624,815 at beginning of 2015.[5] The most remarkable change is the mixed background of the population. In 2014, the ethnicity of the population was as follows: Non-Western (228,556), Western (71,128), and Dutch (316,635), with every indication that this trend will continue.

Physical Form and Conditions

The major physical change in 2015 is that many companies left the city ports and moved westward. A number of the former industrial and port areas, such as Lloydpier, Mullerpier, Entrepotgebied, Wilhelminapier, and Katendrecht have been redeveloped as mixed-use

Figure 10.5 The covered Market Hall designed by MVRDV, which opened in 2014
Source: Photo by Ossip van Duivenbode, courtesy of the City of Rotterdam.

districts with new waterfront amenities. As a result, Rotterdam, long known for being an unattractive city, has begun to attract more highly educated people to the city center. Successful recent experiments such as do-it-yourself renovations by individual homeowners of deteriorated housing stock owned by the municipality and housing corporations has led to a resurgence of decent and affordable housing for young people and families, especially in the city center and surrounding neighborhoods on the north and south bank of the river. Unlike many cities in Europe and North America, Rotterdam regards gentrification (in moderation) as a good thing and actively supports the process. Another interesting development is that the environmental quality of the city has improved over the years. For example, the air quality has improved measurably: particulate matter with a diameter of 10 micrometers or less (PM10) fell from 43 micrograms per cubic meter in 1985 to 25 micrograms per cubic meter in 2008. The health impact measured in increased life expectancy shows an average gain of twelve months per person.[6]

Transformation of the City (1985–2015)

After 1985, there was a new appreciation of the city center. The first step in its transformation was mixed-use development followed by the reintroduction of downtown residents. Prior to 1985, new housing was constructed in large-scale urban expansions mainly in Rotterdam South and in new suburbs surrounding the city center. Quality of life and environmental considerations were not common concepts at that time and the city center neighborhoods were not in demand. It was easier to simply build a certain number of units in new or redeveloped buildings outside the city center. However, in the early 1990s, the city embraced the river again and improved access to the south bank with the construction of a new city icon, the Erasmus Bridge. This was followed by the development of the Kop van Zuid neighborhood on the south bank, a mixed-use development, thus expanding the city center to include both sides of the river.

City Center

The town council looked for ways to get rid of the barren, cold image of the town center. Cultural amenities were missing. In the 1970s, no high-rise construction was permitted and, as a result, few people lived downtown. After 1985, the policies changed, permitting high-rise construction, which led to the construction of several apartment buildings. Within a few years the Rotterdam skyline changed dramatically. Slowly, the city regained allure. Downtown Rotterdam was nicknamed "Manhattan on the Maas." However, life at street level did not improve at first. After the city implemented a comprehensive public space strategy, public life became vibrant. The new skyscraper city now had a "ground scraper" strategy.[7, 8]

With more people living in the city center and better public spaces, the next step was to develop vacant and under-utilized land. In 2014, the covered Market Hall, embedded in a new public space, transformed the city center and garnered international attention (Figure 10.5). A new train station opened, connecting at a beautiful public square and featuring designated lanes for walking and biking. Over 6,000 bikes can be parked below the station. New metro lines to The Hague were built as well as high-speed rail (TGV) connections to Schiphol Airport, Amsterdam, Brussels, and Paris.

Figure 10.6 Green walkways in the city center
Source: Photo by Rotterdam partners, courtesy of the City of Rotterdam.

Rotterdam South (Rotterdam Zuid)

In the 1980s and 1990s, the city's goal was to reverse the trend of people leaving the city. The redevelopment of abandoned port areas near the city center offered the perfect opportunity. Rotterdam Zuid's redevelopment began in 1994 with the Kop van Zuid neighborhood on the south bank. The Erasmus Bridge, built from 1993–1996 became a showcase of the new image of Rotterdam, inspiring renewed civic pride (Figure 10.7). The city center now extends to both sides of the river with bars, restaurants, theatres, schools, office buildings, as well as middle and upper class housing. The Luxor Theater and a new courthouse were also built on the south bank.

In the older neighborhoods of the south bank, the regeneration processes of the 1970s and 1980s were only marginally successful. Within two decades the houses were outdated compared to the new houses built in the surrounding suburbs. In 2011, the municipality of Rotterdam and the national government, along with Rotterdam South's housing associations, educational institutions, businesses, and health care institutions signed the National Program Rotterdam South. The program's goal is to improve the quality of life in Rotterdam South. Their approach is not only to focus on the typical physical and social problems, but also to give attention to the young population, particularly their potential, ambitions, and opportunities. This led to a number of successful initiatives such as the public private partnership to renew the center, "Hart van Zuid."

For the long-term improvement of housing, the municipality, together with housing associations, established a home owners' association in 2010. This organization supports residents by setting up a system with reserves and resources for future management and maintenance of the housing. There are also creative initiatives in public schools, such as judo, philosophy, engineering, care giving, and cooking classes to expand the students' talents and develop new skills, while also expanding their interests and career options. This

Figure 10.7 Erasmus Bridge and part of Kop van Zuid area on the South Bank
Source: Photo by Ossip van Duivenbode, courtesy of the City of Rotterdam.

dual approach to improve both housing and education concurrently and holistically will improve living conditions and the workforce in Rotterdam South.

BoTu (Bospolder Tussendijken)

Between 1985 and 2005, the municipality collaborated with the local housing associations to lead urban and social renewal efforts in BoTu. Existing housing was renovated and new public housing was built, but the retail areas declined. After the economic crisis of 2008, it was clear that the municipality and housing associations could not manage the transformation themselves in mixed-use districts like BoTu. Thankfully a local bank, together with the municipality and the housing associations, formed a new partnership to strengthen the local economy. This public/private partnership became the model for the overall development of the urban district. Citizens and businesses participate actively, without large government subsidies. The traditional parties in neighborhood development, municipalities and housing associations, now play a much more modest role that includes creating opportunities for new private sector participants.

For example, in BoTu, the bank, the housing association, and the city, along with local entrepreneurs and residents, formed the Delfshaven Cooperative. The goal is to create long-term and lasting value through entrepreneurship in the neighborhood. The approach is to empower existing residents and attract new residents who are more educated and with higher incomes. A few large companies from outside the district have invested in the initiative. It was agreed that a certain percentage of revenue goes into a "district fund." The fund supports the local Delfshaven Cooperative that finances entrepreneurial activities aimed at: strengthening the local economy; increasing the attractiveness of the area; and improving the quality of life of residents in the neighborhood. Examples of such funded activities in the district include:

- The Cooperative has started a cooperative development project. Together with residents and local entrepreneurs, ideas and actions are developed to incrementally increase the attractiveness of one of the sub-areas in BoTu (Schans-Watergeusarea).
- A health insurance company plans to offer sports and exercise opportunities, an investment in preventive care. The goal is to see a decrease of 7 percent in health care costs as evidenced by a similar strategy in Utrecht.
- The Cooperative is also working to eliminate blight, and is actively engaged in finding new uses for empty buildings to enhance the economic and social vitality of BoTu.

The Rotterdam Climate Initiative (RCI)

The Rotterdam Climate Initiative (RCI) was created in 2007 as a joint effort of the City of Rotterdam, the Port Authority, the employers' organization (Deltalinqs), and the Environmental Protection Agency (DCMR). It established a goal to achieve a 50 percent carbon dioxide reduction by 2025, while continuing to stimulate the economy and improve quality of life. The RCI goal is fully integrated with Rotterdam planning, policy-making, and actions. The City of Rotterdam has developed an online energy atlas showing the potential for renewables based on an energy potential mapping method.[9] This data is being used in energy scenario planning and for the roll-out of district heating,[10] as well as serving as a roadmap for reaching the city's goal of being a livable and low carbon city.[11]

After the 2005 International Architecture Biennale Rotterdam on flooding, the city focused strongly on resilience and climate adaptation. The "sponge function" of the city is being restored with new measures, which contain rainwater where it falls, stores it, and allows it to drain slowly away. This "blue adaptation" improves the environment and attracts new investments. For example, in "Zomerhofkwartier" (ZoHo) private initiatives such as rain gardens, polder roofs, and rain(a)way paving have been installed with great success. These techniques and tools, along with public initiatives such as a new public square with a storage capacity of 1.7 million liters (450,000 US gallons), will lead eventually to a flood-resilient city district.

Businesses are benefitting from the increased focus on climate adaptation, mitigation and sustainable urban development, as well as from the growing international profile of Rotterdam as a sustainable city. At present, there are approximately 3,600 jobs in the region directly linked to climate change adaptation. Many businesses in the maritime, engineering, and delta technology sectors in Rotterdam have good future prospects as a result of these efforts.

What Went Right?

The city has been, and continues to be, a laboratory for new urban practices and innovative developments. The hands-on approach by citizens, combined with traditional long range planning by the municipality, gave the city an excellent development framework, as well as the ability and means to implement projects quickly.

Modern Architecture and Planning

The continuous expansion of the port westward, coupled with investments by 1920s industrialists, fostered an early interest in modern architecture. Today, the city has the largest cluster of architecture and planning firms in the Netherlands, many with strong international practices. The architecture and built environment faculty of Delft University of Technology is also an asset. The first International Architecture Biennale Rotterdam (IABR) was held in 2003. The 2005 Biennale focused on flooding and was the impetus for Rotterdam's Water Plan 2035 that brought together long-range planning and local solutions, not just for water, but also to improve the overall quality of life in the city. The so-called "Dutch Water Approach" exhibited at IABR 2005 led to the Dutch Dialogues in New Orleans after Hurricane Katrina and to New York's recent Rebuild by Design strategy after Hurricane Sandy. All major plans in Rotterdam now begin by solving water issues while improving social conditions, housing quality, public space, and economic benefits.

Biking and Public Transport

Public transport is within a five to ten minute walk for 97 percent of the population. As in all Dutch cities, biking is a main mode of transportation. Delft, which has close to a 40 percent modal split for biking, has the highest percentage in the world, with Amsterdam not far behind. However, Rotterdam had only a 14 percent modal split in 2005. Building a car-oriented city center and the road system to support the rest of the city and the port functions were the top priority for many years. However, in the last decade Rotterdam has slowly become more bicycle- and pedestrian-friendly with investments in walkways, bike lanes, and biking highways. The city also launched a special program, Child Friendly City, that includes building playgrounds and sport facilities near housing so children can walk and bike safely. A recent study showed that Rotterdam has the highest number of kilometers of bike lanes per 100,000 inhabitants.[12] Improvements to biking infrastructure, combined with more people living in the city, led to a 20 percent increase in the modal split in 2015, which is projected to continue (Figure 10.8).

Figure 10.8 The modal split of biking has increased from 14 to 20 percent since 2005, and is still growing fast. Even in winter, biking is very popular.
Source: Photo by N. Tillie.

Do-It-Yourself (DIY) Houses

The Do-It-Yourself (DIY) housing project, running since 2007, gives young people the opportunity to invest in run-down houses in the city and become active participants in the redevelopment of problematic neighborhoods.[13]

What Went Wrong?

The bombing in May 1940 destroyed the city center. After the war the decision was made not to restore the city, as was done in other European cities, but instead to create a new modernist city with housing located outside the downtown area, which would be reserved for office buildings. This had a disastrous effect on the city, and it has taken many decades to make the city center bustle again with a rich street life.

Little attention was given to the needs of middle- and upper-class city dwellers, and so they relocated to new housing developments outside the city. As a result, by the 1980s, more than 70 percent of inner city housing stock was public housing. When workers advanced in their careers and earned higher incomes, they also left the city. Immigrants and the poor disproportionately occupied the housing left behind. Unfortunately, the city center's public housing, representing 70 percent of the housing stock, was deteriorating. Social problems proliferated, resulting in a diminished quality of life for urban residents. In recent years the percentage of public housing stock in the city center has dropped to

58 percent, which is an improvement, but still 10–15 percent higher than in comparable Dutch cities.

South Rotterdam (Rotterdam Zuid) was to be transformed with new developments like Kop van Zuid, but there is still a large socio-economic gap between the new and old areas on the south bank. The education level of residents in the older areas is relatively low, particularly among immigrants who have language deficiencies. An estimated 30 percent of immigrant students have a language delay upon finishing school. Overall, 20–25 percent of young people in South Rotterdam leave school without basic qualifications. In addition, the south bank has youth unemployment rates that are significantly higher than the city's average. More than 44 percent of all unemployed people in Rotterdam live in South Rotterdam where jobs are scarce. Only 20 percent of Rotterdam's jobs are in the south where 33 percent of the people live. Furthermore, public transportation to reach jobs outside South Rotterdam is inadequate. In South Rotterdam, fewer jobs are available within thirty minutes of public transportation than for residents in the northern part of the city. The 2011 National Program Rotterdam South was charged with finding a solution to this inequity.

Lessons Learned

1   Housing and cultural amenities in the inner city are essential parts of city life. It is not healthy to segregate businesses, cultural amenities, and housing.
2   Achieving city center densification requires that building in the suburbs and countryside comes to an end, that public transport remains cost-effective and accessible, and that the city's transportation modality includes more cyclists and pedestrians and fewer cars. There should be less demolition and more adaptive use of existing buildings, resulting in more sustainable development and efficient use of materials.
3   The Green Research 2008 (*Groenonderzoek* 2008) Report confirmed that more green space in the inner city is needed, as well as a greater diversity of green space and better design and management. Green space is useful for climate adaptation such as water storage and reduction of heat islands. An attractive green infrastructure in the inner city increases quality of life, which retains and attracts residents.
4   Biking, walking and public transport are important features of city life and will be more so in the future. In hilly cities, electric bikes provide another option.
5   A child-friendly city offers quality of life to everyone, young and old.
6   Using an open approach in dealing with challenges, getting everyone involved, and trying new ideas to create positive energy in the city. That leads to quick results, innovative ideas, quick implementation, and a more attractive city.
7   There should be no more top-down, blueprint planning as occurred in the two decades after World War II. Bottom-up initiatives are crucial in planning a city. Bottom-up and top-down approaches together achieve the best results.
8   Collect and use data on the city to understand the functioning of the city, as well as its specific challenges and opportunities. It creates a solid base to interact with stakeholders in the city and together they can detect new possibilities for developments that make the city more attractive.

Prospects for the Future

Rotterdam continues to focus on being a vibrant city with a high quality of life and a strong economy as outlined in the long-term vision plan of 2007. This means attracting well-educated people to the city and improving socio-economic conditions for those who are lagging behind. With the Rotterdam Climate Initiative, a low carbon footprint city and being climate-resilient have become important issues as the city continues to transition to more responsible and sustainable development.

A new district in transition is the CityPorts area (Stadshavens), an area of approximately 1,600 hectares (4,000 acres) between the Benelux Tunnel and the Erasmus Bridge. After the completion of the new seaport Maasvlakte 2, a large segment of port-related industry will move westward, away from the existing ports located just west of the Rotterdam city center. As happened previously, this will open up opportunities for new mixed-use regeneration projects with an emphasis on sustainable, innovative, and modern working and living environments. The city would like to host the 2025 World Expo in Stadshavens.

Using big data in city planning and development is becoming important. Rotterdam is a founding member of the World Council on City Data and uses the Council's standard protocol (ISO37120) to structure its data on city services and quality of life for international comparison. The Smart City Planner was developed to use global and local data to drive performance in the city.[14] It is now linking big data to city planning with the aid of scalar GIS, providing a fast and flexible approach to dealing with present and future urban challenges. According to the City of Rotterdam's innovation policy document, there is a growing need to link technology, data, government, businesses, and inhabitants. Under pressure from global issues such as resource scarcity and climate change, cities are looking for solutions to make their economies more resilient and shockproof. Metropolitan regions are becoming more densely populated, and the pressure to keep these areas livable in the future is high. To attract and retain talent and businesses, it seems crucial for Rotterdam to create an ecosystem where governments, institutions, businesses, and citizens can find each other and work together more effectively. Innovation is crucial for competitiveness, for existing economic sectors, sometimes at the end of their life cycle, as well as for the emergence of new businesses in the new economy. This requires structural changes in the city.

The transition to a new sustainable economy is also referred to as the Third Industrial Revolution by Jeremy Rifkin, or the Circular Revolution. In Rotterdam, the gradual transition to a locally distributed, renewable energy network will change society dramatically in the coming decades. The ability to generate local renewable energy, store it, and exchange it will turn the producer and consumer relationships upside down. It is expected that fundamental changes in communication caused by digital technology and the Internet will spread to the handling of energy, production of consumer goods and other applications in construction, health care, food, transportation, etc. This offers great opportunities for talent development, business, and employment at all levels in Rotterdam, particularly in the high tech industry with the proliferation of urban small and medium enterprises, such as technology companies, creative industries, and design firms.

In other words there is now the prospect of a new economy that is no longer based solely on globalization and big industry, but increasingly on small, locally organized networks of producers and consumers. Due to rising labor costs in low-wage countries, the decline in the cost of innovative digital manufacturing, and the decrease of logistics costs, the local production of goods will be more organized near end users, preferably in places that have a high quality and innovative ecosystem. Metropolitan areas will therefore increasingly develop into economic centers, not only for services but also for the production of goods and, increasingly, their own energy and food. For Rotterdam this could be described as the conversion of Rotterdam from a Labor City into a Maker City.

The Next Economy should not be just the domain of highly skilled nerds, but should provide an inclusive strategy which also offers opportunities for other groups, especially in a diverse, young, energetic city like Rotterdam. Therefore one of the focal points of

Rotterdam's strategy should be education, in order to anticipate the required skills for the next economy, which will likely include everything from vocational studies to universities.

An example of this approach has been applied on the former shipyard of the Rotterdam Dry Dock Company (Rotterdamsche Droogdok Maatschappij) in the port area, now known as the RDM Campus. Today RDM stands for Research, Design and Manufacturing. It has created an environment for research, education, and entrepreneurship in one location. Education is focused on innovation teams that work on real-life problems for private companies. Entrepreneurs can rent business space in the Innovation Dock. There is also a start-up incubator program for training and financing new businesses.[15] Another example is Roffab, an initiative that sets up micro-maker spaces in neighborhoods for children to playfully learn about new technologies like 3D printing. The bottom line is that all inhabitants of the city should be given the opportunity to take part in city life and in this Next Economy. It will be critical to prepare young people with the right education and experience. Innovation is not a goal in itself. It is the driving force behind stepping into the economy of the future. The 2016 International Architecture Biennale "Next Economy" will help Rotterdam make the next steps.

Notes

1 World Council on City Data, *ISO37120: The First Twenty Cities Celebrating Excellence* (Toronto, 2014). Available at: www.dataforcities.org
2 See www.pluspuntrotterdam.nl/cms/Uploads/Lezing_Jacques_Borger_21_april.pdf
3 See www.portofrotterdam.com/nl/Brochures/werkenindehaven.pdf
4 Gemeente Rotterdam, *Economische Verkenningen Rotterdam* (Rotterdam, 2015).
5 See www.stadsarchief.rotterdam.nl/bevolkingscijfers-van-rotterdam-vanaf-1868
6 See www.cephir.nl/files/pdf/Burdorf-HIA-CEPHIR2012.pdf
7 Gemeente Rotterdam, "Rotterdam Urban Vision, Spatial Development Strategy" (2007a).
8 Gemeente Rotterdam, "Visie Openbare Ruimte Centrum Rotterdam" (2007b).
9 S, Broersma, M. Fremouw, and A. van den Dobbelsteen, 'Energy Potential Mapping: Visualising Energy Characteristics for the Exergetic Optimisation of the Built Environment." *Entropy* 15(2) (2013): 490–506.
10 A. van den Dobbelsteen, K. Wisse, D. Doepel and N. Tillie, "REAP2: New Concepts for the Exchange of Heat in Cities." *Proceedings of SASBE 2012* (São Paulo: 2012).
11 N. Tillie, A. van den Dobbelsteen, and S. Carney, "A Planning Approach for the Transformation into Low-Carbon Cities." In S. Lehmann, ed. *Low Carbon Cities* (London: Earthscan, 2014).
12 World Council on City Data, *ISO37120.*
13 N. Tillie, M. Aarts, M. Marijnissen, et al. "Rotterdam People Make the Inner City, Densification Plus Greenification = Sustainable City" (Rotterdam: Mediacenter, 2012).
14 N. Tillie, and R. Heijden, *Rotterdam's Smart City Planner: Using Local and Global Data to Drive Performance* (London, ON: Public Sector Digest, 2015).
15 B. Hooijer and G. Muris, "IRDM Campus: An innovative learning and working environment in the Port of Rotterdam" (Rotterdam, 2009).

11 Ruhr Region Case Study

Michael Schwarze-Rodrian

Introduction

The remaking of the post-industrial cities of the Ruhr region between 1985 and 2015 involved massive changes, a wide range of new strategies and projects, and a steady and still ongoing process to transform the economy and the living conditions in each city and the region at large. The current initiatives are *Sustainable Ruhr Region* and *Knowledge Region Ruhr*. The next big initiative will be *Climate Expo NRW 2022*. Symbolically, the last three remaining hard coal mines in the Ruhr region will close in 2018. However, redevelopment in the Ruhr region did not mean saying goodbye to the past. Rather, over the past thirty years, industrial heritage has been the root and the basis for the future of the Ruhr region. Today, former factories, steelworks, coal mines, mining heaps, and heavy industry train tracks are the anchor points of the Route of Industrial Heritage Ruhr region, a 250-mile tour with 5 million visitors per year, something that was unimaginable in 1985.

A group of independent cities in Western Germany form the Ruhr region, in the state of North Rhine-Westphalia, which includes fifty-three cities and four districts (comprised of smaller towns) with a total population of 5 million. The region covers an area of 72 miles from east to west and 41 miles from north to south (2,950 square miles) (Figure 11.1). It is the largest urban agglomeration in Germany and the fifth largest in Europe. There has never been one dominant or ruling city in the Ruhr region. None of the cities has a major state or federal government center, harbor, or military base. The cities all grew and prospered together with a strong regional industrial base of steel-making and coal mining, and they all shared the problems of the severe decline of that industrial base in the 1980s. Cooperation and competition are skills that entrepreneurs, engineers, and workers in the Ruhr region have learned and incorporated in more than 150 years of industrial development. Similarly, strategic cooperation of the cities has been a key element in the successful regeneration of the Ruhr region.

In 1920, a regional organization with the task of looking after the urbanization of these independent cities was founded, *Siedlungsverband Ruhr Regionkohlenbezirk* (*SVR*). The SVR was the first regional assembly of cities in Germany—a pioneer in regional planning. The organization exists today as the *Regionalverband Ruhr Region* (*RVR*). The RVR is a planning institution financed and politically controlled by the cities of the Ruhr region and based on the laws and regulations of North Rhine-Westphalia. However, it is not a part of state government but is rather a bottom-up instrument for inter-municipal cooperation and to deliver regional strategies and projects. The mayors of the eleven largest cities and the directors of the four districts are voting members in the Regional Assembly Ruhr of the RVR that today includes 138 political parliamentarians, delegated from the city councils.

Figure 11.1 The Ruhr Region and cities
Source: Image courtesy of Regionalverband Ruhr region (RVR).

In the 1980s, the Ruhr region, like most industrial regions in Europe and North America, suffered a precipitous economic decline. The causes were many: structural change in the economy from manufacturing to service; the worldwide crises in the steel industry; declining demand for German coal; global competition for commodity manufacturing, such as iron and steel; and unfavorable conditions for the emergence of new industries. The Ruhr region had to adapt and change or it would continue to decline. For sixty years the Ruhr region has been undergoing structural change with different strategies and policies (some successful, some not) imposed by changing governments (some effective, some not). A regional consensus between local, regional, and national government leaders, the private companies, the unions, and the people has managed to cope with the industrial decline and the resultant transformation of the economy.

A series of structural policies, interventions, and tools—including subsidies and public funding—by the European Union, the Federal Republic of Germany and the State of North Rhine-Westphalia supported the transformation of the Ruhr region, beginning in the 1960s and 1970s. By the 1980s these interventions and financial supports were gradually reviving the changing regional economy city-by-city, project-by-project, and phase-by-phase. The remaking of the cities of the Ruhr region has always been and continues to be a cooperative and pragmatic process, epitomized by "learning by doing."

Then, in 1985, the unexpected happened, as economic forces began to deeply impact the region. The government announced that there would be no continued demand for a strategic German coal reserve in the Ruhr region by 2015. This was followed by the government's decision in 2011 to discontinue atomic energy production in Germany. Finally, RWE, the largest German energy supplier, divested itself of its coal-based and nuclear-based power plants in order to focus on energy network management and renewable energy. The Ruhr region fell victim to these decisions and was greatly challenged to overcome them.

Great strides were made in the transformation of the Ruhr region, but many displaced workers did not find new jobs and not all declining neighborhoods were revived. Long-term unemployment rates—concentrated in poor neighborhoods—remain a concern. Social, economic, and environmental inequity continues to be a challenge. Inequality differs from city to city but it remains linked to the overall prosperity of the Ruhr region. There is a shortfall between the public spending required for economic and physical change and inadequate revenue from local taxes. Finally, the population is changing, becoming more culturally diverse with immigration, and, like other countries in Europe, the population is aging with lower birth rates and longer life expectancies.

Brief History of the Region

The Ruhr River gave its name to the largest industrialized agglomeration in Germany. Three rivers—the Ruhr, the Emscher, and the Lippe—flow east to west into the Rhine River. A medieval trade route, the Hellweg, connected numerous small towns in the Ruhr region before the Industrial Revolution. Larger cities like Duisburg, Bochum, and Dortmund had no more than 5,000 inhabitants at the end of the eighteenth century. The population of the Ruhr region grew with its expanding industrial base from 220,000 in 1818 to 2.6 million in 1905, to the peak of 5.67 million in 1961.[1] The population has declined steadily since the 1960s. This long-term trend was temporarily interrupted between 1987 and 1993, when more than 200,000 immigrants came to the Ruhr region—mainly as a result of the opening of the Berlin Wall.

Locks were built on the Ruhr River between 1773 and 1780 that transformed the river into a transportation channel for the emerging industrial companies. A rich geological hard coal seam comes to the surface along the Ruhr River. People have been collecting coal along the river for centuries. The seam runs north for 10 miles from the river but is deposited deeper and deeper until it reaches 4,000 feet below the surface. The invention of steam engines, pumps, and elevators allowed the mining industry to follow the coal north and go deeper underground. In 1804, 229 coalmines were operating in the Ruhr region.[2] By 1850, there were nearly 500 active coal pits. Overall there were 3,200 coalmines in the Ruhr region. The last three mines will cease to operate in 2018. So many mineshafts have been drilled over the years that the Ruhr region is perforated with holes like a Swiss cheese.

Early development of iron technology in the mid-eighteenth century was followed by major investments in coal mining, steel, weapons industries, and chemical industries. The Krupp Company began iron production in Essen in 1811. Other entrepreneurs and inventors followed, supported by a growing network of railroad lines, beginning in 1843 with the east–west track in the center of the region, the Köln–Mindener Railroad. Ironworks, blast furnaces, and mining towers—combined with water and air pollution—shaped and defined the cities and the urban landscapes. The companies located housing for workers near the coal pits and steelworks. Urban development thus followed and was adjacent to industrial development regardless of the social and health consequences.

Industrial growth was not linear but cyclical due to overcapacity, wars, economic booms and busts, the development of new technology, and the volatility of international markets. The Ruhr region was the armorer of Germany during World War I and World War II. After World War II, the rebuilding effort under the Marshall Plan began to restore the wartorn industrial heart of the Ruhr region. In 1968, the many competing coal mining companies of the Ruhr region, with the political support of the national and state governments, merged into one company: the Ruhr Regionkohle AG, now known as RAG Aktiengesellschaft.[3] However, the decline of heavy industry began not long after with the "coal crisis" of 1975, followed by a series of "steel crises" of the 1970s and 1980s.

A crucial decision was made to build new universities as well as public and private research facilities. Before the 1970s, the only post-secondary education available in the Ruhr region had been for mining engineers.

The Region in 1985

Physical Form and Conditions

The Ruhr region in 1985 consisted of a group of mature industrial cities at the heart of the urban agglomeration, surrounded by an attractive semi-urban and rural fringe. The small towns on the fringe were growing moderately (the beginnings of suburban sprawl), while the larger cities in the center were shrinking in population and employment.

Daily commuting from the fringe increased. Planners in the struggling industrial cities began to re-think their cities and their neighborhoods. In 1985, there was little time for grand regional plans because the ongoing economic crisis in steel and coal had destroyed the grand goal of growing the region to eight million inhabitants as had been forecast in the *1966 Regional Development Plan Ruhr*. Pragmatic planning became the norm, but at the same time many hoped there would be a comeback and that the days of industrial prosperity and full employment would return, following the temporary problems of the economic downturn.

The Ruhr region's cities in 1985 typically had a cultural and political downtown, based around a town hall and traditional shopping streets. Flowing out from the town center were residential neighborhoods with smaller commercial districts serving each neighborhood. Several cities partly converted their downtowns into pedestrian-only zones. At the same time new shopping malls were being developed outside the cities along the B1/40 motorway—first, in Bochum and then in Mülheim an der Ruhr. City centers and suburban shopping malls were in competition with each other, and the economic balance shifted to the shopping malls.

By the mid-1980s there was a growing concern about environmental conditions in the Ruhr region cities. New German laws and regulations set high standards for air pollution that required industrial companies to install better filters and technologies to reduce emissions and clean the skies of the Ruhr region. Contaminated soil was identified in the 1980s as an environmental problem. German environmental laws already protected water quality, air quality, and endangered species, but not soil—and especially not the soil under abandoned factories. Despoiled brownfields thus became a great fear and topic in national, regional, and local media and politics. The Ruhr region, which was beginning to deal with its smog and coal grime in the 1980s, nevertheless remained the dirty corner of Germany and environmentally dangerous.

The long-term coal mining demolished the hydrologic balance of the Emscher River system. After taking out millions of metric tonnes of rocks and coal, the surface of the flat Emscher area sunk, changing the natural drainage directions and capabilities forever. The surface has sunk in places more than 20 meters, leaving great parts of the densely populated urban Emscher area as polder areas, where electric pumps are running to keep it dry. The Emscher River runs between dikes and was misused as an open sewer for more than one hundred years. In the 1980, it became clear that coal mining would soon be finished in the center of the agglomeration, and that it was no longer acceptable to misuse the river. The first discussions about the need to rebuild the whole urban water system started at this time and led to the founding of the International Building Exhibition (IBA) Emscher Park in 1989.

A growing number of closed factories and abandoned industrial sites sat vacant. Owners were not willing to pay for decontamination because of the low sale prices for industrial land. Prospective new owners would not take on the financial responsibility either. In the Ruhr region, the problem was growing with vacant brownfield sites totaling 12,400 acres in 1985.[4] Knowledge of the danger of soil contamination grew worldwide and new strategies for soil-treatment emerged, such as the Superfund program in the US, which were applicable to the Ruhr region.

Another concern emerged in the 1980s, that of historic preservation. Fortunately the demolition of old mining and steel settlements had mostly stopped. There was a newfound national respect for historic towns and neighborhoods, especially the garden cities built for the miners and steel workers. This shift in public opinion and official policy came about partially because of massive protests against demolition in the Ruhr region as well as in other large German industrial cities, such as Berlin and Hamburg. New historic preservation laws and regulations were enacted to go along with the existing environmental protection laws, reflecting a new sensibility for the inherited urban fabric, cultural life, and natural environment. This approach became known as "Integrated and Sustainable City Development."

Demographics

The population of the Ruhr region in 1985 was stagnant at 5.2 million, down 480,000 from the peak of 5.67 million in 1961 (Figure 11.2). There was no expectation of population growth in 1985. Demographic change was not a major topic in the face of the larger problems of economic depression and job losses. However, the collapse of socialism in Russia and Eastern Europe in 1989 was not anticipated. East Germany (the German Democratic Republic, the GDR) and West Germany (the Federal Republic of Germany, the FRG) were still two separate countries in 1985. After the fall of the Berlin Wall in 1989, immigrants from East Germany and other former socialist countries in Eastern Europe made their way to the Ruhr region, which partially stemmed the tide of population loss.

Economy

The economic situation in the Ruhr region in 1985 was dire. The crisis in the coal and steel industries brought together the national and state governments, the cities, the mayors, the unions, the workers, and the managers of the companies to look for new perspectives and solutions. In essence, it was the beginning of a strategy for a complete turnaround.

In order to understand the economy of the Ruhr region in 1985, it is necessary to consider the broad consensus at the time that the cities would not be able to manage the decline and the necessary massive change individually. Local public budgets were too small to meet the needs of the globally changing industrial economy, such as investment to upgrade the infrastructure, for urban regeneration, and for social and educational programs. The regional government, North Rhine-Westphalia, was asked to help with expertise and, most importantly, with funding. Support was provided for physical improvements (e.g., urban redevelopment), social needs (e.g., training for new jobs), technology development (e.g., incubators for startup companies), and for environmental cleanup (e.g., soil decontamination). The state and federal governments also provided financial support to private companies to subsidize coal and steel production costs.

In 1985, the German Chancellor, Helmut Kohl, came to the Ruhr region, accompanied by national and international media, because workers were demonstrating to keep their steel and mining jobs. Steel plants in other parts of Germany, such as Bavaria and the

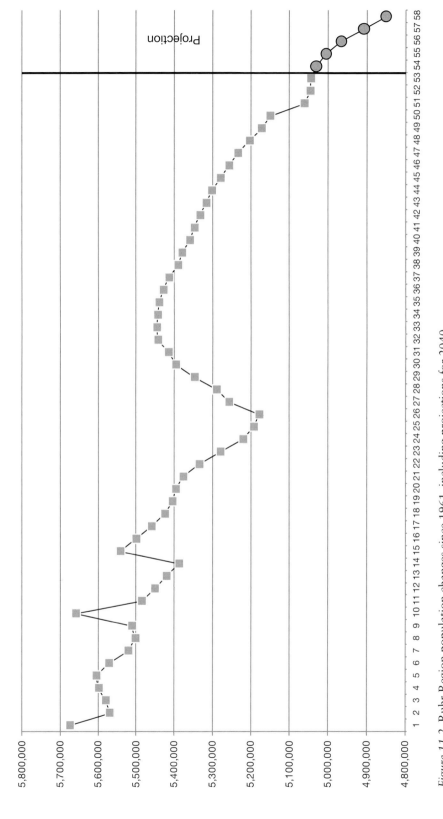

Figure 11.2 Ruhr Region population changes since 1961, including projections for 2040
Source: Image courtesy of Regionalverband Ruhr (RVR).

Saarland, had already shut down. A consolidation process in the German steel industry was underway. Most of the region's blast furnaces had closed. The remaining few were concentrated in the west Ruhr region, at the Duisburg-Rheinhausen plant on the banks of the Rhine River. The unemployment rate was rising and out-of-work workers remained unemployed for longer and longer periods of time.

In November 1987, the media reported on the upcoming closure of the Krupp steelworks in Duisburg-Rheinhausen. It precipitated a 160-day-long strike by workers fighting for 5,300 jobs. On December 10, 1987, a public demonstration became a milestone in the history of the Ruhr region with more than 100,000 people showing their solidarity with the steel workers across all the cities of the Ruhr region. In February 1988, a chain of 80,000 people held hands, connecting the steel plants in Duisburg-Rheinhausen to the Westfalenhütte steel plant in Dortmund.[5] Those public protests resulted in a compromise that included a phased closure of the Ruhr region factories in two stages between 1988 and 1993 and funding to retrain the displaced workers.

New universities in Duisburg, Essen, and Bochum were founded as investments in the new technology economy. It takes twenty to thirty years to be regarded as an established teaching university, just as it would take decades to manage the economic transformation of the Ruhr region. An extended timetable like that does not mesh with the short term of office of elected officials. Nevertheless, in the mid-1980s, the government of North Rhine Westphalia, working with local politicians, unions, and private industry, developed a new economic development strategy, but not without controversial debate about questions such as:

- How can we support technology development and what are the best instruments for a rapid economic success?
- What strong elements of the Ruhr region should be prioritized?
- Should the state and the Ruhr cities invest in the weaker links of the chain?
- What is the best approach to dealing with environmental, cultural and social issues?

The Region in 2015

Physical Form and Conditions

The sky over the Ruhr region is blue again, a campaign promise made by then Governing Mayor of West Berlin Willy Brandt in 1961 that at the time, was seen as highly improbable, if not impossible. But over time air pollution has been greatly reduced and contaminated soils were mapped, cleaned up or encapsulated. Brownfield sites are now being re-used by new and cleaner businesses, and have been converted into cultural facilities, historic landmarks, and parks. The urban landscape has become greener as symbolized by the internationally famous regional park system, Emscher Landscape Park. Abandoned railroad tracks have been converted into a connected network of bicycle trails. The water of the Emscher River is becoming clear again after one hundred years of misuse as an open sewer for industrial pollutants. It will be fully restored by 2020 at a total cost of €4.5 billion.[6] The strategy to develop and revitalize the weaker elements of the region is best symbolized by the International Building Exhibition Emscher Park (IBA) project from 1989 to 1999. Its successes have continued with new strategies and projects for integrated urban development.

Not only did the national and state governments help finance the transformation of the Ruhr region with economic development programs and funding, but the European Union also supported the redevelopment of aging European industrial regions like the Ruhr region through EU Structural Funds. Between 1989 and 2011 a total of €4 billion was invested in EU programs like Resider I & II, Rechar I & II, URBAN I & II, URBACT I & II, Goal II, the European Fund for Regional Development (ERDF), the European Social Fund (ESF), and HORIZON 2020. This effort continues today under the umbrella of EUROPE 2020.[7]

Demographics

In 2015, the population of the Ruhr region was 5.05 million inhabitants at a density of approximately 172 inhabitants per square kilometer compared with 34 inhabitants per square kilometer overall in Germany. Of those, 3.2 million live in the larger cities at the heart of the urban agglomeration and 1.8 million in the suburban and rural fringe.

The population is expected to continue to decline to 4.8 million in 2030 (Figure 11.3), not because people are leaving the Ruhr region, but because of the declining birthrate and the aging population that are endemic to all European countries. Nevertheless, some cities in the Ruhr region have developed proactive programs to attract new residents, particularly younger people with skills.

Economy

The economic transformation of the Ruhr region since the 1980s has been successful. The economy is no longer dependent on or dominated by the old industries. It is diverse with growing service and knowledge-based industries. By the end of 2012, the economic capacity of the Ruhr region included a gross domestic product (GDP) of €151.848 billion, a gross domestic product per job (GDP/job) of €64.891 billion and a gross added value of €135.924 million. The changes to the economy since 1980 are represented by Figures 11.4 and 11.5.

The economic strengths of the region are now in the chemicals, logistics, energy, health care, and emerging technology sectors. It should be noted that it is less a regional economy than part of the global economy. The region's large private companies transformed as well, merging and orienting their businesses toward changes in the global economy. Many companies that are based in the Ruhr region sell their knowledge and products worldwide. While active coal mining in the region will end in 2018, the manufacturing and exporting of mining technology continue. German electric energy production and distribution companies (RWE AG and E.ON Ruhr Regiongas AG) have their headquarters in the Ruhr region. Other major German companies (ALDI Süd and ALDI Nord, Franz Haniel and Cie GmbH, BP Europe SE, Hochtief AG, Schenker AG, and Evonik Industries AG) manage their global businesses from the Ruhr region. In addition, a growing number of small and medium sized enterprises are emerging, based on the historic strength of engineering skills, and supported by research being done at the universities and within corporate laboratories.

The Rheinhausen steel plant in Duisburg, where the massive strikes and historic demonstrations took place in the 1980s, has been converted into a successful logistics terminal, LOGPORT. Two German steel corporations, Krupp and Thyssen, merged in 1999 to become ThyssenKrupp AG, following two years of secret negotiations. The result was to close the Dortmund works and to consolidate all regional steel making in Duisburg. It was a defensive step to combat the arrival in Europe of Mittal, the large Indian steel company that was beginning to acquire European steel competitors. In 2005, ThyssenKrupp located its new global headquarters in Essen on an old Krupp plant site. The closed steel plants in the south of Dortmund were redeveloped into the Phoenix Project, where a new technology center operates on a former blast-furnace site (Phoenix-West) and a new

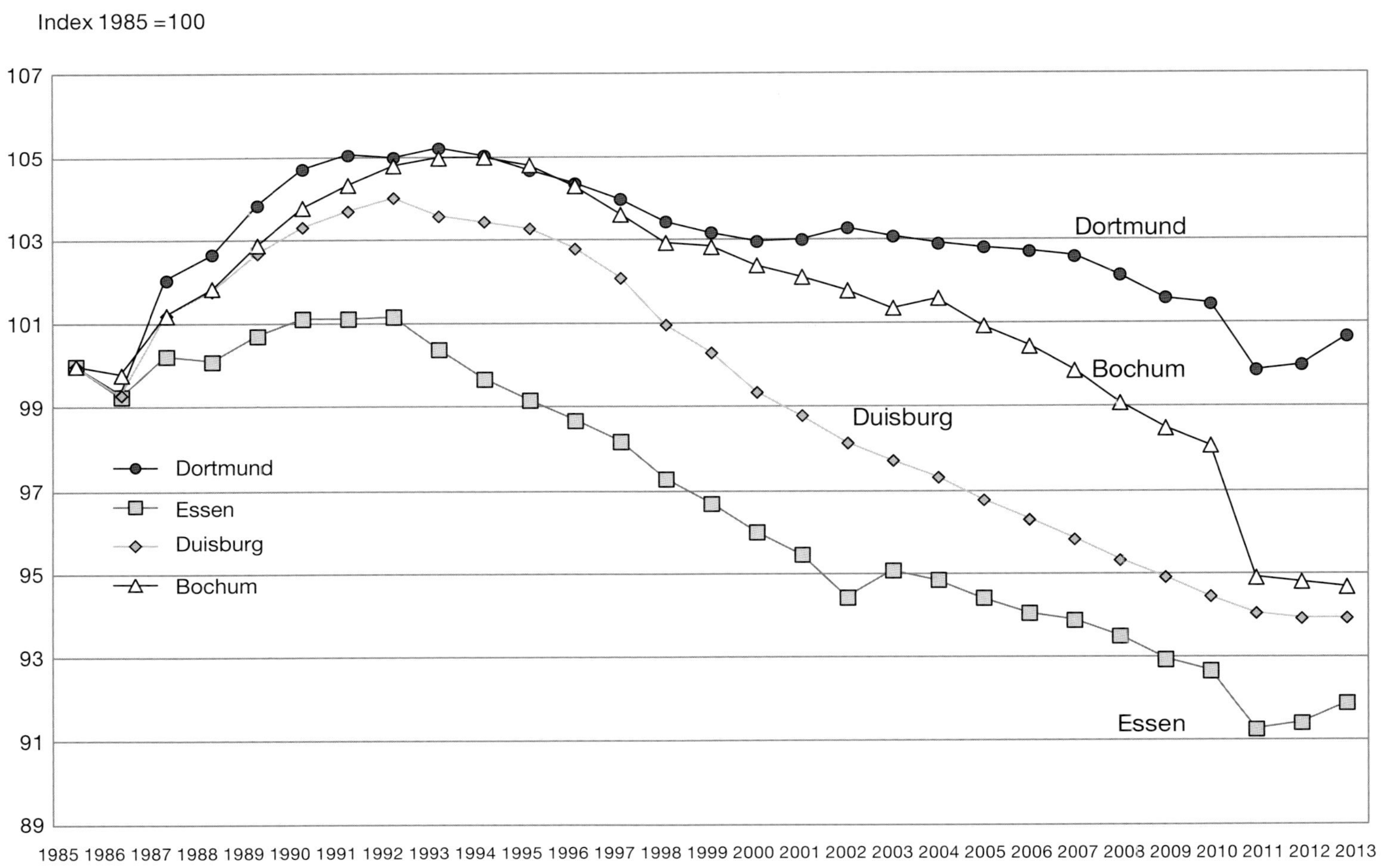

Index 1985 =100

Figure 11.3 Demographic development in the cities of Bochum, Dortmund, Duisburg, and Essen between 1985 and 2013
Source: Image courtesy of Regionalverband Ruhr (RVR).

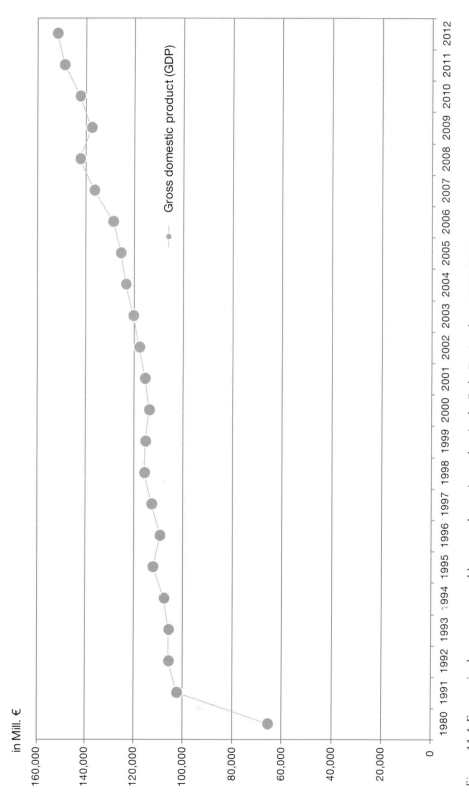

in Mill. €

Gross domestic product (GDP)

Figure 11.4 Economic changes measured by gross domestic product in the Ruhr Region from 1980–2012
Source: Image courtesy of RVR.

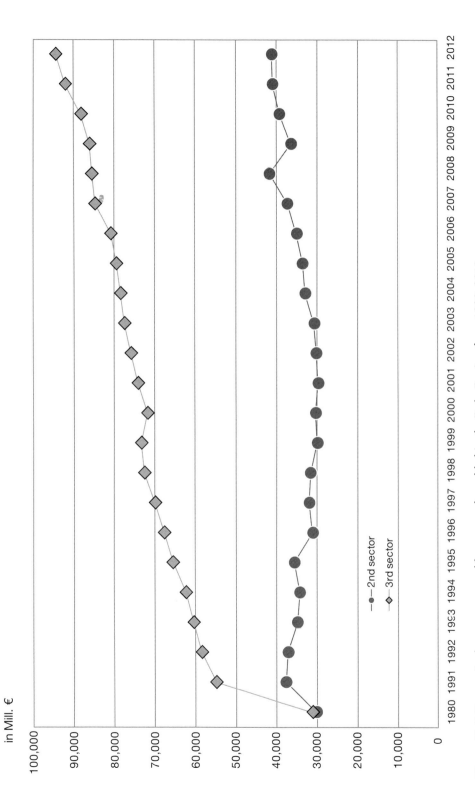

Figure 11.5 Economic changes measured by gross value added in the Ruhr Region from 1980–2012
Source: Image courtesy of RVR.

lake is surrounded by new housing and office buildings (Lake Phoenix). The lake is the pride and joy of Dortmunders, with thousands of people picnicking, walking, biking, and running along the shore on the trails every weekend.

Employment in the Ruhr region in 2015 was 2.21 million, broken down as follows: 10,000 in agriculture and forestry, 597,000 in manufacturing, and 1,609,000 in the service industry.[8] Since 1988, service jobs have exceeded manufacturing jobs, making the service sector the dominant sector in the economy.

Unfortunately the unemployment rate remains high overall in the Ruhr region, but conditions vary from city to city (Figure 11.6). For instance, cities in the Emscher valley are still suffering from the crisis of the 1980s and have not benefited as much from the transformation of the region as have other cities.

In April 2015, the total of unemployed people in the Ruhr region was 279,165, or an unemployment rate of 10.8 percent. The unemployment rate in Gelsenkirchen was 14.5 percent, in Essen 12.2 percent, and in Ennepe-Ruhr region district 7.0 percent. Despite major investments in training and social programs, the concentration of people in poverty has not improved as initially hoped. A new, more focused approach to reducing poverty is just beginning, including opportunities for training and personal development, the integration of different cultures (especially immigrants), and the revitalization of problem urban neighborhoods.

The development of new universities, specifically new universities of applied science, since the 1980s has been a success. In 2014, the Ruhr region had five universities, one art school (Folkwang), and ten universities of applied science with 256,000 students, compared to 112,000 students in 1985.[9] The University Alliance Metropolis Ruhr (UAMR) is a cooperative arrangement between all the universities focusing on achieving international excellence in teaching and research.[10] Cities have begun to embrace the program of the *Knowledge Region Ruhr* to support specialization in "fields of competencies." Several cities have adopted the concept of UniverCity, a strategy to forge strong economic and development links between cities and universities. This regional technology-driven strategy resulted in the development of technology centers and business incubators in the 1980s and 1990s. However, some critics say that not enough substance is coming from them, other than support of small and medium-sized enterprises.

Transformation of the Region (1985–2015)

What Went Right?

Below is a list of successful initiatives and projects between 1985 and 2015 that characterize the transformation of the Ruhr region. Several are explained in more detail following the list:

- Grundstücksfonds Ruhr region (1979)
- Regional Structural Policy of the state of North Rhine-Westphalia (NRW) (1980s)
- Structural Funds of the European Union (EU) (late 1980s)
- International Building Exhibition (IBA) Emscher Park (1989–1999)
- Emscher Landscape Park (1989)
- Renewal of the Emscher River system (1989)
- Ruhr Regiontriennale (2002)
- Thematic Strategies and Partnerships
  - Cities Region Ruhr region 2030 (2003)
  - Ruhr Region Touristic Agency (RTG) (2005)

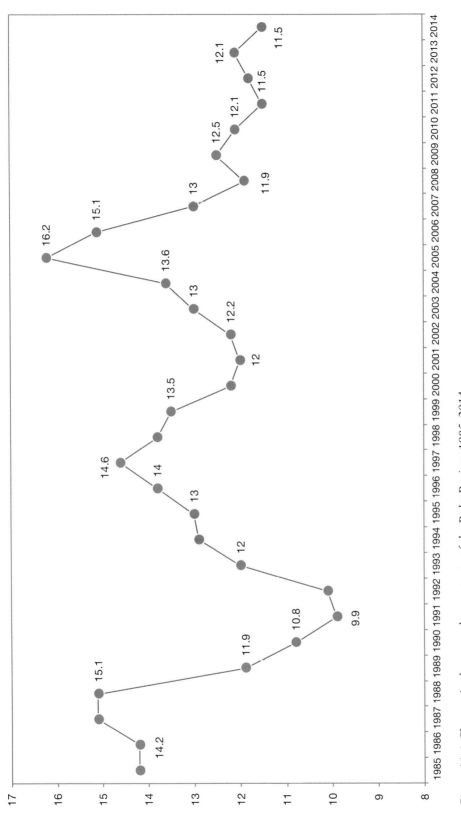

Figure 11.6 Changes in the unemployment rate of the Ruhr Region, 1985–2014
Source: Image courtesy of RVR.

○   Economic Development Agency Metropolitan Ruhr (WMR) (2007)
○   Concept Ruhr (2007)
○   Chance of Change (2008)
○   Knowledge Region Ruhr (2011)
● RUHR REGION.2010—European Capital of Culture (2010)
● InnovationCity Ruhr (2010)
● ClimateExpo.NRW 2022 (2013)

Grundstücksfonds Ruhr

Grundstücksfonds Ruhr, a unique environmental cleanup initiative for the Ruhr region, was created in 1979 by the state of North Rhine-Westphalia. It is a state-driven revolving fund that takes over ownership of contaminated brownfields and develops plans for their future public and private use. It works in cooperation with local city administrations, finances the remediation of the sites with state tax funding, sells parcels to new owners, and returns jurisdiction back to the cities. After 1984, Grundstücksfonds Ruhr began working in the entire state of North Rhine-Westphalia. By 2011, Grundstücksfonds *NRW* had assisted in the remediation of 2,670 hectares of land on more than one hundred sites in its thirty-two years of operation. It is operated today by a state-owned entity, *NRW. urban*. NRW intervenes only at the request of individual cities.[11]

International Building Exhibition (IBA) Emscher Park

The *International Building Exhibition (IBA) Emscher Park* was a unique workshop that operated from 1989 to 1999 to capitalize on the industrial heritage of the Ruhr region. It was a state-owned taskforce under the direction of Professor Karl Ganser. The IBA concentrated on seven activities:

1   Emscher Landscape Park
2   Redevelopment of the Emscher River system
3   Recreation at the Rhein-Herne Ship Canal
4   Industrial monuments and industrial heritage
5   Working in the park
6   Urbanism and new housing
7   New social, cultural, and recreation opportunities.

Seventeen cities in the northern urbanized center of the Ruhr region that were suffering from the decline of the old industries were invited to develop creative projects for an international building exhibition. Emscher Park focused on the missing qualities of urbanism, urban landscape, cultural identity, industrial heritage, and environmental health (especially of the Emscher River). "Change without Growth" became the new vision for the Ruhr region and the theme of the German Pavilion at the 1996 Venice Biennale.[12]

The Emscher Park initiative was limited to ten years and began on day one with an open invitation to professionals and the public to join in the workshop. It had wide participation and support in the Ruhr region—informal and formal, top-down and bottom-up, amateur and professional—including involvement of international advisors and artists. The key stimulants were: a competition of ideas; an open-minded workshop atmosphere; local and regional inter-governmental partnerships; interdisciplinary cooperation; and supportive media coverage. IBA Emscher Park FINALE '99 was a concluding showcase of project presentations, exhibitions, books, conferences, and tours.

Over one hundred projects were completed with a total investment of €2.5 billion: two-thirds public investment and one-third private investment.[13] Quality of implementation and execution was paramount. Significant projects included: Landscape Park Duisburg-North (on a former blast furnace site); Gasometer Oberhause (an exhibition room in a 100-meter-high gas storage tank); Tetraeder Bottrop (a steel tetrahedron sculpture of 60 meters in length on a coal mining hill); Richard Serra's sculpture (Bramme für das Ruhr Regiongebiet); a world heritage coal mining site and artifacts (Zollverein) (Figure 11.7); and the conversion of a former steelworks gas turbine hall into the festival hall (Jahrhunderthalle). These and other projects changed the view of the post-industrial past to positive and hopeful for the future and affirmed the link between city, industry, landscape, history, and culture.

IBA Emscher Park was a major production, professionally planned and managed. It was carried out like a great opera for regional, national, and international audiences. The IBA Emscher Park was and is a best practice for redevelopment. It demonstrated what was possible, that innovation can take place in the Ruhr region, decline includes the elements of a new beginning, and that industrial heritage can function as the identity of the region. Emscher Park was emblematic of the structural change in the Ruhr region and serves as an international example of the remaking of the post-industrial cities in Germany, Europe, and North America, of which the region is justifiably proud.

Emscher Park was a laboratory, a test bed, for innovative management and governance. This was new and uncharted territory for the cities and companies of the Ruhr region in the 1990s. It became a training ground for the whole region. However, Emscher Park was tailored to a specific economic period under historically unique political and physical conditions in North Rhine-Westphalia in the 1980s and 1990s. Although it is a model to be emulated, it cannot simply be transferred wholesale to other regions, cities, or countries. The ideas and methods may apply to other post-industrial cities.

Figure 11.7 Essen-Zollverein, 2011
Source: Photo by author.

Ruhr Regiontriennale

The *Ruhr Regiontriennale* was created as an international cultural festival of the highest quality. Planning and preparations began after the completion of IBA Emscher Park in 1999. Since 2002, the Ruhr Regiontriennale, in three-year cycles, has featured music, dance, and theatre performances and art exhibitions all across the Ruhr region. The venues are industrial sites and factories that are transformed into spectacular settings for cultural events. The intellectual driver of the Ruhr Regiontriennale is the concept of "Kreationen" (creation, or invention) that fosters the interdisciplinary productions of music, drama, and art. Up to eighty performances of thirty productions are performed during each year of the three-year cycle. At the center of the enterprise are regional, national, and international artists in dialogue with each other and with the industrial spaces. The Ruhr Regiontriennale is curated by a new art director every three years.

Gerard Mortier, then Director of the Salzburg Festival and later Director of the Paris Opera, directed the first festival in 2002. Mortier was fascinated by the challenge of transforming industrial buildings and landscapes into locations for performing arts and exhibitions. Jürgen Flimm was the second art director from 2005 and 2008. Willy Decker directed the third Ruhr Regiontriennale (2009–2011). Composer and stage director Heiner Goebels curated the fourth (2012–2014). Dutch director Johan Simons will direct Ruhr Regiontriennale 2015–2017.[14]

Cities Region Ruhr 2030

Cities Region Ruhr 2030 is a voluntary collaboration of the planning directors of the eleven big cities and the four districts of the Ruhr region established in 2003. A steering committee meets every two months to exchange information on current developments in each municipality. *Wirtschaftsförderung metropoleRuhr GmbH* (WMR), established in 2007, is the regional economic development agency. WMR provides the Ruhr region's cities with economic data, strategies and projects.[15] *Concept Ruhr*, also dating from 2007, represents the cooperation of forty-one cities (with nearly 400 projects) to ensure sustainable development practices in the coming decades.[16]

Chance of Change

For many years the German government subsidized coal production costs, thus closing the gap between higher German production costs and lower global market prices for coal. In 2007, the German government, after intense negotiation with stakeholders in the Ruhr region, decided to end the coal subsidies in 2018 due to new EU market rules and the changes in global energy markets. This provided a soft landing for the final years of the post-coal period in the Ruhr region and also allowed time for the necessary interventions in the few remaining coal mine cities. Since 2008, those coal-mining cities have been cooperating in an inter-municipal working consortium, *Chance of Change*, to prepare for the closing of the mines in 2018. The mayors of the cities and the state Minister for Economic Affairs signed a contract in 2014 with the CEOs of the coal mining companies to join in a public/private partnership with the responsibility of closing the mines and the subsequent cleanup, conversion, and development of the sites.[17]

European Capital of Culture 2010

In 2010, the city of Essen was selected by the European Union to become *European Capital of Culture*. Essen's successful motto during the competition against other European cities was: "Change through Culture—Culture through Change." There was agreement among all the cities of the Ruhr region that the Essen bid was to represent the region. If Essen won, the whole region would celebrate as Capital of Culture in 2010. Regional cooperation and trust were again the basis for success in the Ruhr region. Essen, and the Ruhr region, won the competition because of the EU competition jury's recognition of the value of industrial heritage as the basis for economic, social, and ecological renewal. The Essen bid was not just about creating something new for the year 2010, but rather built on the success of the Ruhr Regiontriennale, with the aim of celebrating the industrial sites that had been converted since the 1980s. Nearly 6,000 events were organized for the 2010 Capital of Culture year. Over 10.5 million people visited Essen and the Ruhr region in 2010, affirming for the people of the Ruhr region that their strategy for redevelopment based on industrial heritage was of international significance.[18]

Innovation City Ruhr

Another success was *Innovation City Ruhr*, a regional competition in 2010 to select one urban neighborhood of at least 50,000 inhabitants that would be converted by 2020 into a low energy consumption, energy-efficient, and low climate impact community, including a 50 percent reduction of gas emissions by 2020. The competition was won by the city of Bottrop and its approach has become the exemplar for climate change in the Ruhr region.[19]

What Went Wrong?

Like many post-industrial cities, social and economic equity remains a major issue in the Ruhr region as evidenced by:

- unemployment—too high and too protracted;
- critical financial situation of the cities—large public debt and low tax income;
- historic patterns of poor people living in struggling neighborhoods;
- struggling neighborhoods along the Emscher River;
- physical and social segregation between poor and rich areas.

The conclusion to be drawn after more than fifty years of state-driven and local economic and redevelopment policies in the Ruhr region, including the critical thirty years between 1985 and 2015, is that not all the problems of the local economy and neighborhood development can be foreseen, managed, or solved, even with the best intentions. Economic and urban policies in the cities of the Ruhr region were successful when they were accompanied by job training programs and attempts at social integration, but too many people are still living in poor and unhealthy circumstances, are unemployed, and do not have qualifications for jobs in the new economy. Strategies and programs that combine economic, urban, educational, and social transformations are still needed to meet the social and equity challenges of the Ruhr region.

The decontamination, re-use, and re-integration of the old industrial sites and the regeneration of deteriorated urban neighborhoods may take more time than most had hoped in the 1980s, especially those people at the lower economic levels of society.

IBA Emscher Park was a unique example of regional cooperation and resolve, but there were problems. Some are typical of such undertakings: too much on the agenda and unrealistic expectations for a temporary urban laboratory. The political and public reception of the IBA Emscher Park sometimes wavered during the ten years of the program and there was contention about costs and priorities. Nevertheless, goodwill and open and frank discussion of the controversial issues resulted in the ultimate success and worldwide acclaim of IBA Emscher Park.

Lessons Learned

The remaking of the Ruhr cities required a broad and ongoing consensus for action by local and state entities to transform the cities, the economy, the environment, the infrastructure, social conditions, and cultural life. The shared political strategy was to manage a soft landing with concern for the human scale that avoided a catastrophic crash of the economy and the social fabric of the Ruhr region. The result was a wide range of economic, social, and cultural programs, projects, and interventions, combined with progressive public policies that transformed the region. It was not just one remaking, but rather a continuous process of many pro-active makings, large and small, with a multitude of public and private partners working toward a common goal.

Cooperation

The Ruhr cities that jointly experienced the decline in the 1970s and 1980s joined together in the successful remaking of the Ruhr region. The cities were active players, sharing in both the triumphs and the failures. This ethos was in their DNA, that of cooperation and hard work to solve big challenges. The Ruhr cities are cooperating today in nearly every field of activity. A recent survey identified 370 ongoing inter-municipal activities, from buying fire hoses, to jointly sponsoring cultural activities, to strategic lobbying for support from the regional and the federal governments.[20]

Bad Image Lasts Longer

The image of the Ruhr region and its cities is still associated in Germany with "dirty," "ugly," "dusty," "industrially shaped," and "poor." The region learned that a bad image stays far longer in people's minds than a new and better reality. Germans from other parts of the country still expect to see grime, smoky chimneys, and air pollution as in the 1950s when white shirts could not be dried outside. Mayors and proud residents of the Ruhr region are accustomed to hearing from surprised visitors, "What a green city!" (Figure 11.8).

Prospects for the Future

In addition to shared regional efforts, each Ruhr city continues to make its own plans, from a formal new land use plan (e.g., Duisburg 2027), to a new local climate strategy (e.g., "Climate is a Home Game"—the campaign of the football city of Dortmund), to a new relationship between the university and the city (e.g., Master Plan UniverCity Bochum).

All of the Ruhr region cities are discussing energy efficiency, resource responsibility, climate change, and climate adaptation. The state of North Rhine-Westphalia has organized *ClimateExpo.NRW* to establish best practices for climate adaptation and climate protection in the Ruhr region by 2022.

Figure 11.8 Lake Phoenix in Dortmund, 2014
Source: Photo by author.

Another future project is *RadSchnellweg 1 (RS 1)* that in 2020 will be the first high-speed bikeway in Germany. It will set the standard for German bikeways just as standards were established for the German Autobahn system before World War II. The Ruhr region is also engaged in a public process to produce a new regional land use plan, *Regional Plan Ruhr*, by 2017.

The future aspirations of the Ruhr region include:

- improve social integration and equity;
- integration of green and blue infrastructure;
- cultural integration of the 160 nationalities who live in the Ruhr region;
- *Knowledge Region Ruhr*—integrating all people of the Ruhr region in life-long learning;
- sustainability, energy efficiency, climate-protection, and climate adaptation for a post-fossil fuel, post-carbon Ruhr region.

Notes

1   Detailed data on the history of the Ruhr Region development can be found at: www.
metropoleRuhr Region.de/pl/land-leute/daten-fakten/geschichte.html *(Regional internet portal of the Regionalverband Ruhr Region (RVR)*; www.route-industriekultur.de/fakten-hintergruende/geschichte-und-kultur/geschichte-des-RuhrRegiongebietes.html; website of "Haus der Geschichte des Ruhr Regiongebiets" an der Ruhr Region University Bochum (RUB)) (German Version), available at: www.isb.rub.de/index.html.de; www.isb.RuhrRegion-uni-bochum.de/index.html.en (English version); http://de.wikipedia.org/wiki/Geschichte_des_Ruhr Regiongebiets; www.RuhrRegiongebiet-regionalkunde.de/vertiefungsseiten/introduction.php (RIS Regional Information System – www.RuhrRegiongebiet-regionalkunde.de)

2   "Damals auf dem Pütt." In: *WAZ Extra*. Essen, 16 April 2010. (*Westdeutsche Allgemeine Zeitung*).

3   RAG Aktiengesellschaft "Running the current coal mining business." Available at: www.rag.de and RAG Stiftung "Endowment for the everlasting costs after the active mining 2018." Available at: www.rag-stiftung.de

4   NRW.URBAN (Agency for the Mobilisation of Brownfields), Available at: www.nrw-urban.de; Rolf Heyer, "Flächenrecycling bei gewerblichen Brachflächen. " in: *KommP Special, 3/2012*. See also: www.nrw-urban.de/fileadmin/user_upload/pdf_flyer___journale/downloads/ Flaechenrecycling_bei_gewerblichen_Brachflaechen.pdf

5   Arbeitskampf 1987 bei Krupp Rheinhausen. Available at: www.derwesten.de/thema/krupp-arbeitskampf. See also: www.rp-online.de/nrw/staedte/duisburg/vor-25-jahren-starb-krupp-rheinhausen-aid-1.3054777 and http://de.wikipedia.org/wiki/H%C3%BCtten-_und_ Bergwerke_Rheinhausen

6   Renewal of the Emscher River. Available at: www.eglv.de/wasserportal/emscher-umbau.html and http://de.wikipedia.org/wiki/Umbau_des_Emschersystems

7   EU Funding in North Rhine-Westphalia. Available at: www.efre.nrw.de/1_NRW-EU_Ziel2_ Programm_2007-2013/index.php ; www.efre.nrw.de/0_EFRE_NRW_2014-2020/index.php; www.nrw.enterprise-europe-germany.de/english.htmlb; www.europa.metropoleRuhrRegion.de

8   RVR, "Statistics and Data/Employment." Available at: www.metropoleRuhrRegion.de/ regionalverband-RuhrRegion/statistik-analysen/statistik-trends/erwerbstaetigkeit.html

9   RVR, "Statistics and Data/Knowledge & Education," Available at: www.metropoleRuhr Region.de/regionalverband-RuhrRegion/statistik-analysen/statistik-trends/bildung.html and www.metropoleRuhrRegion.de/land-leute/daten-fakten/bildung.html

10   University Alliance Ruhr Region (UAR). Available at: www.uaRuhrRegion.de/index_en.php

11   Rolf Heyer, (NRW.URBAN) "Brownfield Development" (Presentation 2011). Available at: www.immo.tu-dortmund.de/EIBURS/Medienpool/presentations_conf1/Presentation%20 Heyer.pdf

12   Kunibert Wachten, ed., *Wandel ohne Wachstum? Stadt-Bau-Kultur im 21. Jahrhundert = Change without growth?*/ German Pavilion - Biennale Venice 1996 (Wiesbaden: Vieweg, 1996).

13   IBA Emscher Park, *Erfahrungen der IBA Emscher Park – Programmsteine für die Zukunft – IBA Memorandum III* (Gelsenkirchen: IBA, 1999).

14   Ruhr Regiontriennale. Available at: www.RuhrRegiontriennale.de

15   Business Development MetropoleRuhr Region GmbH. Available at: http://business. metropoleRuhrRegion.de

16   Concept Ruhr Region. Available at: www.konzept-RuhrRegion.de

17   Chance of Change/Mining Site Contract Ruhr Region. Available at: www.konzept-RuhrRegion. de/konzept-RuhrRegion/wandel-als-chance.html and; www.konzeptRuhrRegion.de/fileadmin/ user_upload/metropoleRuhrRegion.de/Konzept_RuhrRegion/Veroeffentlichungen/Verein barung_FINAL.pdf

18   European Capital of Culture RUHR REGION.2010. Available at: http://archiv.Ruhr Region2010.de/en/home.html

19   Innovation City Ruhr Region. Available at: www.icRuhrRegion.de/index.php?id=3&L=1

20   Kooperationsdatenbank Ruhr Region. Available at: http://www.metropoleRuhrRegion.de/ regionalverband-RuhrRegion/kooperationen.html#ko_form

References

Aßmann, K. and Matzner, F., eds. (2010) *Emscherkunst.2010: eine Insel für die Kunst*. Ostfildern: Hatje Cantz.

Aßmann, K. and Matzner, F., eds. (2013) *Emscherkunst.2013*. Ostfildern: Hatje Cantz.

Auer, S. and Maier-Jantzen, H. (2010) *Unter freiem Himmel –Emscher Landschaftspark = Under the open sky*. Regionalverband Ruhrregion, ed. Basel: Birkhäuser.

Bandelow, V. and Moos, M., eds. (2011) *SchachtZeichen: Geschichte, Menschen, Ballone*. Essen: Klartext.

Beierlorzer, H. Boll, J. and Ganser, K., eds. (2013) *IBA Emscher Park Siedlungskultur: Neue und alte Gartenstädte im Ruhr regiongebiet*, 2nd edn. Wiesbaden: Vieweg & Teubner.

Bessen, D. and Grütter, H. (2012) *200 Jahre Krupp – ein Mythos wird besichtigt – Katalog zur Ausstellung im Ruhr region-Museum*. Essen: Klartext.

BMVBS (2011) *Die Zukunft Internationaler Bauausstellungen. Internationale Fallstudien und ein Monitoringkonzept.* Reicher, C. et al., eds., Bundesinstitut für Bau, Stadt- und Raumforschung (BBSR)Werkstatt: Praxis, Heft 74, Berlin: BMVBS.

Boesch, D. (2010) *Grubengold: Mythos Ruhr regiongebiet.* Essen: Klartext.

Bogumil, J., Heinze, R., Lehner, F. and Strohmeier, K. (2012) *Viel erreicht—wenig gewonnen – ein realistischer Blick auf das Ruhr regiongebiet.* Essen: Klartext.

Borsdorf, U., ed. (1994) *Feuer & Flamme: 200 Jahre Ruhr regiongebiet – eine Ausstellung im Gasometer Oberhausen.* Essen: Klartext.

Borsdorf, U., ed. (1999) *Sonne, Mond und Sterne: Kultur und Natur der Energie ; Katalog zur Ausstellung auf der Kokerei Zollverein im Rahmen des Finales der IBA Emscher Park.* Essen: Pomp.

Callwey, ed. (1999) *Internationale Bauausstellung Emscher-Park = IBA: a renewal concept for a region, Topos 26.* München: Callwey.

Dettmar, J. and Ganser, K., eds. (1999) *IndustrieNatur – Ökologie und Gartenkunst im Emscher Park.* Stuttgart: Ulmer.

Dettmar, J. and Rohler, P., eds. (2015) *Der Emscher Landschaftspark, die grüne Mitte der Metropole Ruhr region weitergedacht - Impulse aus dem Forschungsprojekt "Nachhaltige urbane Kulturlandschaft in der Metropole Ruhr region (KuLaRuhr region)."* TU Darmstadt - Fachbereich 15/Architektur, Essen: Klartext.

Emschergenossenschaft (EG), ed. (2006) *Masterplan Emscher Zukunft: Das Neue Emschertal.* Essen: EG.

Engel, K., Großmann, J. and Hombach, B., eds. (2011) *Phönix flieg!: das Ruhr regiongebiet entdeckt sich neu.* Essen: Klartext.

Frohne, J., Langsch, K., Pleitgen, F. and Scheytt, O. (2010) *Ruhr region - vom Mythos zur Marke: Marketing und PR für die Kulturhauptstadt Europas Ruhr region.2010.* Essen: Klartext.

Ganser, K. (1999) *Liebe auf den zweiten Blick: Internationale Bauausstellung Emscher Park.* Dortmund: Harenberg-Verlag.

Golombek, J., ed. (2011) *Schichtwechsel: von der Kohlekrise zum Strukturwandel. LWL-Industriemuseum; Zeche Hannover.* Essen: Klartext.

Günter, B., ed. (2010) *Alte und neue Industriekultur im Ruhr regiongebiet: ein Symposium des Deutschen Werkbunds auf Zollverein.* Deutscher Werkbund, Essen: Klartext.

Günter, R. (1999) *Im Tal der Könige: ein Handbuch für Reisen an Emscher, Rhein und Ruhr region,* 4th edn. Essen: Klartext.

Günter, R. (2010) *Karl Ganser – ein Mann setzt Zeichen – eine Planer-Biografie mit der IBA in der Metropole Ruhr region.* Essen: Klartext.

Höber, A. and Ganser K., eds. (1999) *IndustrieKultur: Mythos und Moderne im Ruhr regiongebiet ; im Rahmen der IBA Emscher Park.* Essen: Klartext.

Huske, J. (2006) *Die Steinkohlenzechen im Ruhr regionrevier: Daten und Fakten von den Anfängen bis 2005,* 3rd edn. Bochum: Deutsches Bergbau-Museum.

IBA Emscher Park (1990) *Machbarkeitsstudie Emscher Landschaftspark,* Emscher Park. Planungsgrundlagen Bd. 1., eds. Schwarze-Rodrian, M. et al. Gelsenkirchen: IBA.

IBA Emscher Park (1996) *Werkstatt für die Zukunft von Industrieregionen Memorandum II der Internationalen Bauausstellung Emscher Park 1996–1999.* Gelsenkirchen: IBA.

IBA Emscher Park (1999) *Erfahrungen der IBA Emscher Park—Programmsteine für die Zukunft IBA Memorandum III.* Gelsenkirchen: IBA.

Kiessler, R., ed. (2007) *Metropole Rhein-Ruhr region: eine Region im Aufbruch.* Oberhausen: Asso-Verlag.

Kiessler, E., ed. (2010) *Metropole Ruhr region Raum für Zukunft* [Ruhr region metropolis: region for the future]. 2nd edn. Oldenburg: Verlag Kommunikation & Wirtschaft.

Kilper, H. (1999) *Die Internationale Bauausstellung Emscher Park: eine Studie zur Steuerungsproblematik komplexer Erneuerungsprozesse in einer alten Industrieregion.* Opladen: Leske und Budrich.

Kommunalverband Ruhr region (1989) *Datenanalyse Emscher Stadtökologie. Bestandsaufnahme und Defizitanalyse ökologischer Daten im Planungsbereich der Internationalen Bauausstellung*, ed. Schwarze-Rodrian, M. Essen: KVR.

Kreibich, R., ed. (1994) *Bauplatz Zukunft: Dispute über die Entwicklung von Industrieregionen.* Essen: Klartext.

Kuhlmann, S., ed. (2010) *B1-A40: die Schönheit der grossen Strasse: ein Projekt im Stadtraum der A40 von Duisburg bis Dortmund.* Berlin: Jovis.

Kultur Ruhr region GmbH. (2004) *Ruhr regiontriennale 2002–2004.* Essen: Klartext.

Kurth, D., ed. (1999) *Laboratorium Emscher Park.* Dortmund: IRPUD; Dortmund: Informationskreis für Raumplanung.

Minister für Stadtentwicklung, Wohnen und Verkehr des Landes Nordrhein-Westfalen (1996) *Internationale Bauausstellung Emscher Park: Werkstatt für die Zukunft von Industrieregionen—Memorandum zu Inhalt und Organisation.* Düsseldorf: MSWV.

Mittag, J., ed. (2008) *Die Idee der Kulturhauptstadt Europas: Anfänge, Ausgestaltung und Auswirkungen europäischer Kulturpolitik*, Essen: Klartext.

Monheim, H. and Zoepel, C., eds. (2008) *Raum für Zukunft: zur Innovationsfähigkeit von Stadtentwicklungs- und Verkehrspolitik*, 2nd edn. Essen: Klartext.

Prossek, A., Schneider, H., Wetterau, B., Wessel, H. and Wiktorin, D., eds. (2009) *Atlas der Metropole Ruhr region: Vielfalt und Wandel des Ruhr regiongebiets im Kartenbild.* Emons Verlag.

Regionalverband Ruhr region (RVR) (2012) *Konzept Ruhr region & Wandel als Chance — Statusbericht 2011–2012.* Ed. Schwarze-Rodrian, M. Essen: RVR.

Regionalverband Ruhr region (RVR) (2014) *Konzept Ruhr region & Wandel als Chance Perspektive 2020*, Ed. Schwarze-Rodrian, M. Essen: RVR.

Regionalverband Ruhr region (RVR) (2015) *Concept Ruhr region & Chance of Change —Perspective 2020*, Ed. Schwarze-Rodrian, M. Essen: RVR.

Reicher, C. and Million, A., eds. (2008) *International Building Exhibition Emscher Park: The Projects 10 years Later*, TU-Dortmund, Fachgebiet Städtebau, Stadtgestaltung und Bauleitplanung. Essen: Klartext.

Reicher, C., Million, A. and Niemann, L. (2011) *Internationale Bauausstellung Emscher Park: Impulse: lokal—regional—national—international.* TU-Dortmund, Fachgebiet Städtebau, Stadtgestaltung und Bauleitplanung. Essen: Klartext.

Reicher, C. and Schauz, T., eds. (2010) *Die Wohnprojekte 10 Jahre danach / Internationale Bauausstellung Emscher Park*, TU-Dortmund, Fachgebiet Städtebau, Stadtgestaltung und Bauleitplanung. Essen: Klartext.

Reicher, C., Kunzmann, K., Polívka, J., Roost, F. and Wegener, M., eds. (2011) *Schichten einer Region: Kartenstücke zur räumlichen Struktur des Ruhr regiongebiets*, TU-Dortmund, Fachgebiet Städtebau, Stadtgestaltung und Bauleitplanung. Berlin: Jovis.

Rettberg, Jan Fritz (2012) *Staatliche Innovationsförderung und die Innovativität von Unternehmen: eine empirische Untersuchung vor dem Hintergrund des Strukturwandels im Ruhr regiongebiet.* Hamburg: Kovač.

Rossmann, A., Ganser, K. and Klemm, B. (21012) *Der Rauch verbindet die Städte nicht mehr: Ruhr regiongebiet: Orte, Bauten, Szenen.* Köln: König.

Rother, T. (2001) *Die Krupps: durch fünf Generationen.* Frankfurt/Main: Campus-Verlag.

Rother, T. (2003) *Die Thyssens: Tragödie der Stahlbarone.* Frankfurt/Main: Campus-Verlag.

Ruhr region.2010 GmbH (2010) *Ruhr region.2010 - die unmögliche Kulturhauptstadt: Chronik einer Metropole im Werden.* Essen: Klartext.

Sack, M. (1999) *Siebzig Kilometer Hoffnung: die IBA Emscher-Park - Erneuerung eines Industriegebiets.* Stuttgart: Deutsche Verlags Anstalt.

Scheuvens, R. and Taube, M., eds. (2010) *Der produktive Park: Denkschrift zum Emscher Landschaftspark ; anlässlich des Europäischen Zukunftskongresses "Unter Freiem Himmel—Under the open sky".* Essen: Regionalverband Ruhr region.

Schwarze-Rodrian, M. (1992a) "Emscher Landschaftspark—Konzept einer regionalen Entwicklungsstrategie." *Stadtbauwelt* 110(24): 1230 ff.

Schwarze-Rodrian, M. (1992b) "Internationale Bauausstellung Emscher Park—Werkstatt für die Zukunft alter Industriegebiete." In: Wentz, M., ed. *Planungskulturen*. Frankfurt/Main: Campus, pp. 120–6.

Schwarze-Rodrian, M. (1996a) *Parkbericht Emscher Landschaftspark*. Kommunalverband Ruhr region. Essen: KVR.

Schwarze-Rodrian, M. (1996b) "Interkommunale Zusammenarbeit: Voraussetzung für die Freiraumpolitik im Ruhr regiongebiet." In: Selle, K. ed., *Planung und Kommunikation*. Hannover: TU Hannover, pp. 220–3.

Schwarze-Rodrian, M. (1999) "Der Emscher Landschaftspark– von der Vision zur Umsetzung." In: *Laboratorium Emscher Park - Städtebauliches Kolloquium zur Zukunft des Ruhr regiongebiets*, Dortmunder Beiträge zur Raumplanung, Bd. 99, IRPUD, Dortmund: TU Universität, pp. 65–70.

Schwarze-Rodrian, M. (2004) "In acht Schritten zum Masterplan—Die Weiterentwicklung des Emscher Landschaftsparks." In: Selle, K., ed., *Kommunikation gestalten—Beispiele aus der Praxis für die Praxis*, Aachen: RWTH – Lehrstuhl für Planungstheorie und Stadtplanung.

Schwarze-Rodrian, M. et al. (2005) *Masterplan Emscher Landschaftspark 2010*, Projekt Ruhr region GmbH. Essen: Klartext.

Schwarze-Rodrian, M. (2008) "Metropole Ruhr region–Strategie voor een duurzame stads–en regionale ontwickkeling." In Metropolen, S&RO, No. 6/2008, Nederlands Instituut foor Ruimtelijke Ordening en Volkshuisvesting (NIROV), Rotterdam: NIROV, pp. 34–9.

Schwarze-Rodrian, M. (2010a) "Regionale Zusammenarbeit bestimmt die Zukunft der Metropole Ruhr region [Regional cooperation shapes the future of the Ruhr region Metropolis. " In Kiessler, E., ed. *Metropole Ruhr region - Raum für Zukunft* [Ruhr region metropolis - region for the future]. 2nd edn, Oldenburg: Verlag Kommunikation & Wirtschaft, pp. 102–8.

Schwarze-Rodrian, M. (2010b) "Ein günstiger Augenblick - Zur Positionsbestimmung des Produktiven Parks." In: Scheuvens, R. and Taube, K./Regionalverband Ruhr region, eds. *Der Produktive Park—Denkschrift zum Emscher Landschaftspark*. Essen: RVR, pp. 76—81.

Schwarze-Rodrian, M. (2011) "Stimulierung der eigenen Stärken - Annäherung an einen au sgesprochen komplexen Forschungsgegenstand." In: Reicher, C., Million, A. and Niemann, L. eds. *Internationale Bauausstellung Emscher Park: Impulse: lokal—regional—national—international*, TU-Dortmund, Fachgebiet Städtebau, Stadtgestaltung und Bauleitplanung, Essen: Klartext, pp. 16–26.

Tenfelde, K. (2005) *Krupp bleibt doch Krupp: Ein Jahrhundertfest: das Jubiläum der Firma Fried. Krupp AG in Essen 1912*, Essen: Klartext.

Urban, T. (2008) *Visionen für das Ruhr regiongebiet: IBA Emscher Park: Konzepte, Projekte, Dokumentation*, Stiftung Bibliothek des Ruhr regiongebiets. Essen: Klartext.

Wachten, K., ed. (1996) *Wandel ohne Wachstum? Stadt-Bau-Kultur im 21. Jahrhundert - Chance without growth?*, Braunschweig & Wiesbaden: Vieweg.

Wirtschaftsförderung metropoleRuhr region GmbH (wmr) (2008) *Konzept Ruhr region—Strategy for sustainable urban and regional development in the metropolitan area of the Ruhr region*, international edition, ed. Schwarze-Rodrian, M., Mülheim an der Ruhr region: wmr.

Wirtschaftsförderung metropoleRuhr region GmbH (wmr) (2010) *Konzept Ruhr region 2010—Umsetzung und Perspektiven*, ed. Schwarze-Rodrian, M., Mülheim an der Ruhr region: wmr.

12 Turin Case Study

Anna Prat and Simone Mangili

Introduction

Located on the western edge of a fertile plain that stretches from the western Alps to the Adriatic Sea, Turin is the capital of the Piedmont Region and, with population exceeding 900,000, the largest city in north-west Italy (Figure 12.1). The wider Turin Metropolitan City includes 2.3 million people[1] with a GDP of €58 billion in 2011.[2] The anchor of a primary city-region, Turin has important relationships with nearby Milan and Genoa, as well as with Lyon and Geneva.

Turin's history stretches from Roman times to the birth of the Italian state and the modern day. The city can boast having been the seat of the Savoy kingdom and a Baroque capital, the political and military driver of Italian reunification in the mid-nineteenth century, and the first capital of the Italian state. For much of the twentieth century Turin was the industrial capital of Italy and home to an enormous concentration of automotive and mechanical manufacturing firms and related industries. Together with Milan and Genoa, north-west Italy formed the "industrial triangle" that drove Italy's post-war economic miracle.

Today Turin is recognized for its scientific, engineering, manufacturing, and military vocations, a strong legacy of social activism, a progressive political and intellectual tradition and a significant artistic and cultural heritage. As the regional economic engine, Turin boasts extensive infrastructure including an international airport, intermodal cargo port, and high-speed rail links to Milan and eventually, with the construction underway of the high-speed European corridors, to other major cities across Europe. Turin is also the regional center for a variety of highly-skilled and highly-valued services, home to two universities counting approximately 100,000 students and is increasingly a jumping-off point for tourism throughout the Alps and the Langhe region.[3]

Like many other twentieth-century industrial cities, Turin experienced an unprecedented period of concentrated economic, population and physical growth from the beginning of the century to the 1970s. As increasing globalization ushered in an era of industrial decline, the city was left struggling with the legacy of the Fordist economic model, including its physical implications in a post-industrial context and the social and political dimensions of mass migrations. The challenges generated by these economic and social transformations, including the loss of a quarter of the city's population, were immense. And yet, through concerted and sustained remaking processes, Turin has made great strides reinventing itself and its economic *raison d'être* over the past three decades.

Turin's history is in fact marked by explicit city-making and re-making processes, from the city building of the Middle Ages to the capital making of the Savoy kingdom, the

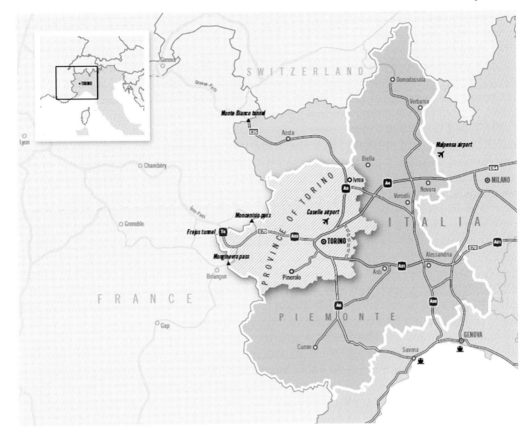

Figure 12.1 Map of Turin in Europe, Italy, and the Piedmont Region
Source: Map by Chiara Lucchini, courtesy of Urban Center Metropolitano Torino.

industrialization of the twentieth century and the innovation city of today. Building on this dynamic history and learning from the past thirty years of remaking Turin, the city is once again proving resilient and mobilizing to adapt to twenty-first-century challenges.

Brief History of the City

Turin's name is thought to derive from the original settlers of the area, the Gallo-Ligurian Taurini people. Rebuilt as the Roman fort city Castra Taurinorum in approximately 38 BC, after the collapse of the Roman Empire, it fell under the alternating sway of numerous regional powers and for the remainder of the first millennium did not gain in stature relative to other cities in the region. In 1046 AD, the city came under the rule of the bishopric of the Counts of Savoy, which would become the longest ruling monarchy in Europe. Under the Savoy regime the city's population began to grow but a true watershed moment came when Emmanuel Philibert moved the capital of the Duchy of Savoy from Chambery, France, just across the western Alps to Turin in 1563.[4] From this point forward, as the capital of the Savoy Empire for nearly 400 years, Turin gained significant political, cultural, and economic power.

It was in the seventeenth and eighteenth centuries that the city's historic core was developed and expanded in the Baroque style of the day, including much of the monumental architecture still in existence today. From their new capital, the Savoy regime so effectively consolidated their power that by the late nineteenth century they were in a position to lead the campaign to unify Italy, and in 1861, Turin became the first capital of the newly formed Italian state. This privileged position was short-lived. In the late nineteenth century Turin experienced another watershed moment in its history, a turn of events that would mark the city physically, economically, demographically, and psychologically for the next 100 years. That turning point was the founding of FIAT (Fabbrica Italiana Automobili Torino) in Turin in 1899, which ushered in an era of tremendous growth and full-scale industrialization (Figure 12.2).

FIAT and the broader automotive and mechanical manufacturing sectors and related industries grew exponentially, such that over the next seventy-five years the city was transformed. With the support of the Italian state, which recognized the national automaker as a strategic asset for the production of all kinds of military vehicles, FIAT survived World War I and then the Great Depression. Though FIAT suffered huge losses during World War II as its plants became strategic targets, the receipt of "an astonishing 38 percent of the German Marshall Fund's allocation to the entire Italian engineering sector," fueled FIAT's recovery and positioned it to become the driver of Italy's post-war economic miracle.[5] By the 1960s, FIAT accounted for 80 percent of Turin's industrial production, and employment in FIAT's Turin plants grew from roughly 45,000 in 1951 to 115,000 in 1971, not including approximately 30,000 white-collar workers employed by FIAT in the city.[6] In addition to the automotive sector, Turin's manufacturing base grew to include other transportation-related components, metal processing and energy sectors, as well as the more traditional textile sector.

As manufacturing and employment soared, the urbanized area of the city consequently grew dramatically, doubling in the thirty years from 1880 to 1910.[7] Growth continued at an unprecedented rate throughout the century and the urbanized area of the Turin Metropolitan Area nearly tripled between 1920 and 1990.[8] Fueled by massive migration

Figure 12.2 FIAT Mirafiori plant in 1945 before the city grew to surround it
Source: Image courtesy of Archivio Storico della Città di Torino.

from the less economically developed Italian South, the city's population increased from just over 350,000 to a peak of approximately 1.2 million in 1974.[9] The 1950s and 1960s saw the greatest migration, with average annual figures reaching over 50,000 per year.[10] By the end of the 1960s, Turin had Italy's third largest concentration of southern-born Italians, with a southern-born population surpassed only by Naples and Palermo.[11] Public administrations struggled for many years to provide services for new immigrant communities: housing conditions languished and schools had to operate two to three shifts per day in order to accommodate the growing student population (Figure 12.3).

Large tracts of land were occupied by FIAT's production facilities as well as by those of related industries such as steel and tire production. Transportation infrastructure was greatly expanded; the rail and road networks grew to connect Turin to the surrounding industrial and agricultural basins as well as other regional hubs. Working-class neighborhoods proliferated throughout the city and especially around the major industrial areas to the south, west and north of the city, while middle- and upper-class residential areas expanded in the center of the city and in the eastern hills.

This era also saw unprecedented growth in the cultural, education, and service sectors as well as significant steps towards internationalization. Hosting the Universal Exhibitions in 1884 and 1902, and the World's Fair of 1911, propelled Turin to global recognition. The city later mounted a huge celebration on the centennial of the founding of the nation, the International Labor Exhibition of 1961, also known as Expo '61. Expo '61 spurred the development of a United Nations campus, beginning with the establishment of the UN International Labor Organization (ILO) headquarters on the bank of the Po River in 1964, followed in 1968 by the opening of the UN International Center for Interregional Crime and Justice Research Center (UNICRI) nearby.[12] At the same time the universities expanded and Turin consolidated its role as the anchor of the broader Piedmont region in terms of institutions and services.

Figure 12.3 Temporary housing to accommodate the burgeoning workforce
Source: Image provided by Fondazione Istituto Piemontese A. Gramsci.

Such tremendous growth did not come without significant cost. Massive industrialization came hand in hand with environmental contamination and the expansion of the city into agricultural hinterlands, while migration on an unprecedented scale fueled social tensions. The same forces that were driving growth were also stretching the city's social fabric thin and Turin became ground zero for Italy's student, labor and political battles of the 1960s and 1970s. While heated confrontations between the labor and student movements and industrial powers culminated in massive strikes, political assassinations and terrorist attacks scarred the city and the nation. As the situation escalated, the global economic shocks of the 1970s, specifically the 1973 oil crisis, sparked the beginning of a national economic restructuring process that hit Turin's manufacturing base particularly hard. FIAT's restructuring in response to national and global forces signaled once again a watershed moment in the city's history.

The City in 1985

Physical Form and Conditions

Industrialization had transformed the physical city beyond recognition over the course of the twentieth century. The urbanized area grew at an almost uncontrollable pace as residential neighborhoods sprung up around new industrial plants large and small. To put this growth into perspective, the number of industrial areas within the city limits doubled over the course of the two decades following the adoption of the 1959 master plan, and grew five-fold in the first-ring suburbs (Figure 12.4). Taking Turin and the first-ring suburbs together, industrial areas occupied nearly a quarter of the total land area by 1980.[13]

Two other phenomena were having a direct impact on the physical transformation of the metropolitan area: the first was the progressive industrialization of the inner-ring suburbs over the course of the 1960s and 1970s; the second was the abandonment of large-scale industrial plants and facilities located in Turin, beginning in the late 1970s and through the 1980s. The industrialization of the inner-ring suburbs was in large part due to the relocation of mostly small to medium-sized industrial firms relocating from Turin to expand or upgrade production facilities. Relocation away from Turin left significant voids in the city's physical fabric, yet it was the concomitant closure and abandonment of the largest plants in the city that marked the turning point for Turin. For the most part, these larger plants were not being relocated to the suburbs where they would have continued to provide local employment, but rather were closed as a result of shifting national and international manufacturing geographies.[14]

By 1985, the closure of large-scale industrial plants and the abandonment of these areas were quickly becoming a dominant feature of the urban landscape. In 1982, production at FIAT's iconic Lingotto plant, perhaps the most recognizable symbol of Turin's industrial history was shut down. While attempts to quantify the scale of abandoned and disused lands vary significantly, by some estimates in 1989, 100 million square feet (10 million square meters) of abandoned industrial space scarred the urban landscape (Figures 12.5a and 12.5b).[15]

Many high-density residential areas had been hastily built around industrial sites with few public spaces and services. These neighborhoods typically housed working-class families, and local services often mirrored the production rhythms and cycles of the plants themselves. They often lacked more traditional neighborhood centers and were perceived as cold and isolated, given their limited communication and integration with the historic and institutional core of the city. Shutdowns, mass layoffs, and suburbanization left areas of social and economic blight across the city.

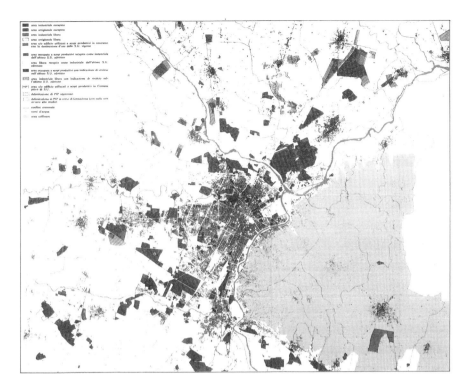

Figure 12.4 Distribution of industrial areas in the municipalities of the Turin metropolitan area in 1980
Source: Reproduced from the Relazione Illustrativa, Vol. III, La Struttura del Piano, by Gregotti Associati Studio (1993).

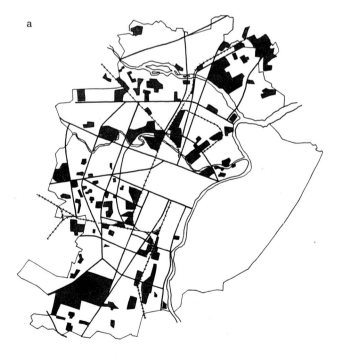

Figure 12.5 (a) Turin's main industrial areas in 1971
Source: Image provided by Dansero (1993).

b

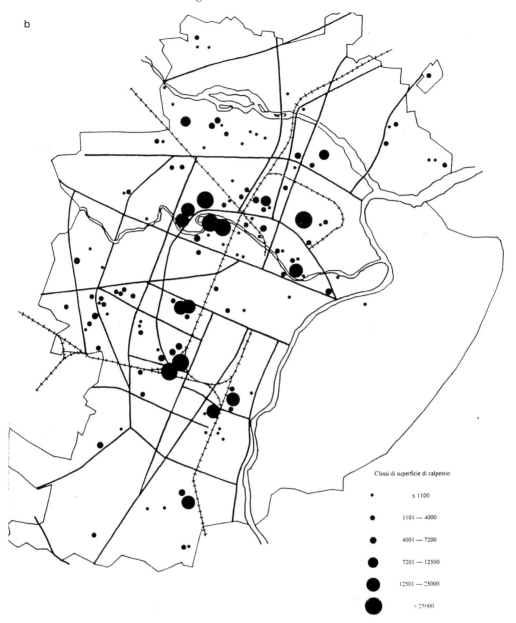

Classi di superficie di calpestio

•   ≤ 1100

•   1101 — 4000

●   4001 — 7200

●   7201 — 12500

●   12501 — 25000

●   > 25000

Figure 12.5 (b) Square meters of abandoned industrial areas in 1989
Source: Image provided by Dansero (1993).

The extent of social, economic and physical decline was such that even the historic center—
the baroque jewel representing the artistic patrimony of the city—had fallen into disrepair.
Once the symbol of Turin's regal past, the large public squares which characterized the
historic city were overrun by cars and the streets were choked with congestion, street crime
had become more common, and the ornate buildings were covered in soot and visibly
deteriorating. The spatial dimensions of social inequity became increasingly discernible in
the physical fabric of the city.

Demographics

Unparalleled rise and fall in population accompanied Turin's spectacular economic growth and decline. Fueled by immigration during the post-war economic boom, the city's population doubled over roughly forty years to peak at over 1.2 million in 1974.[16] As the prospects for Turin's manufacturing sector began to wane, by the mid-1970s so did the city's population. Over the two decades from 1971–1991 Turin's population shrank by 206,000, and then by another 97,000 in the ensuing decade to 2001 (Table 12.1).[17] The city's population reached a low point of just fewer than 900,000 in 2002 and has seen only minor growth since. Given the dominance of manufacturing in Turin's economy, the labor force was typically less educated than those of Italy's other major economic centers. Compared to Milan, Bologne and Rome, for instance, Turin continued to have significantly fewer high school and college graduates in 1991.[18]

Just as Turin's population growth during the boom years mirrored the industrialization of the city itself, increased industrialization of the first- and second-ring suburbs had driven commensurate population growth there. Consequently, Turin's population loss beginning in the mid-1970s coincided with suburban population growth and may well have reflected the shift in location of employment opportunity; while Turin shed over 300,000 people; the suburban population grew by approximately 150,000. Yet while suburbanization accounted for a good deal of the demographic shift, the overall population of the metropolitan area began to decline in the 1980s and the net population loss would change the city's social landscape dramatically.

Economy

Throughout the twentieth century, Turin's economy became increasingly specialized, to a point where heavy industry, specifically the automotive and transportation sectors and an array of related industries supplying energy, materials, products, design and technologies, progressively squeezed out more traditional sectors of Turin's economy, including the textile and clothing sector. Assembly plants, steel foundries, processing and production facilities for tires and other rubber components, electrical and mechanical components, paint, and finishes dominated the economy. The dominance of the automotive industry left Turin's economy particularly vulnerable to the oil shocks of the 1970s, which dealt a major blow to industrial production throughout Italy.

In addition to the oil crisis, several internal and external factors together conspired to reduce the competitiveness of Turin's economic structure. Social tension due to poor wages, job insecurity, and lack of affordable housing had been steadily rising throughout the 1960s and 1970s, resulting in major strikes and various factory shutdowns, costing

Table 12.1 Demographic evolution of the Turin Metropolitan Area from 1971 to 2001

Years	City of Turin (a)	Metropolitan area excluding Turin (b)	Metropolitan area (a) and (b)	-(b/a) (%)
1971–1981	−51	93	42	>100
1981–1991	−155	42	−113	27
1991–2001	−97	15	−82	15

Note: Absolute variation in the resident population over the decades.
Source: Adapted and translated from: Molina (2003). The metropolitan area referred to by Molina is composed of 52 municipalities and reflects the first definition of the metropolitan area given by the Piedmont Region in 1972.

industry dearly in lost labor hours. Meanwhile a national policy re-orientation favoring investment in Italy's underdeveloped South allowed FIAT to take advantage of national financial incentives to shift production and escape labor tensions.[19] Finally, because of the internationalization of its industrial firms, Turin was "one of the areas most heavily affected by economic globalization processes and the competitive stresses which they generate."[20]

By 1985, Turin was deep in the throes of economic decline: over the decade from 1981–1991 Turin's metropolitan area shed approximately 90,000 industrial jobs.[21] A major FIAT plant closure in 1980 resulted in the loss of 23,000 jobs in just one year.[22] Turin's de-industrialization process had in fact begun even earlier, with the shift of industrial production from within Turin's city limits to the first-ring suburbs, and subsequently to its second-ring suburbs. This process saw the share of total employment in industrial firms shift from being highly concentrated (over 80 percent in 1951) within Turin to being almost equally split between Turin and the surrounding suburbs in 1981. The manufacturing sector's share of total employment in Turin's overall economy fell below 45 percent by 1981.[23]

Compounding the loss of its more traditional economic sectors, Turin was simultaneously failing to capture growth in other economic sectors in which Italy overall was excelling, specifically in tourism. In 1986, unemployment in the province of Turin reached 11.6 percent.[24]

The City in 2015

Physical Form and Conditions

Turin's twentieth-century industrial identity and its legacy of physical decline are hardly discernible today: the gray, dull city of industrial plants, dormitory neighborhoods, and automobile supremacy is no more. Major public sector intervention in the 1990s and 2000s concentrated on remediation and redevelopment of industrial brownfields, renovation of the historic core of the city, upgrading of the transportation system, and regeneration of marginalized and peripheral neighborhoods.

Change began with the 1993 election of Mayor Valentino Castellani and his administration's adoption of a new city master plan in 1995, which focused on redefining land uses across the city, but particularly along the north–south rail corridor bisecting the city and the four major industrial areas along it. In conjunction with a major project by the national railroad authority to expand track capacity along the rail corridor, the master plan called for the tracks to be buried underground and the surface to become a six-lane artery into the heart of the city. By re-zoning the four major redevelopment areas for residential, commercial and open space, the plan intended to spur private-sector redevelopment and densification of the urban core through new neighborhood development. New development would be supported by the reorganization of the transportation system.

In the decade from 2000–2010, over 60 million square feet of abandoned industrial space were remediated, converted and repurposed, primarily along the "Central Spine" (Figure 12.6).[25] Examples of remediation and conversion include the former steel foundries and tire production plants that are now occupied by a green business park and the new Dora Park neighborhood, as well as the Lingotto retail, conference and convention center. Recent examples of new transit-oriented, multi-functional areas include the new Intesa San Paolo headquarters designed by Renzo Piano at the Porta Susa rail station and the new Piedmont Region high-rise designed by Massimiliano Fuksas at the Lingotto metro station, both of which are to serve as anchors for new development in the respective areas. Meanwhile, modern architecture by world-renowned designers has sprung up across the city.

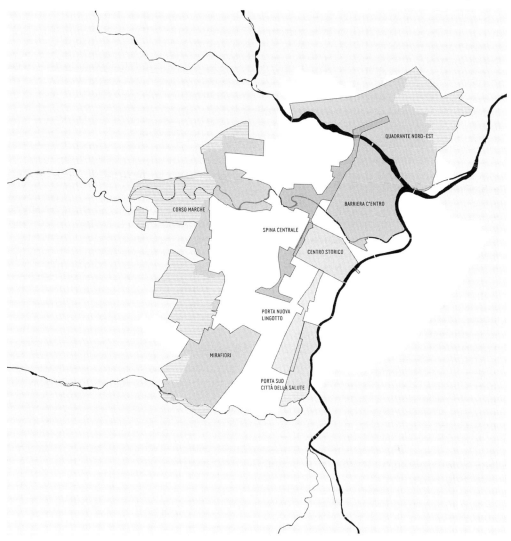

Figure 12.6 "Central Spine" and other strategic redevelopment zones
Source: Images produced by Urban Center Metropolitano Torino.

Transportation networks built to serve more industrial interests have been reinvented to serve a far more integrated metropolitan area. In the process of developing high-speed rail connections with Milan and other cities, the city's historically minor Porta Susa train station has been transformed into an ultramodern international rail hub that will eventually connect Lyons and Paris with Milan, Venice and even Budapest. Burying the tracks along the urban portion of that corridor has removed a major physical barrier dividing the city from north to south for over a century and, when completed, will help mend the urban fabric along that seam. The city's first subway line was inaugurated during the 2006 Winter Games and now connects the westernmost reaches of the city with the city center and southern areas of the city.

As vast tracts of land were being reclaimed, city leaders also turned their attention to social tensions in the city's underserved neighborhoods. These tensions had many causes including mass layoffs and discontent with labor contracts, limited cultural integration of new migrants, and inadequate public services. With the availability of dedicated funding for urban renewal projects from the European Commission, the Castellani administration launched a complex and inclusive neighborhood revitalization initiative under the banner "Periphery Project." Breaking a local tradition of top-down planning driven by industrial and real estate interests, consultation of local residents ensured interventions catered to local needs. Projects varied from the redevelopment of public spaces to the establishment of neighborhood markets and from the development of community centers and recreational facilities to streetscape and housing improvements.

Meanwhile the city's historic core has seen a true renaissance. A once run-down, automobile-dominated and unsafe area with few accessible public spaces has been restored to an attractive, safe, and vibrant cultural hub. Throughout the 1990s and in the lead-up to the 2006 Winter Olympics, public investment sparked a wave of private investment in the once derelict residential buildings of the historic core, prompting a positive feedback cycle that led to the recovery and renovation of this invaluable asset. Many historic and former industrial buildings, including the symbol of the city, the Mole Antonelliana, have been converted to contemporary cultural uses and landmarks have been restored. Newly pedestrian streets and public art have revived squares and commercial areas. Neighborhood craft, food and clothing markets ensure heavy foot traffic during the day while trendy restaurants and bars invigorate a city once known for the absence of night and street life. District heating networks and traffic restrictions in the historic center have improved energy efficiency and reduced air pollution.

While great emphasis was placed on the revitalization of the city itself, Turin in 2015 is a more functionally integrated, polycentric metropolitan area. Major commercial and retail centers, cultural assets, public services and institutions are less centralized than they once were. Population shifts from Turin to surrounding municipalities fueled housing starts and increased the total urbanized area significantly with respect to 1985. As large peri-urban greenfield sites were developed into new residential districts and commercial centers, what were once peripheral neighborhoods became centers of newly urbanized areas. Urbanized land in the Turin Metropolitan Area increased by 15 percent in the period from 1990–2006.[26]

Demographics

By the early 2000s, thirty years of population decline had finally slowed and the city even saw a slight increase (.08 percent) from approximately 872,367 in 2001 to 902,137 in 2011.[27] The recent stabilization and slight growth are in large part due to the influx of foreign immigrants, who comprised nearly 15 percent of the city's population in 2014 compared to roughly 55,000 or 6 percent in 2001.[28] Immigration has generally been most prominent from southeastern European and northern African countries; the four countries most represented by the foreign-born population today are Romania, Morocco, Peru and China, with 39.5 percent, 14.2 percent, 7.2 percent and 7.1 percent of the total respectively.[29]

Though immigrants to Turin and the metropolitan area in recent years have typically been low-skilled workers, the past decade has seen a significant increase in the foreign student population as well. Today foreign students make up 15 percent of the student body at Turin's Polytechnic University and nearly 6 percent at the University of Turin—significant increases over the previous decade.[30] The composition of the labor force has changed apace with de-industrialization: low-skilled jobs (as a percentage of total) have decreased from 57.3 percent in 1971 to 33.7 percent in 2001, and higher-skilled jobs increased from 23.7 percent to 42.2 percent in the same period.[31] Notwithstanding this shift in the labor market and the presence of two major universities, at just 13.7 percent in

2007, Turin continues to have one of the lowest percentages of college graduates of any major European city, and ranks eighth among major Italian cities.[32]

Perhaps even more concerning is the age composition of the population. While fertility rates in Italy have been below replacement levels since 1980, Turin, along with other northern Italian cities, has among the lowest fertility rates in the world. This is true notwithstanding the influx of foreign youth, which by 2011 accounted for almost a quarter of the under-30 population.[33]

Despite a more than threefold increase in the demand for social services since the recent economic downturn, Turin ranks second among metropolitan provinces in per-capita spending on social services. At a time when national fiscal austerity has imposed strict belt-tightening, growing demand has placed increasing pressure on the city's extensive non-profit sector.[34]

Economy

Throughout the 1970s, the weight of the industrial sector in Turin's economy had been declining in favor of the wider metropolitan area. The local impacts of shifting regional geographies were compounded by the global shift in manufacturing towards emerging economies. Meanwhile the continued integration of European economies into a single market (i.e. the Single European Act of 1992) increased international competition and saw national and European market share for Italian manufacturing decrease.[35] By 2012, the manufacturing industry's share of total employment had dropped even further to just under 25 percent, while services had grown to account for 65 percent. The added value of manufacturing in Turin's economy meanwhile decreased from 32 percent in 2000 to less than 20 percent.[36]

Notwithstanding continuing decline, in 2012, manufacturing still accounted for a higher share of employment in Turin than in all other Metropolitan Provinces and the Piedmont Region still registered the highest number of automotive sector firms of any region of Italy. In fact, manufactured products account for over 98 percent of total exports and the Turin Province continues to rank second only to Milan in exports.[37] The construction sector contributed significantly to economic growth in the lead-up to the financial crisis of 2008, but has since been suffering, as the local real estate market has generally. The finance and insurance sectors continue to be pillars of Turin's economy: Italy's largest bank by market capitalization is based in Turin while the insurance sector accounted for about 17 percent of the national market in 2011. In contrast to a national contraction in the banking industry, the Turin Metropolitan Province saw an increase in the number of banking institutions from 1996 to 2012.[38]

Turin's economy has substantially diversified over the past fifteen years. New economic specialization, specifically in high-tech and innovation-oriented sectors such as information technology and electronic engineering, biotechnology, aerospace engineering, nano-technology, and material sciences is driving the formation of new firms and start-ups at a surprising rate. In 2013, the Turin area was ranked third among Italian metropolitan provinces with the highest number of innovative startups, and third again in the number of firms in the information and communication technology sector.[39] The city is also home to successful business incubators including the University of Turin's biotechnology center and the Polytechnic Institute's I3P incubator, which ranked fifth in Europe and fifteenth worldwide, according to the University Business Incubator index in 2014.

Other sectors have gained ground in Turin's economy including film, the arts, tourism and hospitality services, and event planning and management. A concerted and sustained public and philanthropic effort to invest in the culture sector in the province has yielded significant results: total spending has topped €200 million every year since 2001. Major international events such as the Salone del Gusto (international food expo), the Salone del Libro (international book expo), the Torino Film Festival, and Artissima (one of the largest art fairs in Europe) are a few examples of large-scale events drawing tens of thousands of visitors to Turin annually and biannually. Consequently tourism in the metropolitan area nearly doubled between 1997 and 2012, reaching 3.8 million hotel stays.[40]

Though the overall shift from a manufacturing base towards a service-sector oriented economy has been impressive, the financial crisis of 2008 shocked the city once again. The crisis accelerated certain global economic restructuring processes with severe national and local repercussions. Turin's continued reliance on its industrial sector, more so than other metropolitan provinces in Italy, makes it particularly vulnerable to shocks in global demand. After moderate growth throughout the 2000s the city was thrown into a double-dip recession mirroring that of the Piedmont Region, which saw regional GDP decrease over 7 percent in 2009–2010 and over 2 percent in 2012–2013.[41] Unemployment in the Province of Turin had recovered from a high of nearly 11 percent for much of the 1990s, reaching just over 4 percent in 2006. Since the financial crisis of 2008, however, the unemployment rate has been steadily climbing and in 2014 it reached 12.9 percent. More troubling still is the extremely high rate of youth unemployment among 15–24-year-olds, which in 2014 was almost 50 percent.[42] Four years after the onset of the crisis, over 10 percent of the city's population were living in poverty.[43]

Transformation of the City (1985–2015)

What Went Right?

National Reform to Local Governance: An Escape from Politics as Usual

The story of Turin's transformation is one of a concerted, collective response by the city's leadership to confront, over the course of three decades, a structural economic crisis and the physical, economic, and social impacts of rapid de-industrialization. The transformation must be understood within the broader regional context of European integration and the national context of political reform in the wake of the 1991–1992 bribery scandals, which saw over half of Italy's parliamentarians indicted (*Tangentopoli*).[44] Legislation passed in 1993 allowing the direct election of mayors, giving mayors greater power over cabinet appointments. It complemented a 1990 law conferring to municipalities some limited discretion over local taxation and allowing the privatization of municipal services. These reforms increased transparency and local authority, ushering in a new era of accountability essential for facing Turin's enormous challenges.

The period leading up to these reforms was a particularly tumultuous one for Turin's politics. Corruption scandals spelled the end of the Novelli administration in 1985 and plunged the city into political turmoil until finally the indebted city was placed in receivership by the central government in 1992.[45] The election in 1993 of Mayor Valentino Castellani signaled a third watershed moment in the city's politics. A professor of telecommunication engineering, Mayor Castellani was a political outsider elected on a center-left platform of change. The Castellani administration inherited a city in the throes of economic and population decline, a city in need of deep re-thinking of the Fordist model of economic development, which had sustained growth for almost a century. On the brink of economic collapse and facing tough choices the city's leadership and powerful elites developed bold strategies to arrest decline and reverse course.

The 1995 Master Plan and Public-Private Partnerships for Redevelopment

The transformation of the city began with its physical renovation. Upon adoption of the new master plan in 1995, the Castellani administration led negotiations to develop public-private partnerships to undertake the massive efforts of demolishing disused industrial structures, remediating contaminated areas, concentrating redevelopment plans and re-building the four areas of the "Central Spine." Partnerships included private owners of disused facilities, private property developers, the City of Turin, the Piedmont Region, the Italian National administration, the European Commission (URBAN program), Turin's largest private foundations (the Compagnia di San Paolo and the Fondazione CRT), and the State railroad company (Ferrovie dello Stato). The partnership approach to the city's redevelopment was revolutionary in a city previously dominated by industrial interests and party politics. The ability to work across agencies and sectors, to pool resources and share responsibility, was the key to success in many of Turin's transformative projects.

Strategic Planning and Reinventing the City

In addition to healing the physical scars of the industrial era, city and civic leaders faced an almost existential crisis, the solutions to which would require creative thinking, openness to self-examination and a suspension of disbelief towards new approaches and processes. The big question that city leaders faced was simple but profound: if the automotive sector moved to other parts of Italy, Europe, and the world, and Turin were no longer Italy's industrial giant, what would Turin become?

Mayor Castellani initiated a strategic planning process in 1998 to answer this fundamental question, to develop a vision for Turin's future, and the strategies and actions required to realize that vision. The process saw the engagement of a broad segment of civil society over the course of two years in a rich and complex dialogue that succeeded in building a new vision: a *City of Action*, a place with the ingenuity and capacity to imagine and realize, very concretely, its future. The plan was in fact as much outward-looking as it was inward-looking, an attempt to convince itself and the outside world that Turin was a city with extraordinary potential, one capable of reinventing itself and building on skills and traditions developed over centuries to propel itself into a new future.

While certain assets were evident, such as a strong technical vocation and an impressive design and engineering capacity, others were less so and the strategic plan proposed cultivating certain assets that had previously been ignored and undervalued, most notably in the arts, culture, and entertainment sectors. The city's administration and civic leaders bet that, with concentrated investment, these assets could be developed into vibrant economic sectors capable of driving and supporting economic growth. Turin has indeed made great strides in this arena, developing dozens of museums and cultural events drawing visitors from across Italy, Europe and the globe. Less tangible results include the conscious re-branding of the city and the reconstruction of city identity and pride: the Turin sections of international travel guides are now more likely to refer to a dynamic, sophisticated and undiscovered corner of Italy rather than a rusting post-industrial city.

The 2006 Winter Olympic Games and the Renewal of the Historic Core

Another bold element of the city's first strategic plan was the proposal to nominate the city to host the 2006 Winter Olympics. Though the Turinese had always had a close connection with the Alps, to the outside world this aspect of Turin's identity was vastly overshadowed by its industrial legacy. The Olympics represented an opportunity to shrug off the image of the city's industrial past and embrace that of a modern, vibrant, and innovative city. This was as important a message to the rest of the world as it was to the Turinese themselves, who had not seen their city in that light for over a century.

The lead-up to the Games saw major public investment, not only in new athletic and housing facilities but also in new infrastructure and the renovation of the historic core of the city in an attempt to restore the city's past splendor. The Games also represented a common goal towards which many of the projects undertaken to physically heal the city and to improve the quality of its infrastructure, as well as the investments made in the development of cultural assets, could be focused. By many accounts the 2006 Winter Games proved a resounding success in showcasing the city to the throngs of international visitors and remote spectators.

The Second Strategic Plan: Knowledge City

In 2004, the incoming administration of Mayor Sergio Chiamparino determined that there was still work to be done to accomplish the economic restructuring begun by the Castellani administration and thus launched the city's second strategic planning process. Extensive economic analysis determined a need to continue to focus energy on the culture and tourism sectors, but also to bet heavily on the knowledge economy by investing in technological innovation: the vision crystallized around the concept of a Knowledge City, one in which highly skilled workers add value at the highest rungs of the economic ladder in advanced manufacturing, specialized services, and the arts.

As a result of the ambitious plan, various research and innovation centers took shape that are a critical part of Turin's innovation ecosystem today.[46] Building on the successful realization of the Winter Games, Turin continued cultivating expertise and recognition for hosting large-scale international events, such that in 2011 Turin hosted the country's most important celebration of the 150th anniversary of the birth of the nation. Meanwhile, renewed emphasis was placed on creating metropolitan agencies in order to improve service integration and delivery throughout the metropolitan area: municipal waste disposal, transportation, water and sewage, and energy provision were each spun off into quasi-private authorities and "smart city" technologies began to be integrated into urban systems.

Capacity Building

At home and abroad, Turin's model of urban transformation and economic diversification through physical reclamation and strategic planning is generally considered a great success. The capacity for self-analysis and the ability to look inward and outward simultaneously, as well as to contemplate long-term visions, is a significant result in and of itself. Likewise the ability to mobilize stakeholders and local leaders, and to develop broad coalitions, is a further indication of a successful process.[47] Campbell suggests that this collective experience results in city learning and the development of citywide social capital, what he calls "a unique and highly productive process of learning that lasted more than two decades."[48]

Though not all of the ideas generated during the strategic planning process were ground-breaking, and some were fully implemented while others only partially or not at all, the general consensus among internal and external observers is that strategic planning has been a pillar of Turin's remaking process. In fact, strategic planning has been adopted by cities large and small throughout Italy largely due to the success of Turin's first strategic planning plan. That process culminated in the establishment of a non-profit entity, Torino Internazionale, tasked with supporting the implementation of the strategic plan, monitoring outcomes, and periodically renewing the vision and actions. In addition to being the repository of a good deal of the two-decade learning process, the organization continues to play a central role in promoting, evaluating, and shaping development strategies.

What Went Wrong?

Incomplete Physical Transformation

While the physical transformation of the city proved within reach given the availability of large-scale public investment and strategic partnerships, projects not completed during the boom years still languish today. One example is the partially completed roadway intended to cover the central spine rail corridor, which still traverses the northern part of the city like an open wound. Notable quality of life issues such as alarming air quality due to the prevalence of diesel vehicles and certain geographic and climatological phenomena also persist to this day. And while the city made concerted efforts to revitalize lower-income neighborhoods, large communities of foreign-born residents and first generation non-citizens are often spatially segregated in lower-income neighborhoods and poorly integrated into the social and economic fabric of the city. While the Olympic Games were a great success on many fronts, limited reuse of infrastructure and facilities have left a lasting mark on various parts of the metropolitan city and the alpine environment.

Limited Engagement of Non-Governmental Actors in the Economic Restructuring Process

The city council-led remaking process between the mid-1990s and 2000s was most effective in creating change in those areas where the public sector was primarily responsible for implementation, particularly in driving the physical transformation and promoting specific economic sectors. The prevailing conviction among city leaders in the early years of the remaking process was that a transition to a specialized economy focused on cultural programming and tourism could, if successful, be sufficient to drive city-wide economic growth. Given a lack of evidence to support these presumptions, investments may have been too narrowly focused in these sectors in an era when public sector funding was still a significant resource.

The business community played only a marginal role in the agenda-setting process and consequently was largely extraneous to it. This lack of engagement may have been the result of the historic dominance of FIAT in the industrial community, which left little room for, or tradition of, the engagement of other players. Notwithstanding this context, the economy is indeed far more diverse than it was in the days of FIAT dominance, and new sectors including the creative economy, science and innovation, and international convention and event planning have gained significant ground. Domestic tourism has also grown tremendously though there is plenty of room for growth in the international arena. As a result, Turin in 2015 is a much more dynamic city, one connected to innovation networks in Europe and internationally.

Yet the recent economic downturn reveals that economic restructuring is by no means complete. The transition to value added activities such as advanced manufacturing and advanced services has proven more difficult to incentivize and sustain than the physical transformation of the city. In the wake of the 2008 financial crisis, it became evident that perhaps too much investment had been focused on making the city more attractive and not enough on retaining and attracting investment in diverse economic sectors, as firms were once again closing or leaving. Lack of investment in game-changing projects during the boom years, such as for a large research facility capable of changing the long-term prospects of the health and life science sectors, illustrates the limits of the strategies employed.

In addition to the direct economic impact suffered since 2008, the alienation of the business community and the lack of attention to renewing the welfare system in the process risked the dissipation of valuable social capital built over the previous decade. Increasing economic inequality meanwhile threatens the social cohesion of the city.

Going it Alone

Given the scale of the physical, economic and cultural challenges facing Turin's leadership, attention was understandably focused on the transformation of the city proper. While both the first and second strategic plans identified metropolitan governance as a strategic direction, and despite the fact that the key economic and urban challenges had already taken on metropolitan dimensions, with the exception of certain key service sectors, such as water and energy, city leaders made limited progress in sustaining effective metropolitan cooperation and governance. Part of the difficulty may have been the city's inability to consistently engage the national government and the Piedmont Region to create a shared vision of the central role of the metropolitan area as the economic powerhouse of the entire region. Notwithstanding very effective cooperation in the run-up to the Olympic Games, city leaders also had limited success building effective collaboration strategies with the City of Milan.

Lack of Sustained Attention to the Social Dimensions of Crisis and Change

Considering the city's transformation began as a response to the post-industrial economic crisis of the late 1970s and 1980s, the remaking process placed primary emphasis on restoring the city's economic prospects. While economic restructuring would undoubtedly be the foundation of the city's broader recovery, the crisis also aggravated existing social ills and generated new ones. Inadequate access to affordable housing, an increasingly vulnerable aging population, and rising inequality, for instance, generated needs for social services the city was not prepared to meet. Notable efforts to improve quality of life and increase social equity through neighborhood revitalization initiatives and more efficient and effective public services did help in confronting some of these issues. Yet, in a city with a long tradition and dense fabric of socially oriented organizations and institutions, the policy response was fragmented and few sustained public-sector strategies to address the social dimensions of crisis emerged.[49]

Public Indebtedness

Turin's major transformation projects required significant public-sector investment funded in part through the issuance of public debt. Given the dependence of municipal finances on transfers from central government to the regions, and from regions to cities, shortfalls created by reductions in national transfers since the imposition of austerity measures have left Turin on a difficult financial footing when trying to balance significant debt obligations with the provision of basic services. Between 2009 and 2012, net transfers to the city decreased by over 75 percent due to austerity measures. While transfers accounted for 35 percent of the city's total budget in 2009, they decreased to less than 8 percent of total budget in 2012, though spending actually increased by 1.5 percent over the same period.[50] In one of Italy's most indebted cities, with a total debt burden exceeding €3 billion in 2013, the situation has reached alarming proportions and hampered the city's ability to maneuver through the crisis.

Lessons Learned

Building on the tremendous progress to date, the next phase of Turin's economic restructuring and physical transformation will require:

- adoption of a rigorous, evidence-based approach to economic analysis capable of envisioning new economic models and investment streams;
- leveraging limited public resources through broad-based partnerships in support of market-oriented initiatives and new growth coalitions;
- development of mutually-supportive inter-municipal cooperation to maximize efficiency and project a common vision for development;
- valorization of local cultural diversity in the development of international talent and entrepreneurial networks;
- reinforcement of resilient systems and civic networks capable of adapting to evolving economic and social realities;
- sustained commitment to collective learning processes and continued exchange with practitioners and thought leaders.

Prospects for the Future

The heady atmosphere of the Olympic Games and inaugurations of museums and international events waned with the onset of the European financial crisis, as did the collective enthusiasm and the creative capacity to collaborate on strategic projects, which so characterized the 1990s and 2000s. However, Turin is better positioned today to confront the current challenges of economic structuring as a result of the extensive physical and cultural transformations, and the partial economic transition, of the past two decades.

Incoming Mayor Piero Fassino launched a third strategic planning process in 2012 in a move to respond to the latest crisis by reactivating the collective agenda setting process. Fruit of an extensive consultation process of the thirty-eight municipalities comprising the morphological urban area (MUA) and a broad spectrum of community and business leaders, the city's third strategic plan, "Metropolitan Turin 2025," identifies two primary strategies to accelerate economic recovery and diversification. The first is to increase metropolitan governance in order to promote greater efficiency in service delivery and improved coordination of public investment. The second is to unleash economic growth by improving the conditions for, and facilitating the development of, entrepreneurship and innovation. Emphasis is placed on projects aimed at attracting and retaining talent and investment, growing the innovation ecosystem, reducing public-sector bureaucracy, and developing strategic cross-sector partnerships and networks.

Recent national reform of local government has the potential to be very supportive of the strategies of the third strategic plan. On January 1, 2015 a new level of administration —the Metropolitan City—replaced the provincial administrations of ten major cities in Italy, including Turin (Figure 12.7). This long awaited reform is intended to accelerate decentralization by conferring greater authority for economic development and inter-municipal cooperation on major urban areas.

The establishment of the Metropolitan City government reinforces the metropolitan dimension of the plan and gives teeth to some of the more structural metropolitan governance projects. Yet in some ways the implementation could be complicated by the reform, which agglomerates a much larger area than the MUA (315 municipalities, including significant rural and mountainous areas). The formal recognition of the driving

Figure 12.7 Map of the new Metropolitan City of Turin and proposed areas of increased cooperation
Source: Image courtesy of the Metropolitan Conference.

role of the Turin MUA by the Metropolitan City could therefore prove a critical factor in overcoming local political fragmentation and establishing the systems and tools, at an appropriate scale, required to obtain the economic benefits of metropolitan integration.[51]

Most importantly, today's remaking efforts must include the broadest possible coalition of non-governmental actors, from all walks of civil society and spanning the entire business community, in order to harness the full creative and implementation capacity of the metropolitan area. In contrast to previous remaking efforts, successful implementation of the catalytic projects aimed at spurring innovation and cultivating value-added economic sectors will require sustained non-governmental leadership. The extensive engagement of private and third sector actors in the third strategic planning process has already generated significant momentum in mobilizing new leaderships and coalitions. The ability of Turin's political leaders to empower diverse leaders, facilitating and enabling innovation rather than driving it, could prove to be the most important ingredient in creating the third strategic plan's "City of Opportunity".

Notes

1   ISTAT, "Popolazione residente per età, sesso e stato civile al 1° Gennaio 2014." ISTAT, Superfici delle unità amministrative al 2011.
2   In 2011, the GDP of the Province of Turin was over €58 billion. Istituto Giuglielmo Tagliacarne, *Atlante della Competitività delle Regioni e delle Province* (Torino: Unioncamere, 2014).

3   Data obtained by the Piedmont Region directly from the University of Turin and the Turin Polytechnic University. Data set accessed on March 18, 2015 at: www.ossreg.piemonte.it/doc_01_02_01.asp

4   Encyclopaedia Britannica Online, "Turin." Accessed March 14, 2015. Available at: www.britannica.com/EBchecked/topic/609705/Turin

5   Astrid Winkler, "Torino City Report." *Center for Analysis of Social Exclusion, Case Report 41* (London: CASE, 2007).

6   Ibid., 11–12.

7   Provincia di Torino, "Trasformazioni Territoriali della Provincia di Torino." *Quaderni del territorio, Area Territorio, Trasporti, e Protezione Civile*, n. 2. (Torino, 2009), 18.

8   Ibid.

9   Bancadati Rapporto, "Giorgio Rota" su Torino 2014, *Resident Population in the City of Turin 1971–2013*, data from the Statistics Office of the City of Turin and ISTAT, 2014.

10 Winkler, "Torino City Report," 13.

11 A. Cardoza and G. Symcox, *A History of Turin* (Torino: Einaudi, 2006), 249.

12 B. Dente, and E. Melloni, *Report per la ricerca sul tema "Internazionalizzazione dell'area metropolitana"* (Milan: Istituto per la Ricerca Sociale, 2014), 27–8.

13 E. Dansero, *Dentro ai vuoti. Dismissione industriale e trasformazioni urbane a Torino* (Torino: Libreria Cortina, 1993), 64.

14 Ibid., 70–1.

15 E. Manzo, *La Città che si Rinnova. Architettura e scienze umane tra storia e attualità: prospettive di analisi a confronto* (Milan: Franco Angeli, 2012), 144.

16 Calculated based on census data from ISTAT and Comune di Torino.

17 Stefano Molina, *Popolazione torinese: ieri, oggi e domani* (Torino: Fondazione Giovanni Agnelli, 2003).

18 M. Maggi and S. Piperno, "Turin: The Vain Search for Gargantua," Istituto di Ricerche Economico Sociali del Piemonte, Working Paper no. 124/1999 (1999), 10.

19 Winkler, "Torino City Report," 15. According to Winkler, the number of labor hours lost due to strikes surpassed 15 million by 1969.

20 Maggi and Piperno, "Turin," 14.

21 Ibid., 12.

22 Winkler, "Torino City Report," 15.

23 Maggi and Piperno, "Turin," 12.

24 Istituto di Ricerche Economico Sociali del Piemonte, *Relazione sulla situazione economica, sociale e territoriale del Piemonte* (Torino: Rosenberger & Sellier, 1988). Original data from ISTAT.

25 Ibid.

26 Provincia di Torino, "Trasformazioni Territoriali," 29.

27 ISTAT, 2011, 2014.

28 ISTAT, 2014 and 2001. City of Turin, *Annuario 2001*.

29 City of Turin, *Informa Casa, Studi e Statistiche*. Available at: www.comune.torino.it/informacasa/studi_statistiche/processi_demografici/stranieri_torino.shtml

30 Dente and Melloni, *Report per la ricerca*, 6.

31 S. Belligni and S. Ravazzi, *La politica e la città. Regime urbano e classe dirigente a Torino* (Bologna: il Mulino. 2012), 48.

32 Data originates from various sources and is drawn from research conducted by the EU-Polis group of the Polytechnic Institute of Turin for Torino Internazionale in 2013. Exact figures from Eurostat Urban Audit data contained in report entitled "Investment Attraction".

33 Ibid. Report entitled "Renewal of the Welfare System,"

34 Ibid.

35 Winkler, "Torino City Report," 16.

36 Data originates from various sources and is drawn from research conducted by the EU-Polis group of the Polytechnic Institute of Turin for Torino Internazionale in 2013. Report entitled "Traditional v. New Economic Sectors."

37 Ibid. Report entitled "Investment Attraction."

38 Ibid. Report entitled "Traditional v. New Economic Sectors."

39 Ibid. Report entitled "Start Up."

40   Ibid. In this case the metropolitan area referred to is that designated by the Piedmont Region as the ATL1 in its original definition of local tourism agencies, which comprised Turin and the surrounding suburbs.
41   Data extrapolated from "Piemonte in Cifre 2014" produced by Unioncamere Piemonte based on data from Prometeia Srl.
42   ISTAT, 2014.
43   Centro di Ricerca e Documentazione Luigi Einaudi, *Rapporto Giorgio Rota 2014. Semi di Fiducia* (Torino: Centro Einaudi, 2014), 169.
44   S.Z. Koff and S.P. Koff, *Italy: From the First to the Second Republic* (London: Routledge, 2000), 2.
45   Winkler, "Torino City Report," 18.
46   Ibid., 59–61.
47   Dente and Melloni, *Report per la ricerca*.
48   T. Campbell, "Torino as a Learning City." In *Comparative Domestic Policy Paper Series 09* (Washington, DC: The German Marshall Fund of the United States, 2009), 15.
49   Belligni and Ravazzi, *La politica e la città*, 68.
50   City of Turin accounting summary (Rendiconto per l'esercizio 2012 e 2013 della Città di Torino).
51   R. Ahrend et al., "What Makes Cities More Productive? Evidence on the Role of Urban Governance from Five OECD Countries," OECD Regional Development Working Papers, 2014/05 (Paris: OECD Publishing, 2014). Available at: http://dx.doi.org/10.1787/5jz432cf2d8p-en

References

Ahrend, R. et al. (2014) "What Makes Cities More Productive? Evidence on the Role of Urban Governance from Five OECD Countries." OECD Regional Development Working Papers, 2014/05, Paris: OECD Publishing. Available at: http://dx.doi.org/10.1787/5jz432cf2d8p-en
Bagnasco, A. and Olmo, C. (2008) *Torino 011, biografia di una città.* Torino: Urban Center Metropolitano Torino.
Bagnasco, M. and Castellani, V. (2014) *Per fare il sindaco. Idee, storie e strumenti.* Vol. 9, La Buona Politica. Audino.
Belligni, S. and Ravazzi, S. (2012) *La politica e la città. Regime urbano e classe dirigente a Torino.* Bologna: il Mulino.
Campbell, T. (2009) "Torino as a Learning City." *Comparative Domestic Policy Paper Series 09.* Washington, DC: The German Marshall Fund of the United States.
Cardoza, A. and Symcox, G. (2006) *A History of Turin.* Torino: Einaudi.
Centro di Ricerca e Documentazione Luigi Einaudi (2014) *Rapporto Giorgio Rota 2014. Semi di Fiducia.* Torino: Centro Einaudi.
Dansero, E. (1993) *Dentro ai vuoti. Dismissione industriale e trasformazioni urbane a Torino.* Torino: Libreria Cortina.
Dansero, E., Giaimo, C., and Spaziante, A. (2001) *Se i vuoti si riempono. Aree industriali dismesse: temi e ricerche.* Firenze: Alinea Editrice.
Dente, B. and Melloni, E. (2005) "Il piano strategico come strumento di 'governance' locale: il caso di Torino." *Amministrare*, 3: 385–420.
Dente, B. and Melloni, E. (2014) *Report per la ricerca sul tema "Internazionalizzazione dell'area metropolitana".* Milan: Istituto per la Ricerca Sociale.
Istituto Giuglielmo Tagliacarne (2014) *Atlante della Competitività delle Regioni e delle Province.* Torino: Unioncamere.
Istituto di Ricerche Economico Sociali del Piemonte (1988) *Relazione sulla situazione economica, sociale e territoriale del Piemonte.* Torino: Rosenberger & Sellier.
Koff, S. Z. and Koff, S. P. (2000) *Italy: From the First to the Second Republic.* London: Routledge.
Maggi, M. and Piperno, S. (1999) "Turin: The Vain Search for Gargantua," Istituto di Ricerche Economico Sociali del Piemonte, Working Paper n. 124/1999.
Manzo, E. (2012) *La Città che si Rinnova. Architettura e scienze umane tra storia e attualità: prospettive di analisi a confronto.* Milano: Franco Angeli.
Molina, S. (2003) *Popolazione torinese: ieri, oggi e domani.* Torino: Fondazione Giovanni Agnelli.

Provincia di Torino (2009) "Trasformazioni Territoriali Della Provincia di Torino," *Quaderni del territorio, Area Territorio, Trasporti, e Protezione Civile*, no. 2. Torino.

Regione Piemonte (2012) "Monitoraggio del Consumo di Suolo in Piemonte," *Assessorato all'Urbanistica e Programmazione Territoriale, Beni Ambientali, Edilizia e Legale*. Torino.

Winkler, A. (2007) "Torino City Report", *Center for Analysis of Social Exclusion, Case Report 41*. London: CASE.

Conclusion

Donald K. Carter

In 1973, when American sociologist Daniel Bell published his seminal book, *The Coming of the Post-Industrial Society: A Venture in Social Forecasting*, none of the ten cities in this book was in serious decline. Bell correctly predicted in 1973 that mature economies, such as in the US and Europe, would transition from manufacturing-based to service-based. What he did not forecast was the unequal distribution of results. Cities in the US and Europe that relied on basic industries and commodities, such as steel, aluminum, glass, coal, ship building, and automobile manufacturing, lost out in the global shift of industrial jobs to low-cost producers in Asia and South America in the 1980s. In addition, modernization and labor-saving technology in industry led to better productivity and fewer manufacturing jobs. On the other hand, cities that had more diverse economies and that were knowledge-based did not suffer the same disastrous declines, even during periods of worldwide recession.

The ten cities in this book are emblematic of many other post-industrial cities that were hard hit in the 1980s, such as Youngstown, Ohio, and Gary, Indiana, in the US, and Glasgow, Scotland, and Nantes, France, in Europe. Some were given up for dead thirty years ago and many are still struggling, but the resilience and determination of the leaders and citizens of these ten cities are the story behind the story. As the reader will have discerned, there are commonalities in the successful transformation of the ten cities from 1985 to 2015. This concluding chapter will elucidate those commonalities and summarize the lessons learned from the case studies.

What the Ten Cities Had in Common in 1985

In addition to being manufacturing-based and typically focused on one or two major industries, the ten were second-tier cities in terms of population, political power, and financial influence. As the decline played out in these post-industrial cities, its effects were not experienced in the financial and capital cities of their countries. Displaced workers moved to more affluent and diversified areas, bolstering the economies in those regions, such as London, Paris, Washington, DC, and the fast-growing cities of the US South and West. Regions like the Midlands in the UK and the Midwest in the US began to shrink in population, jobs, wealth, and influence.

Physically the cities had much in common on the positive side: historic downtowns and neighborhoods; abundant potable water; rivers and ports; density to support transit; major universities and medical centers; and rich cultural assets such as parks, museums, and the arts. They also had much in common on the negative side: air, water, and ground pollution;

industrial vacancy and brownfields; aging populations; loss of young educated people to other regions; deteriorated infrastructure; increased poverty; race, class, and equity issues; suburban sprawl even in the face of economic decline of the central city; neglect by the national government; financial and mental depression; and lack of a vision or strategy for economic recovery.

What the Ten Cities Had in Common in 2015

Optimism has replaced the despair and resignation that existed thirty years earlier. Populations have stabilized. Their economies have become more diversified. Economic development issues are being addressed regionally. Public and private interests have converged. Signature projects and programs have become emblematic of regeneration. Cultural assets have been preserved, celebrated, and enhanced. Tourism, of all things, has increased as the global image of each city has been enhanced by these turn-around efforts. In a word, they are resilient. However, struggles remain in all the cities, especially around social issues.

Four National and Global Concerns that Impact Post-Industrial Cities

Before taking up *lessons learned* from the ten city case studies, it is worth briefly discussing several concerns that impact the cities in this book that are national, even global, in scope and that are beyond the capabilities of cities or regions in North America and Europe to solve on their own. These are universal concerns affecting all cities, not just post-industrial cities, and include, among other things, *energy*, *water*, *immigration*, and *equity*. They are discussed below, with equity dealt with in more detail.

Energy

Energy is a global market, with haves (Saudi Arabia) and have-nots (Japan). Cities are at the mercy of the global market, e.g., the reliance of European cities on Russian natural gas and the regional strife between Russia and Europe that often ensues. Several authors in this book cite the worldwide oil crises of 1973 and the early 1980s as precipitating economic decline in their cities. Coal is losing market share to natural gas, affecting national economies and cities differently. Some countries (Germany) are de-commissioning nuclear power plants. Others in Scandinavia are seeking net zero energy status. Alternative energy sources (solar, wind, hydro, bio, and geo) are increasingly being employed. These global and national forces are for the most part outside the purview or control of cities, except for employing sustainable practices such as retrofitting inefficient municipal buildings to green standards, adopting progressive building codes, and creating central energy districts. Yet the cost of energy is a major determinant of the cost of living in cities, especially impacting lower-class families. Furthermore, in the global competition for jobs, higher energy costs or another oil crisis will put some cities at a marked disadvantage.

Water

Here, post-industrial cities are in a strong position. The case study cities in this book are all water-rich, having been established along rivers, lakes, and seas to take advantage of water transportation initially, and later in the nineteenth and twentieth centuries to supply the heavy industries that clustered there. In 2015, in the US, large regional disparities in fresh water supply exist—with a decade-long drought in the Southwest and California, compared to states in the Midwest and Great Lakes regions where 20 percent of the world's supply of fresh water exists. Fortunately, the Midwest is also the location of most of the post-industrial cities in North America.

Europe is likewise well supplied with fresh water, including the five case study cities in this book. Other regions of the world are less well endowed with water, such as parts of India, Pakistan, China, and Africa. In the twenty-first century, fresh water has become as important as energy in the development of cities. This bodes well for post-industrial cities.

Immigration

Immigration is one of the hottest political issues in the US and Europe. National elections focus, sometimes hinge, on debates about illegal immigration. In the US, the primary focus is on Hispanic immigration from Mexico and Central America, and to a lesser extent from the Caribbean and Asia. In Europe, the immigration crisis has different aspects depending on the receiving country and origin of immigrants: Germany (Turkey); France and Italy (North Africa and Africa); United Kingdom (Asia, West Indies); and the Netherlands (Surinam, Morocco). The addition of the former communist countries of Eastern Europe to the European Union also produced immigration issues as workers, especially from Poland, moved to Western European countries where they compete with nationals in those countries for jobs and housing. The massive flow of immigrants from war-torn Syria to Europe in 2015 is the most recent example, resulting in political crisis and economic stress from the Balkans to Scandinavia.

On the other hand, a close reading of the case studies in this book shows that population decline, or at best stagnation, is a common problem across all ten cities. These post-industrial cities have aging populations, low birth rates, and have experienced the loss of younger educated adults to other cities and regions. Without immigration (legal or illegal), their populations and workforces would have declined even further. But immigration comes at a price. Many immigrants arrive with little education or wealth. They bring different religions, languages, and lifestyles, making assimilation difficult and burdening the welfare and public school systems. As a result, immigrant communities become segregated from the larger society, accompanied by crime, poverty, discrimination, alienation, mistrust, and in some cases violent outbreaks. Cities are where these issues play out, but it is at the national level where immigration policy is made, leaving cities at the mercy of national and international politics.

Equity

The most pressing social issue in the US and Europe is equity and it is national in scope. As described in the Introduction, the 2013 Remaking Cities Congress identified equity as the overriding issue coming out of the Congress workshops.

The study of equity, and its opposite, inequality, has led to such American classics as *How the Other Half Lives*, by Jacob Riis (1890), *Let Us Now Praise Famous Men*, by James Agee and Walker Evans (1941), and *The Negro Family: The Case For National Action*, by Daniel Patrick Moynihan (1965).

Two recent best-selling books, one from France and one from the US, tackle the inequality issue head on. French economist, Thomas Piketty, published *Capital in the Twenty-First Century* in 2013. Harvard sociologist, Robert Putnam, published *Our Kids: The American Dream in Crisis* in 2015. Both concluded that unequal distribution of wealth results in entrenched inequality in social and financial outcomes for lower-class populations, and that the global income gap between rich and poor is increasing.

Other recent publications on inequality from across the political and research spectrum include: *More than Just Race: Being Black and Poor in the Inner City*, by William Julius Wilson (2009); *Searching for the Uncommon Common Ground: New Dimensions on Race in America*, by Angela Glover Blackwell, Stewart Kwoh, and Manuel Pastor (2009); *Coming Apart; The State of White America, 1960–2010*, by Charles Murray (2012); *Inequality: What Can Be Done?*, by Anthony Atkinson (2015); *Segregated City: The Geography of Economic Segregation in America's Metros*, by Richard Florida (2015); *The Great Divide: Unequal Societies and What We Can Do About Them*, by Joseph Stiglitz (2015); and *The Globalization of Inequality*, by François Bourguignon (2015).

It is fair to say that these authors correlate poverty with family dysfunction, poor health outcomes, underachieving schools and children, loss of community cohesion, alienation from society, crime, drugs, and deteriorated and segregated housing—all resulting in lack of opportunity for upward mobility. Discrimination by race, ethnicity, and immigrant status further exacerbates the struggles of poor families, especially in raising children, the most vulnerable members.

Putnam, in *Our Kids*, illustrates this with case studies that show the dichotomy of rich families (includes middle-class families) who live in upscale safe neighborhoods, and have the time, means, background, expertise, or supportive networks to raise competent and successful children, contrasted with poor families (includes working-class families), often single mothers with children, who live day-to-day in rundown and dangerous neighborhoods, and have little time, means, background, expertise, or supportive networks to increase their children's prospects. Putnam further makes the argument that the US now has four classes: rich white families; rich minority families; poor white families; and poor minority families. Rich white and rich minority families (with parents with college degrees) have similar successful child-rearing practices, while poor white and poor minority families (with high school diplomas or less) experience similar diminished educational and career outcomes for their children.

The other authors cited above come to similar conclusions for both the US and Europe. Most are also in agreement that social equity is a problem to be dealt with primarily at the national level. However, they do not agree on the means to achieve equity. Debates rage over whether poverty is cultural (personal failing) or structural (societal failing), and whether early childhood education, vocational training, supportive family services, affirmative action, welfare to work, addiction counseling, housing subsidies, and other social programs are effective in the long run. Piketty sees transfer of wealth as the primary means to achieve equality. Is there now a permanent "underclass" or "culture of poverty" of poor whites and poor minorities in the US as posed by Murray and Wilson? Similar instances of intransigent poverty can be seen in the immigrant enclaves outside the high-income central cities of Europe. How this all plays out on the national stage in each country will have a profound impact on the future of cities, but it is beyond the ability of cities themselves to solve.

Lessons Learned from the City Case Studies

Each city case study in this book has a section on *lessons learned*. Some lessons were repeated in nearly every chapter, while others less so. Without duplicating those accounts in detail, below is a summary of lessons learned. The reader is encouraged to revisit each chapter for in-depth accounts.

It Takes Time

None of these city transformations happened overnight. It took decades of hard work, false starts, successes, mistakes, and regrouping. Note the uneven trajectory of changes over the thirty years covered in each case study, 1985 to 2015. Work is ongoing in each city on visions for the next ten to thirty years.

The Scale is Metropolitan

Bruce Katz, author of the Foreword to this book, proclaims in his 2013 book, *The Metropolitan Revolution: How Cities and Metros Are Fixing Our Broken Politics and Fragile Economy*, written with Jennifer Bradley, that regions in the US are where the action is and will be in the future. In their view, the US government, in perpetual political gridlock and incessant budget wrangling, has turned away from tackling urban problems.

In Europe likewise, despite trickle-down funding from the EU and national governments, regions are increasingly where initiatives have to be taken and funded. The best example of regionalism in this book is the Ruhr case study, but Pittsburgh, Bilbao, and Buffalo also offer valuable lessons. On the other hand, the cities of Detroit and Turin have had to go it alone without much regional participation. Liverpool is struggling with city-region governance issues as the result of devolution of municipal powers from the central government to the regions.

You Need a Long Term Vision

Unfortunately it often takes a dramatic economic downturn or a natural disaster for city leadership to come together for a collective vision on rebuilding and transforming the city. Each case study documents the moment in time when such action was taken. Examples include: Strategy 21 in Pittsburgh in 1985 after the collapse of Big Steel; Bring Back New Orleans in 2005 after Hurricane Katrina; Detroit Future City Strategic Framework Plan in 2013 following the crisis in the auto industry; the strategic plan for the Revitalization of Metropolitan Bilbao in 1991 following the loss of steel and ship-building jobs and the environmental degradation of the Nervion River; and the Torino Urban Master Plan in 1995 following the 1993 receivership of the city and the election of its first directly-elected mayor.

Be Bold, Take Risks

Cities in distress often look for a "silver bullet" to turn things around, perhaps attracting a new industry or company, or building a new sports stadium, hosting a major event, or creating an iconic building or attraction. These can work if combined with an overall vision of how the silver bullet becomes part of a long-term strategy. They can also fail if they are stand-alone efforts not tied to regeneration. Compare the success of the 1992 Summer Olympics in Barcelona that propelled the revitalization of that city to the 2014 Sochi Winter Olympics where a year later Sochi is characterized as a "ghost town."

The most famous example of a successful silver bullet is the Guggenheim Museum in Bilbao (1997). However, the Calatrava-designed museum in Milwaukee (2001), the winter Olympics in Turin (2006), the International Building Exhibition (IBA) Emscher Park in the Ruhr (1989–1999), and being named European Capital of Culture (Rotterdam, 2001; Liverpool, 2008) were projects and events that enhanced the international perception of those cities and also provided a basis and rationale for economic recovery.

You Can't Do It Alone

The five US case studies document the increasing use of public/private partnerships (sometimes known as PPPs or P3s). This is a relatively new economic development technique developed in the US since the 1960s. Essentially, city governments work with private philanthropic foundations, for-profit developers, and not-for-profit developers to finance and implement projects. Tools include land write downs, tax abatement, low interest loans, grants, tax credits for historic preservation and low-income housing, and tax increment financing. These efforts are often matched with national and state funding. As a result, projects typically have multiple public and private investors as well as public and private benefits. Such partnerships have been employed in neighborhood revitalization, brownfield remediation and redevelopment, office buildings, housing, retail, cultural amenities, and public open space. Often as many as ten to fifteen funding sources are cobbled together to make a project happen.

This is less so in Europe, although the beginnings of PPPs can be seen in the five European case studies. Private philanthropy, a major force in the US in transforming cities (for instance, Kresge in Detroit), is mostly non-existent in Europe. However, the partnering of private industry and developers with city agencies is becoming more prevalent. Liverpool is a good example.

Leadership is Important

Leadership can be individual or collective. The election of Mayor Valentino Castellani in 1993 was a watershed moment for Turin. He presided over the 1995 and 1998 master plans that included the bid for the 2006 Winter Olympics. Another example of individual leadership is Dr. Karl Ganser who led the acclaimed International Building Exhibition Emscher Park (IBA) from 1989 to 1999 that transformed the landscape and perception of the Ruhr. Strong mayors in Pittsburgh (Tom Murphy) and in Milwaukee (John Norquist) are examples of dynamic risk-taking US leaders.

Collective leadership is evident in Europe (Bilbao and Ruhr, for example), but especially in the five US cities where government, philanthropy, and private companies work closely together in public/private partnerships (formal and informal) on visioning and implementation. Universities are also a major part of the leadership groups in all the city case studies.

Citizen Engagement Is Also Important

Top-down leadership was the norm after World War II on both sides of the Atlantic. Attempts at citizen participation and community consultation did not begin until the 1960s, initially driven by social unrest, racial conflict, the anti-war movement, and public demonstrations. Poor people were particularly disenfranchised. Starting in the 1970s, however, outreach to citizens became institutionalized in many cities, sometimes mandated by national policy and funding requirements. By the 1990s, planning processes and community charrettes (workshops) involving the public as well as community leaders became standard practice in many cities, particularly those in distress like the ten cities in this book. Sometimes there was disruptive conflict in these processes (Turin, Rotterdam, Detroit, and New Orleans, for example), but consensus was usually achieved and bold ideas emerged that could be embraced by all. It is now hard to imagine a master planning process in the US and Europe that is not inclusionary.

Diversify the Economy

Steelmaker Andrew Carnegie, the Scottish immigrant to Pittsburgh who created one of the largest industrial empires in history, once said, "Put all your eggs in one basket, and then watch that basket." That may work for a private business, but the case studies in this book illustrate the fallacy of such a strategy for cities. All the cities in this book have had to deal with what happens when both the eggs and the basket disappear. For the last thirty years they have striven to replace high-paying jobs in basic industries like steel, aluminum, coal, oil, and auto and ship building, with jobs in technology, finance, medicine, education, service, tourism, and value-added manufacturing. Pittsburgh with its two powerhouse universities, world-renowned medical center, and major banks, is perhaps the best example of a diversifying post-industrial economy over the last thirty years. Nevertheless, industrial companies and jobs remain significant economic factors in the case study cities. Milwaukee, for example, has committed to "reindustrialization as an attitude," using its assets of water, industrial talent, skilled workers, and physical infrastructure.

Strengthen the Central City

The emptying out of the central city was one of the outcomes of the economic decline of post-industrial cities in the 1980s in the US and Europe. Unfortunately sprawl continued outside the central cities even in the face of job losses and population outmigration to other regions and countries. Municipal property and income taxes declined. Disinvestment in the downtowns and urban neighborhoods followed. Infrastructure was neglected. Nevertheless some cities such as Milwaukee, Pittsburgh, Bilbao, Rotterdam, and Turin invested heavily in the central city in the 1990s and 2000s and were transformed. Others, such as Detroit (pejoratively referred to as the "hole in the donut") and Buffalo were unable to focus on regeneration of the central city until recently, but the signs are positive.

The issue of equity re-emerges here related to neighborhood redevelopment, segregation, and gentrification in the central city. Two forces are at work: first, isolation and concentration of the poor, minorities, and immigrants in social housing projects in a few districts of each case study city; and second, displacement of those poor families in regeneration efforts leading to gentrification. The first force, isolation and concentration of families in poverty are root causes of the social dysfunctions recounted above by Putnam and others. The second force, regeneration of poor neighborhoods, although well-meaning, often ends up reducing the stock of affordable housing and displacing poor families unless done strategically by providing affordable replacement housing and services for the displaced. This issue is further complicated by racial and class discrimination, both overt and subliminal. The stated goal of regeneration is to create stable, mixed-income neighborhoods, but in fact the concentration of poverty just moves to another district in the city that then deteriorates, creating another cycle of isolation. The case study cities in this book are all confronted with this issue. Some progress has been made in creating mixed income neighborhoods where affordable units are protected from gentrification forces, but more needs to be done.

Invest in Culture, Heritage, and Quality of Life

Not only is investment in commercial and housing development in the central city important, so too is investment in culture, heritage, and quality of life. Liverpool, Detroit, and New Orleans celebrate their musical heritage and the Ruhr its industrial and natural resources heritage. Historic preservation is an economic development tool used by all the cities in this book. New public parks and bikeways have been constructed. Every city with a waterfront is converting brownfield sites and unused railroad lines and docks to parks and trails combined with mixed-use development. Most cities have built museums and sports stadiums in the last thirty years such as the iconic museums in Bilbao and Milwaukee. The Cultural District in downtown Pittsburgh is exemplary of both a quality of life and a cultural investment that is supported by a public/private partnership of government, private foundations, corporations, and the general public.

Public transportation continues to be an asset that is valued and invested in, especially in European cities where there is appropriate residential density and walkability to provide a ubiquitous and well-used transit system. On the other hand, in second tier cities in the US, like the five in this book, public transit systems are not robust and are underfunded. Many poor neighborhoods are under-served. Subsidies from federal and state governments provide for capital investment and operating expenses, but not to the degree in Europe, and certainly not to the degree needed.

Invest in Education

An educated workforce is essential to the economic health of a city. The cities in this study all suffered a "brain drain" in the 1980s as professionals and skilled workers left for better prospects. Rebuilding, refreshing, and retaining that intellectual base are a high priority in the current vision plans of each city. The Ruhr created three new universities in the 1980s where none existed previously. Delft and Erasmus Universities are important factors in Rotterdam's recovery as are the urban universities in the other case study cities. Pittsburgh is investing in K-12 public education with college scholarship programs for high-achieving graduates. There is increasing interest on both sides of the Atlantic in vocational education using the successful German apprenticeship model of combining school attendance with on-the-job training. Finally, efforts, both local and national, are being made to close the "digital divide" that impacts the education and employability of working class and poor people in a technology-driven economy.

Develop Sustainably

The environmental movement has accomplished much since the days of Rachel Carson (*Silent Spring*, 1962) and the first Earth Day, 22 April 1970. Its impact on the built environment has been profound, including energy-efficient buildings, alternative forms of energy, holistic storm water management practice, recycling, energy districts, multi-modal transportation, transit-oriented development, urban ecology, and urban growth boundaries. In the US, attention is being paid to urban infill development and to densifying existing neighborhoods, not only to save energy and prevent further sprawl, but also to invigorate their transit systems. Walkable neighborhoods contribute to better public health outcomes and better public safety. There is measurable social return on responsible redevelopment. Finally, global climate change has added additional concerns, especially for low-lying coastal cities like New Orleans and Rotterdam and flood-prone cities like Bilbao. Strategic vision plans and urban master plans must now take account of these natural forces and integrate best sustainable design practices in development plans. The new buzz word in planning is "resiliency," i.e., planning in advance for economic, man-made, and natural disasters.

Good Planning and Urban Design Matter

Redevelopment mistakes were made in the US and Europe after World War II in the name of modernism. The rebuilding of Rotterdam after the extensive bombing in the war is a case in point. Historic traditions were cast aside in favor of efficient housing blocks and office towers, but with few amenities such as shops and open space, not only in Rotterdam but across war-torn Europe, including Liverpool. In the US, the same miscues were made in the 1960s and 1970s in the name of Urban Renewal, a euphemism for slum clearance and displacement of poor families—with the same end result as in Europe. In addition urban highways were blasted through the hearts of neighborhoods to support the suburbanization of the US. The intentions of community leaders and planners in the US and Europe were good, but the tools and designs they employed were devastatingly bad. Cities have been recovering from those ill-considered projects ever since. Pittsburgh has three such Urban Renewal areas from the 1960s that only in the last ten years have begun to be transformed into livable neighborhoods again. Buffalo, Detroit, Milwaukee, and New Orleans have similar urban renewal projects from the past to overcome. The lesson learned is that the traditional neighborhoods that existed before World War II remain the best models for today. They are dense, mixed-use, transit-friendly, with schools, shopping, and services within walking distance.

A Final Word

The case studies in this book are encouraging. The cities have come back and are being remade. But much remains to be done. Changes will not come about overnight, as the case studies illustrate. Cities are evolutionary and are in it for the long haul. Their horizon is not one year or ten years or even thirty years, but one hundred years. Hopefully the lessons learned over the past thirty years as described in these pages will inform the next evolution of post-industrial cities.

References

Agee, James and Evans, Walker (2001) *Let Us Now Praise Famous Men.* New York: Mariner Books.
Atkinson, Anthony B. (2015) *Inequality: What Can Be Done?* Cambridge, MA: Harvard University Press.
Bell, Daniel (1973) *The Coming of the Post-Industrial Society: A Venture in Social Forecasting.* New York: Basic Books.
Blackwell, Angela Glover, Kwoh, Stewart and Pastor, Manuel (2009) *Searching for the Uncommon Common Ground: New Dimensions on Race in America.* New York: W. W. Norton & Company.
Bourguignon, François (2015) *The Globalization of Inequality.* Princeton, NJ: Princeton University Press.
Carson, Rachel (1962) *Silent Spring.* New York: Houghton Mifflin Company.
Florida, Richard (2015) *Segregated City: The Geography of Economic Segregation in America's Metros.* Toronto: Martin Prosperity Institute.
Katz, Bruce and Bradley, Jennifer (2013) *The Metropolitan Revolution: How Cities and Metros Are Fixing Our Broken Politics and Fragile Economy.* Washington, DC: Brookings Institution Press.
Moynihan, Daniel Patrick (1965) *The Negro Family: The Case for National Action.* Washington, DC: United States Department of Labor, Office of Policy Planning and Research.
Murray, Charles (2012) *Coming Apart: The State of White America, 1960–2010.* New York: Crown Publishing Company.
Piketty, Thomas (2013) *Capital in the Twenty-First Century.* Cambridge, MA: Harvard University Press.
Putnam, Robert D. (2015) *Our Kids: The American Dream in Crisis.* New York: Simon & Schuster.

Riis, Jacob (1997) *How the Other Half Lives*. New York: Penguin Classics.

Stiglitz, Joseph (2015) *The Great Divide: Unequal Societies and What We Can Do About Them*. New York: W. W. Norton & Company.

Wilson, William Julius (2009) *More than Just Race: Being Black and Poor in the Inner City*. New York: W. W. Norton & Company.

Contributors

Juan Alayo is an international consultant on strategic city planning. Until December 2013, he was Development Planning Director at BILBAO Ría 2000, a public urban regeneration company. Between 1990 and 2005 he worked at the consulting firm Arup, in London. He graduated in Architecture and Urban Design from the University of Navarra and has an MSc in Advanced Architectural Studies from University College London.

Erik Bichard is Professor of Regeneration and Sustainable Development at the University of Salford in England. His career has been devoted to the field of sustainable change in urban environments. He is a regular contributor to the media and has written two books: *Positively Responsible*, and *The Coming of Age of the Green Community*.

Luc Boot works at the Mayor's office in Rotterdam and is manager of the Metropolitan Region Rotterdam – The Hague. He works at improving the economic performance by stimulating cooperation between governments, research institutes, businesses and civil society. He received his Master's degree in Regional Economics from the Erasmus University in Rotterdam.

Donald K. Carter is Director of the Remaking Cities Institute, Carnegie Mellon University (CMU) in Pittsburgh. He is also Track Chair of the Master of Urban Design program in the School of Architecture. Prior to joining CMU in 2009, Don was President of Pittsburgh-based Urban Design Associates. He is a Fellow of the American Institute of Architects and a Fellow of the American Institute of Certified Planners. He was Co-Chair of the international 2013 Remaking Cities Congress. Don earned a Bachelor of Architecture from CMU and did post-graduate studies in urban design and regional planning at the University of Edinburgh, Scotland.

Maurice Cox, newly appointed Planning Director for the City of Detroit is an urban designer, architectural educator and former mayor of the City of Charlottesville, VA. He most recently served as Associate Dean for Community Engagement at Tulane University's School of Architecture and Director of the Tulane City Center, a university-affiliated practice operating at the intersection of design, urban research and civic engagement throughout the New Orleans community.

Iris Dudok is a Senior City Planner for the City of Rotterdam and directly advises various city councilors in Rotterdam. Her focus is the National Renewal Program Rotterdam South, Inner City and transferring knowledge into day-to-day planning solutions. She received her Master's degree in Planning at the University of Amsterdam.

Geraldine Gardner is the Director of Urban and Regional Policy at the German Marshall Fund of the United States. At GMF, Gardner manages a network of US and European urban leaders focused on peer-to-peer learning and research initiatives. Geraldine received her Master's degree in urban planning from the University of California, Los Angeles.

Garbiñe Henry is Director of Social Innovation at the University of Deusto. She has previously held management positions and management consulting companies for eleven years. She holds a BA in Political Science and Sociology, Urban Sociology specialty from the University of Deusto (1995) and a Master's in Business Administration (2003).

Bradshaw Hovey is Co-Director of the Urban Design Project at the University at Buffalo. He has extensive experience in urban politics, community planning processes, citizen participation, and public information. Bradshaw was a primary author or editor of six major plans including Buffalo's waterfront, downtown, and citywide comprehensive plans. He has a doctorate in Urban Design and Planning from the University of Washington.

Bruce Katz is a vice president at the Brookings Institution and founding director of the Brookings Metropolitan Policy Program. He is co-author of *The Metropolitan Revolution* (Brookings Press, 2013). Bruce is a graduate of Brown University and Yale Law School and a visiting professor at the London School of Economics.

Dan Kinkead is Director of Projects for Detroit Future City. He is an architect, and urban designer. Prior to joining Detroit Future City, Dan was design principal at Hamilton Anderson Associates in Detroit and urban designer at SOM in New York. Dan received his Master of Architecture in Urban Design from Harvard University and Bachelor of Architecture from the University of Kentucky.

Alan Mallach is a senior fellow at the Center for Community Progress in Washington, DC. A city planner, advocate and writer, he is nationally known for his work on housing, economic development, and urban revitalization. He is a member of the College of Fellows of the American Institute of Certified Planners, and holds a BA degree from Yale University.

Simone Mangili is currently Head of Projects and Operations for the association Torino Internazionale where he manages metropolitan strategic planning processes. His international experience ranges from real estate consulting and development to designing public engagement processes and building private-public partnerships for the development of parks and green infrastructure. Simone holds a Bachelor's in Community, Regional and Environmental Studies from Bard College and a Master's in Regional Planning from Cornell University.

Beatriz Plaza is Professor in Urban and Regional Economics at the University of the Basque Country. She graduated in Economics from the University of the Basque Country and obtained her MBA from Iese Business School. She has a PhD in Economics from the University of the Basque Country. Her research interests include: cultural policy as development policy; urban regeneration; economic impact of museums; cultural branding; regional policy; measurement and economic analysis of regional economics; cultural economics.

Peter M.J. Pol is an urban economist for the City of Rotterdam and program manager for the Master City Developer. Peter works actively in urban and regional networks improving urban development at the local and regional scale. He completed his PhD on urban development around high-speed railway stations in Europe. Peter works part-time for the Erasmus University for which he has carried out a large number of international comparative urban research projects in the field of urban economics.

Anna Prat is Head of Large Scale Urban Projects for the City of Torino and Director of the Association Torino Internazionale in charge of city strategic planning. Her prior experience includes developing urban projects for Finpiemonte Spa, the investment arm of the Piedmont Region, as well as for consulting groups in Europe, including Ove Arup, Locum Destination and Ecosfera. Anna received her architecture degree from the Polytechnic University of Torino and a Master's in Urban and Regional Planning Studies from the London School of Economics.

Michael Schwarze-Rodrian is the head of the Department of European and Regional Networks Ruhr and the EU Representative of the Regional Association Ruhr (RVR) in Germany. He is a landscape planner who planned and implemented the Emscher Landscape Park and who moderates local and regional networks for a sustainable Metropolis Ruhr.

Robert Shibley is Director and Dean of the School of Architecture and Planning at the University at Buffalo. An internationally renowned scholar and practitioner in architecture, planning and urban design, Robert is passionately devoted to knowledge-based place making. He holds a Master of Architecture in Urban Design from The Catholic University of America and a Bachelor of Architecture, as well as a Bachelor of Science in Psychology, from the University of Oregon.

Jacqueline Taylor has a PhD in the History of Architecture and Art, with a specialty in race and gender. Jacqueline has taught at the University of Virginia, Virginia Tech, and Tulane University. Her current book manuscript explores the democratic and social implications of modern architecture for an aspirational African-American community.

Rachel Teaman is Communications Officer for the School of Architecture and Planning at the University at Buffalo, where she also serves as editor of the *B/a+p Magazine*. She is a graduate of the University of Maryland College Park with a Master of Arts in Public Affairs Reporting and of the State University of New York at Geneseo with a Bachelor of Arts in English Language and Literature.

Nico Tillie is a researcher and teacher of landscape architecture and sustainable development at Delft University of Technology, and lectures around the world. Nico is completing a PhD in liveable low carbon cities. He is an urban planner for the City of Rotterdam and Vice President of the World Council on City Data (WCCD).

Roland van der Heijden is a city planner for the City of Rotterdam. His focus is on the point where sustainable urban development and Geographical Information Systems meet. He also lectures at the Institute for Housing and Urban Development Studies in Rotterdam. He received his Master's degree in Planning from the University of Nijmegen.

Larry Witzling is a Principal at GRAEF Inc. He has served on urban design and development projects involving strategic planning and consensus building in more than fifty communities. His work focuses on a variety of issues, including urban design, growth management, environmental planning, rural design, sustainable planning, and economic development.

Index